MAN

of

WAR

MAN
of
WAR

The Fighting Life Of
ADMIRAL JAMES SAUMAREZ
from the American Revolution to the Defeat of Napoleon

Anthony Sullivan

Frontline Books

MAN OF WAR
The Fighting Life of Admiral James Saumarez, from the American Revolution to the Defeat of Napoleon

This edition published in 2017 by Frontline Books,
an imprint of Pen & Sword Books Ltd,
47 Church Street, Barnsley, S. Yorkshire, S70 2AS

ISBN: 978-1-52670-651-5

CIP data records for this title are available from the British Library

For more information on our books, please visit
www.frontline-books.com
email info@frontline-books.com
or write to us at the above address.

Printed and bound by CPI Group (UK) Ltd, Croydon, CR0 4YY
Typeset in 10.5/12.5 point Palatino

Contents

List of Maps

Acknowledgements

I would like to thank the staff of the National Archives, Kew, the staff of the Ipswich branch of the Suffolk Records Office and the Societe Guernesiaise for their help in the preparation of this book. I would also like to acknowledge the work carried out by the Navy Records Society and thank the staff of the British Newspaper Archive, whose efforts in digitising over 200 years of British news history helped piece together the details of Saumarez's life not covered in his personal papers, Admiralty archives or Sir John Ross's original biography. At Frontline Books I would like to thank Martin Mace, John Grehan, and Stephen Chumbley. Finally I would like to offer my thanks to Paul Killick for his advice and support during the writing of this book.

Prologue:

Gibraltar – 12 July 1801

Stung by their unexpected defeat and the loss of one of their ships in battle against the French on 6 July 1801 the British sailors had worked tirelessly for five days and nights to repair their badly damaged ships. Hulls were patched up, rigging replaced and masts and spars repaired. Several British ships were still taking on ammunition when the French squadron across the waters at Algeciras was spotted preparing for sea on the morning of 12 July and it was not until that afternoon, two hours after the enemy had left port, that the British ships were finally ready to put to sea. Passing a harbour wall lined with cheering spectators, a band on shore playing 'Britons Strike Home', the squadron headed out into the Bay of Gibraltar in line ahead, the 80-gun flagship *Caesar* leading the 74s *Venerable*, *Superb*, *Spencer* and *Audacious* into battle. Off Europa Point a small boat with two men aboard dressed in white hospital gowns was observed pulling towards the squadron. As the boat drew up alongside the flagship it became clear that the two men were members of *Caesar*'s crew who been wounded in the earlier battle and had been convalescing in hospital. Seeing the squadron preparing to put to sea they had asked permission to rejoin their ship. When this had been refused they had escaped from the hospital, found a boat and rowed out to *Caesar* in order to fight alongside their crew-mates.

Aboard his flagship the British admiral was anxious. Having lost the previous battle through a flaw in the wind which had frustrated his attack and left one ship aground and in enemy hands, Sir James Saumarez was eager for a victory to restore both British honour and his own reputation. However, the French squadron that he had fought across the Bay of Gibraltar in Algeciras on 6 July had been strengthened with the arrival of several Spanish ships including two First Rates of 112 guns each, *Real Carlos* and *Hermenegildo*. Whilst seriously outgunned, Saumarez had the utmost faith in the abilities of his officers and men and felt sure that victory would soon belong to the British. However, it immediately became clear that his hastily-repaired and poorly-sailing ships would soon lose contact with the faster-sailing enemy. Thankfully the British had one undamaged ship that had missed the previous battle, having been out on patrol, and Saumarez now ordered *Superb* to give chase to the enemy. Hoisting more sail Captain Keats' ship soon disappeared into the night, her stern lights concealed in match tubs, her other lights shaded.

At 11.00pm, as Keats was walking the quarterdeck along with his surgeon, Benjamin Outram, the massive Spanish three-decker *Real Carlos* suddenly appeared out of the darkness on *Superb*'s larboard bow, lights shining brightly from her gunports and cabin windows. Moments later *Hermenegildo* was sighted a little ahead of her compatriot. As *Superb* drew alongside *Real Carlos* Outram was ordered to his station below decks. At a range of around 300 yards Keats hauled up the foresail, took in the top gallant sails and unleashed the first of three broadsides with his larboard guns against the much larger Spanish ship. The third broadside brought *Real Carlos*'s fore topmast crashing down and as the sail touched the forecastle guns their flashes set it alight, the flames raced up and along *Real Carlos*'s rigging and she was soon ablaze both fore and aft. Observing that the Spanish ship was now on fire, Keats left her to her fate and headed off in pursuit of the French ship *St Antoine*, trailing at the rear of the combined squadron. Neither the Spanish nor the British had any distinguishing lights and in the confusion *Real Carlos*'s crew had begun firing blindly in all directions, missing *Superb* but hitting the other Spanish three-decker *Hermenegildo*, which immediately returned fire. Her crew distracted by the fire now devouring their ship, *Real Carlos* soon ran into *Hermenegildo* which she also set on fire.

Watching the battle from his flagship Saumarez could see the flames engulfing the two Spanish First Rates, illuminating their colours, the sea around the two ships glowing red. In that instant he knew a British victory had been secured.

By the time *Superb* had forced the surrender of *St Antoine* the rest of Saumarez's squadron had caught up with Keats' ship and were finally able to join in the action, pursuing the enemy as they attempted to sail back to Cadiz. Just after midnight the flames spreading through *Real Carlos* reached her magazine and she blew up. *Hermenegildo* was destroyed in a similar fashion some fifteen minutes later. The light from these two huge explosions, which had killed almost 2,000 Spanish sailors, was visible in Gibraltar and their effects could be felt as far away as Cadiz. *Caesar* was soon enveloped in a cloud of thick, acrid smoke that lay on the surface of the water and quickly spread throughout the ship, alarming some of her crew who mistakenly believed that their own ship was on fire.

Having abandoned their pursuit due to a lack of wind, the following morning Saumarez's squadron returned to Gibraltar. Once again the harbour wall was lined with spectators, eager for a glimpse of the victorious ships and their French prize. The royal standard had been hoisted and as *Caesar* came to anchor a 21-gun salute was fired from King's Bastion. On 15 July there was a firework display and the following day the Governor hosted a celebratory dinner. As the reports coming out of Cadiz were beginning to make clear, the destruction of two Spanish First Rates and the loss of nearly 2,000 men was a blow from which the already-strained relationship between Paris and Madrid could not recover. To the surprise of no one, barely a week after the battle the Spanish dissolved their tempestuous alliance with France. Eight months later Britain and France signed a peace treaty that ended the French Revolutionary Wars.

A portrait of Admiral Lord de Saumarez based on a work by the artist Samuel Lane. (Anne S.K. Brown Military Collection, Brown University Library)

Chapter 1

Childhood and Early Career: March 1757 – March 1775

Situated just thirty miles off coast of France and once part of the Duchy of Normandy, the island of Guernsey has been attached to the English crown for almost 1,000 years. The Bailiwick of Guernsey also covers the neighbouring islands of Alderney, Sark and Herm. Guernsey's capital, situated on the east coast, is St Peter Port. With its large deep-water harbour the capital is also a major port that today handles both local and international trade. Throughout most of the eighteenth century the principal occupations on Guernsey, as on Jersey, were privateering and smuggling. Mostly aimed at French trade, in the 1780s these activities drove the governor of Cherbourg to attempt several invasions. In the 1760s Guernsey was a sparsely populated island. Much that is today built over was then open fields. St Peter Port had no street lights or pavements and the roads also served as open sewers. Some roads in the capital were little more than cart tracks, the tall buildings either side of High Street leaning so close to one another that their roofs almost touched. Although the island was attached to the English crown, one would hardly think it walking round the island. The two main languages spoken were Guernesiais (an archaic form of French) or Norman French. There were neither English newspapers nor a post office on the island and travel to the mainland could take several days.

Guernsey's principal families lived in the capital close to the Royal Court either on Smith Street, the High Street or the Pollett. Amongst these families the de Sausmarez's were one of the oldest and most distinguished, tracing, as they could, their ancestry all the way back to the Normans. Earlier members of the family included a bailiff, several rectors and a dean. Their recently completed family home, a large three-storey Georgian townhouse in dressed granite, reflected the saumarez's status, expressing as it did 'a certain grandeur new to St Peter Port'[1.]

1

Matthew Saumarez, born in October 1718, was the fourth son of Matthew de Sausmarez, a colonel in the militia and part-time privateer. Matthew's elder brother, Philip Saumarez, sailed as first lieutenant with Commodore Anson on his journey round the world in 1740–4 and later captained the 60-gun *Nottingham* prior to his death at the Second Battle of Cape Finisterre in October 1747. His younger brother, Thomas, also served in the navy and, as captain of the 50-gun *Antelope*, captured the French 64 *Belliqueux* in a much-publicised action off Lundy Island in November 1758. Matthew studied medicine becoming a surgeon at the Town Hospital where he treated the upper echelons of St Peter Port society. Whilst the de Sausmarez's were justifiably proud of their ancestry this was a period of renewed tensions with France and Matthew, Philip and Thomas all dropped the 'de' and the second 's' from their family name in order to sound more English.

In 1743, three years after the birth of his first child Susannah and the subsequent death of his wife, Susan Dumaresq, Matthew married Cartaret, the nineteen-year-old daughter of James le Marchant, another prominent member of St Peter Port society. Their first child, Philip, was born in 1750, their second child, Anne, in 1752 and their third child, John, arrived in 1755. James Saumarez was born on 11 March 1757 at the family home and baptised two days later at the Town Church. His younger siblings were Thomas (b.1760), Charlotte (b.1763), Richard (b.1764), Nicolas (b.1766), Mary (b.1768) and Cartaret, the Saumarez's last child who was born in 1770. Beginning his education at Dame School in St Peter Port, from around 1764 to 1767 James studied at Elizabeth College, alongside his elder brother John. Elizabeth College was not a well-run school at that time and the quality of its education was poor. Whilst Saumarez always said his brother was a much better scholar of Latin and Greek, he did develop a love of poetry. Impressed by a recital of several lines from Milton's *Paradise Lost* when no more than eight years old, a friend of the family sent the young Saumarez a copy of the *Golden Verses of Pythagoras* that he had soon committed to memory.

Entertained from a young age by stories of his uncle's daring exploits at sea and with his older brother Philip already serving in the Royal Navy, it was no surprise to James's father that he professed a desire to enter the same profession. His Majesty's ships often stopped off at St Peter Port to pick up provisions and Matthew, a former naval surgeon, often entertained captains and other officers at the family home. In September 1767 Matthew persuaded Captain Lucius O'Brien to enter Saumarez's name in the books of his ship, the 28-gun frigate *Solebay*, as a captain's servant alongside his relatives Durell Saumarez and Nicholas Dobree. Although signed on to *Solebay* Saumarez did not actually go to sea. Admiralty rules dictated that youngsters like Saumarez could not become midshipmen until they were fifteen, but midshipman were also required to have served aboard a ship for six years before taking the lieutenants' exam. This resulted in a practice known as 'book time' which, although not officially sanctioned by the Admiralty, was widespread. Saumarez's name remained in *Solebay*'s books until 30 June 1770 during which time he completed his education at a school near Greenwich, possibly to improve his English. James was only at this school, recommended to his father by a friend of the family, for around ten months before Matthew, seemingly disappointed by the quality of education his son was receiving, travelled to London and took him home.

Unfortunately at this important point in Saumarez's naval career the record becomes a little murky. Ross states that Saumarez now joined *Montreal*, James Alms, and that on 9 August 1769 the ship sailed for the Mediterranean from Portsmouth. Of course in 1769 Saumarez was still on the books of *Solebay* and *Montreal*'s log shows that on that particular date the ship was not at Portsmouth but was in fact cruising off the Italian coast, roughly thirty-five leagues off Genoa under the command of Captain Philip Cosby. If we assume that this is an error of dates by Ross and that he meant 1770 not 1769 we are still presented with a problem as from 27 July to 20 August 1770 *Montreal*, now commanded by Alms, was at anchor at Spithead.

On 9 August 1770 the 60-gun *Pembroke*, Phillip Durell, arrived in Mahon Harbour, Minorca, en route to Marseilles. It is unclear how Saumarez had made his way out to the Mediterranean but on 14 August, the day of *Pembroke*'s departure from Mahon, Saumarez was entered into her books as a captain's servant. *Pembroke* was the flagship of Commodore Proby, a friend of the family who had sailed as a midshipman with Saumarez's uncle Philip. The commodore having been forced home due to ill health, on 28 September 1770 Saumarez moved yet again, this time joining the 32-gun *Winchelsea*, Captain Samuel Goodall, at anchor at Leghorn Road. Saumarez would remain aboard Goodall's frigate for the next sixteen months. Goodall, in company with most Royal Navy captains, was eager for the youngest members of his crew to keep up with their education whilst at sea and so he allowed Saumarez and his other 'youngsters' frequent access to his Great Cabin, both to write and to study the books in his small library; various copies of the *Spectator* and Samuel Johnson's *Idler* magazine along with a few stray volumes on Roman history. On 8 November Saumarez took the first major step on his naval career when he was entered in *Winchelsea*'s books as a midshipman.

Following his promotion Saumarez moved in with the other midshipmen sharing *Winchelsea*'s cockpit, a space situated just forward of the officers' quarters on the lower deck that was also used as an operating theatre during battle. In common with all Royal Navy ships, the midshipmen were berthed next to the marines who were deliberately positioned between *Winchelsea*'s officers and her crew. A ship's crew was split into as many divisions as there were lieutenants aboard ship and each division was split into sections led by the ship's midshipmen and mates. Saumarez was now responsible for 'the good order and discipline'[2] of the men in his section; ensuring that they did their duties, had clean clothing and that those who were unwell were recorded on the sick list and reported to the ship's surgeon. During a battle the midshipmen were charge of the gun crews and they had to ensure that the long guns and all their associated equipment – handspikes, rammer, worm, sponge – were in good order. At noon Saumarez and *Winchelsea*'s other midshipmen practised taking the ship's position with their sextants. (Their recordings would later be checked by Goodall.) At various times they also took soundings, oversaw the signalling and, most exciting of all, they were in charge of the ship's boats. Any spare time a midshipman might have was usually spent studying subjects such as navigation, gunnery and seamanship and, just as important, learning the various social graces required of a young officer. Prior to leaving home Saumarez's father had presented him with a purse containing fifteen guineas. Matthew trusted that his son, who was not yet fourteen years old, would use this money wisely but told him that he could draw on his banker whenever low on funds. It gave Saumarez's father great pleasure to notice the irregularity of these drafts, for they proved few and far between.

On 16 December *Winchelsea* sailed for Gibraltar. Cruising from Cape Trafalgar off the south-west coast of Spain to Leghorn (Livorno) in Italy, *Winchelsea* spent the next fourteen months in the Mediterranean. The ship was variously at anchor at Tangier, Gibraltar, Malaga, Cadiz and Genoa. In February 1772 *Winchelsea* was ordered home, but Saumarez, eager to see his friends and family after two and a half years at sea, was informed by his captain that he was being transferred to the 28-gun *Levant*, Samuel Thompson, as both Goodall and his father thought he should remain at sea in order to complete his education as a midshipman. Saumarez's time aboard *Winchelsea* had made a deep impression on the young officer; in later life he would talk of Captain Goodall with great affection and was deeply saddened by his death in 1801.

Saumarez transferred to his new ship on 15 February. The following day *Levant* sailed from Gibraltar and dropped anchor at Port Mahon.

Ordered into the Gulf of Smyrna to protect British trade at the height of the Russo-Turkish war of 1768–74, *Levant* sailed from Minorca three days later and arrived at Smyrna (modern day Izmir) on 25 March 1772, following a brief stop off at Malta. She would remain at anchor at the Aegean port for the next fourteen months. Saumarez's would later refer to his time in Smyrna as a 'blank in his existence';[3] however, it was not without incident. In August a fire broke out near the governor's house and *Levant*'s boats assisted in removing bread and rice from the town's storehouses. Saumarez would most likely have been in command of one of these vessels. By the time the fire was finally extinguished it had ripped through the port, destroying an estimated 10,000 houses. Still recovering from this disaster, in December Smyrna was attacked by 2,000 soldiers led by the governor of Booroonabad, Ayvas Aga. Smyrna's governor, Caro Osman, was forced to flee but returned later that month with 12,000 cavalry to retake the town.

On 29 May 1773 *Levant* weighed anchor and departed Smyrna for Minorca. Having spent ten weeks at anchor in Port Mahon *Levant* sailed for Gibraltar, arriving there on 16 September. In February 1774 Saumarez's ship was ordered to the Tagus but after six weeks in Portugal was recalled to the Aegean due to a heightening of tensions in the region. *Levant* returned to Smyrna almost a year to the day after she had left on 28 May. Having spent a further four months at Smyrna, in September *Levant* sailed for England via Gibraltar, finally arriving back at Spithead on 29 March 1775. Two weeks later Saumarez was discharged along with the rest of *Levant*'s officers and crew and returned home having spent the best part of five years away at sea.

Chapter 2

Lieutenant Suamarez:
August 1775 – August 1778

Having now spent more than six years in the navy (including his 'book time' aboard *Solebay*), Saumarez was eligible to take the lieutenants' exam, his next step on the ladder of promotion. Introduced by the Admiralty in 1677, the exam was a tough and thorough test of a midshipman's abilities and there was no guarantee of success. On 9 August 1775 Saumarez made his way to the Navy Office, a neat and fairly plain-looking building not far from the Tower of London on the corner of Crutched Friars and Seething Lane. Called to his examination, the young midshipman presented the journals he had kept aboard *Winchelsea* and *Levant*, together with certificates from Captains Goodhall and Thompson, confirming to his examiners, Captains John Campbell, Abraham North and the Comptroller of the Navy, Maurice Suckling, that he was more than twenty-one years of age and had been at sea for more than seven years. As Saumarez was well aware, the minimum age required to sit the lieutenants' exam was twenty but due to his two years of 'book time' aboard *Solebay* he was not yet nineteen when he appeared before Suckling, Campbell and North. However, the deceit over his age was far from unusual, especially in an era where there were no birth certificates, only locally held records of baptisms. Nelson, for example, was the same age as Saumarez when he passed his own lieutenants' exam. Having asked Saumarez a series of questions to test his seamanship, Admirals Suckling, Campbell and North were soon satisfied that the young officer could 'splice, knot, reef a sail, &c' and was 'qualified to do the duty of an able seaman and midshipman'. There had not been any exams for several months whilst Suckling accompanied his fellow lords commissioners on their annual tour of the dockyards and by the end of the day twelve 'young gentlemen' (almost three times the usual number) had gone out into the world as passed midshipman. Saumarez was lucky: he was one of the first candidates to be seen and the first to have his name entered in the books.

Having passed his lieutenants' exam Saumarez was not immediately promoted as there was no ship was available. However, war with the American colonies had broken out in April of that year and Commodore Sir Peter Parker was assembling an expedition to sail to America to assist the army in putting down the rebellion. Admiral Keppel had been a friend of Saumarez's uncle, Philip, serving with him under Anson during his voyage around the world and he recommended Saumarez to Parker. Following a successful interview with the Admiral in London, Saumarez travelled to Sheerness to embark on Parker's newly-commissioned flagship, the 50-gun *Bristol*, as a passed midshipman on 9 October 1775. From Sheerness *Bristol* travelled to Spithead where, on 19 December, Parker hoisted his broad pendant. On 29 December *Bristol* sailed for Cork in company with *Actaeon* and *Deal Castle*. Arriving off Cork on 6 January Parker's squadron met up with the rest of the expedition bound for South Carolina; six frigates, two bomb vessels and thirty transports bearing seven regiments of infantry and two companies of artillery under the command of Earl Cornwallis and Brigadier-General John Vaughan.

The expedition sailed from Cork on 12 February 1776 but had not been out of port long before it encountered foul weather. During the stormy voyage across the Atlantic Saumarez came to the attention of Cornwallis, who had embarked aboard *Bristol* with his aide, Lord Chewton, just prior to sailing. Impressed by the attention with which the young officer undertook his duties, Cornwallis offered Saumarez a commission in his own regiment, the 33rd Foot, a regiment that would soon gain a reputation as one of the finest units in the British Army. Flattered by Cornwallis's proposal and perhaps tempted by the thought of having such a powerful patron Saumarez went below to inform his fellow officers of the news but they immediately chided him for having considered abandoning the senior service in order to turn soldier. Suitably rebuked, when Saumarez next spoke to Cornwallis it was to decline his offer.

Delayed by the bad weather, which had caused several transports to part company, the expedition did not reach North America until 3 May 1776, three months after it had first set out. At Cape Fear, North Carolina, the ships and transports were met by General Clinton who had travelled down from Boston with around 2,000 men. Ships damaged in the gale were repaired and once the missing transports finally re-appeared the expedition set off again to find a more suitable base for operations and on 4 June anchored off Charleston.

Charleston is shielded by two islands, Sullivan's Island to the north and James Island to the south. Beyond an underwater bar the channel into the harbour turns north towards Sullivan's Island. It was here that the Americans had hastily constructed a fort to defend the harbour. Built from a local wood known as cabbage-tree that was almost impervious to shot, Fort Sullivan, though still unfinished, controlled the entrance to the harbour and would have to be taken if the expedition was to proceed.

Soundings having been made and marker buoys laid out, on 7 June the frigates and transports safely crossed Sullivan's Bar but it was necessary to transfer the guns of *Bristol* to an East Indiaman in order to get this larger ship into the main channel. On 9 June Clinton's troops landed on James Island. It had been understood that the inlet between the two islands would be fordable but even at low tide the water was seven feet deep, this meant that Clinton's troops could not co-operate in the attack on Fort Sullivan which would now be limited to a naval bombardment. On 25 June the 50-gun *Experiment* arrived from Britain and she too had to have her guns removed in order to pass over Sullivan's Bar. Having spent a few days aboard *Friendship*, one of the transports that had been fitted out with carronades, on 26 June Saumarez requested permission to return to *Bristol*. After a short delay caused by unfavourable winds the attack was fixed for 28 June.

At 10.30am on the morning of 28 June the squadron weighed anchor and moved into position. Parker's plan was for *Bristol*, *Experiment*, *Active* and *Solebay* to station themselves directly opposite the fort supported by the bomb vessel *Thunder* with *Friendship* further out to sea and the frigates anchoring up stream to prevent attacks from fireships and to enfilade the enemy position. However, whilst manoeuvring into position these three frigates, *Sphinx*, *Syren* and *Actaeon* ran aground, *Sphinx* and *Siren* were got off in a few hours with the rising tide but *Actaeon* remained aground, took no part in the action, and was later ordered to be burnt. Before her magazine caught fire and she blew up, the Americans managed to board her and removed her flag, the ship's bell and some other trophies.

The attack on Fort Sullivan began at 11.15am and continued, with little interruption, until 9.00pm. As the bomb vessel *Thunder* lobbed her shells against the fort *Bristol*, *Experiment* and *Solebay* carried out a heavy and continuous carronade. However, it soon became apparent that these ships had anchored too far out, reducing the effectiveness of their guns, meanwhile, most of *Thunder*'s shells either fell into a large pit dug inside the fort behind the defenders or were swallowed up by the sand in front of the fortifications. To increase its range the mortar was overcharged

8

and eventually the mortar bed broke, disabling the weapon and damaging the ship.

Several times during the battle *Bristol*'s quarterdeck was cleared of her officers. The ship's master was wounded in his right arm and Captain Morris was struck several times but refused to go below, only relenting when a shot took his arm off. Saumarez, in charge of one of the gun crews on the lower deck, had a narrow escape when an enemy shot entered the gun port, killing three of the sailors under his command. After the battle Saumarez wrote to his parents explaining how he had 'prepared for whatever fate providence designed me'[1] but to his great surprise he escaped the carnage around him unscathed. At around 4.00pm the springs controlling *Bristol*'s anchor chains were shot away and Parker's flagship drifted out of position, her stern suddenly exposed to raking fire which now poured into the ship. Called up to the quarterdeck, the midshipman Saumarez was stood next to, Darley, was struck by a shot which took his head clean off, soaking Saumarez in his friend's blood. Another anchor with a spring attached was let go and the ship was eventually brought under control

By 9.00pm darkness had descended across the harbour, Parker's ships had almost expended their shot and with his men dead on their feet the admiral finally ordered a withdrawal. The engagement, which had lasted almost eleven hours, had resulted in a great deal of slaughter for little gain. Aboard *Bristol* there were thirty-six killed and fifty-eight wounded. Parker's flagship ended the battle with nine roundshot embedded in the main mast and her mizzen mast so shattered that the day after the battle it fell over the starboard side of the ship. Aboard *Experiment* there were twenty-three killed and fifty-six wounded. Her captain, Alexander Scott, lost his left arm but survived the battle. Captain Morris was removed to the hospital ship *Pigot*, but died from loss of blood on 5 July. At the height of the battle Parker had been standing on *Bristol*'s poop ladder as shot and splinters flew about him, stoutly refusing the pleas of his officers to go below. Eventually he was struck in the buttocks by a large splinter, suffering the indignity of having the backside of his breeches torn off.

The battle had produced several death vacancies. Morris was succeeded by *Bristol*'s first lieutenant, Toby Caulfield, and on 11 July Saumarez was made an acting lieutenant aboard Parker's flagship. Saumarez would be involved in many other battles throughout his career but this, his first, a battle that had cost the life of his captain, a fellow midshipman and several crewmen under his command, witnessed mainly from the terrifying confines of a gun deck, was an experience that would stay with him for the rest of his life.

The attack on Fort Sullivan was not resumed; instead the fleet sailed to New York, arriving there on 14 August. On 22 August Saumarez assisted in the disembarkation of 20,000 British soldiers aboard seventy-five flat-bottomed boats and eleven batteaux at Gravesend Bay prior the Battle of Long Island and he also assisted in the landings made at New Rochelle on 28 October during the Battle of White Plains. Having been appointed aide-de-camp to Lord Howe, the commander-in-chief of the British Army in America, Saumarez conveyed Lord Cornwallis and his staff ashore prior to the British landings that followed the capture of Fort Lee in November 1776. Whilst employed in the disembarkation of the troops from Britain there was an unexpected meeting with his younger brother Thomas who had joined the 23rd Foot (Royal Welch Fusiliers) earlier that year, purchasing a second lieutenancy whilst still only fifteen years old. Saumarez was at British army headquarters on Staten Island in November when a report came through that the American garrison at Fort Washington, almost 3,000 men, had surrendered to Howe's army. Saumarez returned to his ship to inform Parker of this news but at first Parker did not believe him and thought the report false.

On 6 September 1776 Rear Admiral Shuldham shifted his flag to *Bristol* and Saumarez went with Parker to the 50-gun *Chatham*, at anchor off New York, as his flag-lieutenant (aide-de-camp). Entering the ship's books as a supernumerary, Saumarez was given command of *Lady Parker*, an American prize now acting as a tender to Captain Ford's *Unicorn*. In December 1776 *Chatham* led a squadron that included the 50-gun ships *Preston*, *Centurion*, *Renown* and *Experiment* and transports bearing 7,000 troops in an assault on Rhode Island and Saumarez, along with the squadrons other lieutenants, assisted in the disembarkation of troops in flat bottom boats at Newport on 8 December. *Chatham* remained at Rhode Island until 18 February 1778 when she sailed for England, but Saumarez's time in North America had not yet come to an end for the day before *Chatham* was due to depart he was appointed commander of the galley *Spitfire*, then at New York, with instructions to return to Rhode Island.

Impressed by the American vessels he had encountered which, with their shallow draft, were ideal for use in shallow waters, Howe had begun assembling a small squadron of such galleys in late 1776. *Crane* and *Dependence* were American vessels captured together on the Hudson River in October 1776, *Cornwallis* and *Alarm* were both commissioned in 1777 and *Spitfire* was brought down from Boston in January 1778. Travelling to New York, Saumarez found his new vessel in the King's Yard and, having taken charge from her former commander, Lieutenant George Scott, began fitting her out. On 23 February he received twenty-three seamen from *Mercury* and ordnance from *Elephant*. The next day the ship received barrels of salt pork, beef, oatmeal and beer. On 26 February the boatswain and carpenters arrived aboard ship and on 28 February a sergeant and eleven marines joined the vessel from *Preston*. Eager to put to sea, Saumarez weighed anchor that same day, sailing in company with *Sphinx* and six merchantmen up the coast towards Rhode Island. On 2 March the convoy was hit by strong gales and they put in at Huntingdon Bay. The following day *Spitfire* lost sight of *Sphinx* and contact was not re-established until 4 March.

The convoy spent eleven days beset by bad weather in Huntingdon Bay, *Spitfire's* crew were kept busy taking on additional stores, regularly checking the anchor for damage and clearing snow from the decks. Setting off on 13 March the convoy finally anchored off Rhode Island, joining the nine vessels of the Royal Navy commanded by Lord Howe aboard his flagship, the 64-gun *Eagle*. On 19 March three men from *Spitfire* were sent to hospital and next day marine Christopher Budd received two dozen lashes for abandoning his post and theft. On 24 March Howe left for the Delaware and Commodore Griffiths took over command of the Rhode Island Station.

On 27 March the frigate *Lark*, stationed off Point Judith, signalled that she had spotted an enemy vessel attempting to put to sea. Griffiths sent the frigates *Maidstone* and *Sphinx* to give chase and the following morning they discovered the American frigate *Columbus* aground and under bare poles. *Spitfire* now arrived from Rhode Island having been towed out of harbour by the squadron's boats and Saumarez provided cover for *Maidstone's* pinnacle as it attempted to move in and destroy *Columbus*. Lieutenant Vashon and his men were fired at from several field pieces that the enemy had managed to bring up and four seamen were badly injured. *Spitfire* and *Sphinx* returned fire with several rounds of grapeshot whilst *Maidstone's* boat crew boarded *Columbus* and set fire to her. The rebels managed to save the powder from the magazine but their ship was destroyed. After an hour the enemy cannon were finally silenced and *Spitfire* was towed out of range of musket fire that was now coming in from the shore. Five men aboard Saumarez's vessel had been injured in the engagement and the galley had received some slight damage. Twice that day Saumarez had been forced to cut his anchor cable. A kedge anchor and a cable were sent across from *Nonsuch* and on 4 April Saumarez received two anchors and a cable from the store ship *Grand Duke*. On 11 April *Spitfire* arrived in the Sakonnet Passage, anchoring alongside the galley *Alarm* and the sloop *Kingfisher*.

On I May, whilst struggling to maintain her station in high winds and strong seas, *Spitfire* ran aground. The American rebels brought up a field

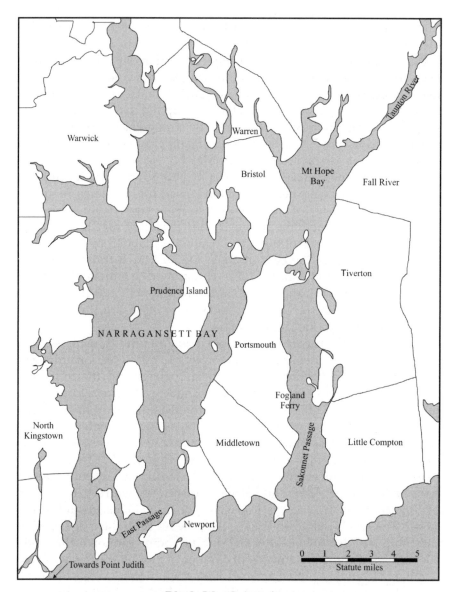

Rhode Island, America.

piece but Saumarez's vessel was successfully warped free of the shoal before the enemy cannon could cause any damage. Anchoring off Fogland Point, the following day *Spitfire* received a spare yard from *Kingfisher* and returned to her station. Griffiths now ordered Saumarez to cruise Sakonnet Passage to defend the eastern shore of Rhode Island from rebel attack and to prevent any rebel vessels from putting to sea.

He was however, to avoid being drawn into a chase that would take him away from his station.

On 24 May *Spitfire* was attacked by three whaleboats that had come from off Point Judith. Expecting *Spitfire* to be unarmed, they were surprised when the galley turned and headed straight for them, firing several shots at the American vessels as they made off in the opposite direction. At 3.00pm *Spitfire* anchored off Newport and that evening Saumarez went ashore and participated in a raid on the towns of Warren and Bristol. In Warren General Pigot and his army of 500 men from Newport set fire to a store house, a corn mill and several houses and destroyed 125 flat-bottomed boats, an armed galley and a privateer of 14 guns. At Bristol military stores together with a large part of the town were destroyed. Under covering fire from *Flora* and two galleys, *Pigot* and a vessel recently captured from the Americans that was rather confusingly also called *Spitfire*, the troops re-embarked on the boats and returned to Newport, bringing with them sixty-six prisoners.

On 27 May Saumarez's galley anchored in Sakonnet Passage in company with *Unicorn*, *Sphinx* and *Alarm*. On 30 May firing was heard in the direction of Fall River in the north-east. Sailing up Mount Hope Bay Saumarez discovered an enemy field piece firing on 100 men of the 54th Foot who were attempting to destroy a sawmill and several large boats. Whilst *Spitfire* and the enemy gun exchanged fire the 54th continued with their raid. They destroyed the sawmill, a corn mill, the boats and around 15,000 feet of lumber before safely re-embarking on the ship's boats under the protection of Saumarez's vessel.

On 13 March 1778 America had concluded a treaty with France which was considered by Britain to be a French declaration of war. Sailing from France in April 1778 with a fleet of twelve ships of the line and four frigates Admiral Comte d'Estaing arrived off Narragansett Bay on 28 July. Three days earlier the squadron at Rhode Island had received orders from Lord Howe to 'make war upon, take or destroy any part of the French squadron lately arrived on the coast'.[2] They were also instructed to burn their own vessels to stop them falling into enemy hands.

On 28 July the alarm was raised when two French ships of the line and two frigates entered Sakonnet Passage. *Cerberus* was run on shore and Cloberry Christian, captain of the sloop *Kingfisher*, ordered the galleys *Alarm* and *Spitfire* to relocate to Fogland Ferry. The following day two enemy ships appeared off Fogland and Saumarez and d'Auvergne were ordered to run their ships ashore and burn them. Saumarez brought *Spitfire* ashore within a cable length of *Alarm* and began offloading guns and stores. With *Kingfisher* and *Alarm* now ablaze, Saumarez set fire to his own vessel.

13

Chapter 3

Lieutenant to Post Captain: August 1778 – February 1782

In the days following the arrival of the French fleet off Rhode Island, *Juno, Lark, Orpheus* and *Flora* were all burned to prevent them falling into enemy hands. The guns, powder and stores taken from *Spitfire* and the vessels subsequently burned by the British were used to stiffen Rhode Island's defences; their crews, around 1,000 men, were formed into a division under Brisbane and Saumarez was given command of an advanced post manned by sailors and marines.

On 8 August 1778 d'Estaing moved his fleet into Newport Harbour and the following day landed some of his 4,000 troops on Conanicut Island, the French soldiers joining the 10,000 American troops who had already crossed from the mainland into Rhode Island. The British garrison at Rhode Island, roughly 6,000 men, was now hemmed in to the north and south. Having been delayed from sailing from New York by contrary winds, Lord Howe's fleet, thirteen ships of the line, appeared off Point Judith on 9 August and Saumarez was sent to Howe's flagship *Eagle* with dispatches. On his return he was making his way across a field behind the beach when the French fleet arrived offshore and immediately opened fire on the coastal batteries. The corn either side of Saumarez was flattened by ball and grapeshot but he somehow emerged unscathed from the barrage.

Having recalled the troops landed the previous day D'Estaing sailed out to meet Howe. As the two fleets steered southwards the weather deteriorated and a violent storm broke out. The storm, which lasted for two days, scattered the fleets and severely damaged d'Estaing's flagship, *Languedoc*. The British returned to New York and, having regrouped off Delaware, the French limped into Newport on 20 August. Having quickly come to the conclusion that the British were unlikely to surrender in the foreseeable future, d'Estaing, who had only recently transferred from the army to the navy and lacked experience in fleet command, immediately deferred to his junior and somewhat insubordinate captains when they informed him that the squadron would need to sail to Boston for repairs. Informing a stunned General Sullivan, the commander of the American forces at Rhode Island, that he could offer no further assistance, on 22 August d'Estaing sailed for Boston.

On 28 September Saumarez was at Staten Island, along with fellow galley captain Philip d'Auvergne, for his court martial following the loss of *Spitfire*. The trial took place aboard Hyde Parker's flagship *Royal Oak*, and was presided over by Parker with twelve senior captains in attendance. Saumarez's evidence, a report written to Captain Brisbane a few days after the loss of his vessel, was presented to the court and he was then asked a series of questions regarding the burning of *Spitfire*. Saumarez told the court that he had run *Spitfire* ashore within a cable's length of *Kingfisher* with the intention of burning her as he felt that that was the only course of action available to him. Although a court martial was standard procedure following the loss of any Royal Navy vessel, Saumarez must have still been relieved when the court found that he had acted correctly in order to prevent his galley falling into enemy hands.

Saumarez's service in North America had now come to an end and on 12 November 1778 he sailed home aboard the store-ship *Leviathan* along with fellow officers d'Auvergne, Dalrymple, Smith, Hudson, Brisbane, Symons and Graeme. As *Leviathan* approached the English Channel on 14 November she was caught in a violent storm and at one stage was taking on fourteen inches of water an hour, her men continually at the pumps. On 24 November the ship lost her main topsail in sight of the Eddystone Lighthouse. Blown off course *Leviathan* was almost lost on the rocks off the Scilly Isles and Commander Tathwell had to continually wear his ship to avoid running aground. It was a narrow escape; these dangerous rocks had already caused one of the worst maritime disasters in the history of the Royal Navy. In 1707 four ships of the line under command of Sir Cloudsley Shovell had been lost at this same spot with the loss of over 1,400 lives.

Following this near-disaster *Leviathan* arrived safely at Plymouth on 26 November from where Saumarez eventually found passage back to Guernsey. His first visit home in many years was, alas, not a happy one for he learned of the death of his father, drowned along with eight other passengers and crew when the Guernsey packet, *Providence*, had sunk off Weymouth on 29 March 1778. A body, badly disfigured but taken to be Matthew's, was one of the five recovered from the water along with the ship's captain, Stephen Mourant. Three months later Matthew's

15

actual body, identified by his watch, was discovered lying amongst the rocks off Swanage.

In May 1779 Saumarez was appointed sixth lieutenant of the 74-gun *Edgar*, Captain Elliot, a newly-commissioned ship then fitting out at Woolwich. Having received his letter of appointment Saumarez had to wait for a vessel to take him to England but he finally found a passage in the frigate *Ambuscade* when his friend, Captain Charles Phipps, stopped off at Guernsey on 12 June on his way out to join Admiral Hardy's Channel Fleet. On 19 June *Ambuscade* spoke to *Southampton* off Portland Bill and Phipps discovered that Hardy's fleet had already sailed from Spithead. There was no time to drop Saumarez off at Portsmouth as originally intended and instead Phipps headed out to meet Hardy's fleet which was eventually discovered on 20 June, sixty miles to the west of the Scilly Isles. *Victory*'s first lieutenant, John Borlase Warren, was made master and commander of the French sloop *Helena*, captured by Phipps on 22 June, and Saumarez joined *Victory* as her third lieutenant, entering the ship's books as a supernumerary.

On 6 July *Victory* returned to Torbay to re-provision but was back cruising off Ushant less than two weeks later. On 4 September the Channel Fleet's flagship sailed for Spithead where she remained until 22 October. A month later she returned to Spithead from Torbay and on 8 February 1780 she dropped down to Portsmouth to be repaired, have additional carronades fitted to her poop deck and forecastle and her hull copper sheathed. On 18 May 1780 Hardy had a heart attack and died. He was replaced by Admiral Francis Geary and on 9 July *Victory* retuned to Channel service, cruising off Cape Finisterre and then Ushant until 15 August. The following month Geary was replaced by Vice Admiral Francis Drake and *Victory* returned to Torbay where she remained until 4 October. Following another cruise off Ushant and Cape Finisterre, Saumarez requested permission to return home, having been at sea for several months. He had only just stepped ashore at Portsmouth when he was approached by a messenger bearing news of a major French attack on Jersey. Angered by the privateers operating from the island attacking shipping travelling along the coast, this was an attempt by the French to gain control of the island. However, the attack was poorly organised and resulted in defeat. At the height of the battle the death of the British commander, Major Pierson, spurred his troops on to fight harder, while the death of the French commander, de Rullecort, had the opposite effect on the French troops who quickly gave up the fight and fled.

In March 1781 Vice Admiral Hyde Parker hoisted his flag aboard *Victory*, at anchor at Spithead, with Saumarez now promoted to the ship's second lieutenant. Saumarez had proved a very capable lieutenant, a fact readily attested to by any of the senior officers he had served under so far during his brief but already very active career. If Saumarez had a fault it was that he was very thin-skinned and did not take criticism well. One morning Parker, an old and irritable admiral whose humour was not improved through suffering from gout, found fault with some aspect of Saumarez's watch. When he later invited Saumarez to dinner his second lieutenant, still brooding over the admiral's earlier comments, refused the offer, leading Parker to exclaim 'What! Can't you put up with the fractious disposition of an old man?'[1]

In June 1781 Parker was appointed commander of the North Sea Fleet and he shifted his flag to the 74-gun *Fortitude*, taking several key officers including his first and second lieutenants, Waghorn and Saumarez, with him. From the earliest days of the American War the Dutch had been supporting the colonists in their struggle for independence by shipping arms and goods from Holland and on behalf of France. Finally, on 22 December 1780 Britain had declared war on the Dutch Republic and the Royal Navy had begun blockading the Dutch coast and sending ships out to protect convoys in and out of the Baltic. Receiving intelligence that a Dutch fleet had evaded the blockade and put to sea from the Texel, on 3 June Parker sailed from Portsmouth with a squadron of six ships of the line, *Princess Amelia*, John Macartney, *Bienfaisant*, Richard Brathwaite, *Buffalo*, William Truscott, *Preston*, Alexander Graeme, and *Dolphin*, William Blair. Off the coast of Norway on 16 July Parker was joined by the 74-gun *Berwick*, John Ferguson, and the frigates *Belle Poule*, Philip Patton, and *Tartar*, Robert Sutton. Ferguson's squadron had been cruising the Baltic for almost two month and had barely enough water and provisions for ten more days so Parker put in at Fleckkerøy, Norway, for supplies.

Only recently installed as commander of the North Sea Fleet, Parker had yet to get to know his officers properly and he had had little chance to put his men through their paces (the fleet had only been made to form a line of battle two or three times). However, of more concern to Parker was the state of his ships. Although his flagship *Fortitude* had only recently been launched and was well-manned, she was rather small for a 74 which made her uncomfortable in rough seas. The 66-gun *Buffalo* had been built in the 1740s and, considered unfit for fleet action, had been serving as a store ship. Hurriedly pressed into service and rigged for a ship of fifty guns her lower deck was only equipped with 18-pounders. *Princess Amelia* was an old, outdated three-decker of 80 guns, the 44-gun *Dolphin* had had her twenty lower deck guns reduced from 18-pounders to 12-pounders and the thirty-year-old 64-gun

Bienfaisant had also had her lower deck armament reduced. These old, outdated ships had also had their masts and yards shortened to reduce the strain on their hulls.

On 28 July Parker's squadron met with a British convoy in the Kattegat, under escort by the 38-gun frigate *Latona*. That evening the cutter *Surprise* arrived with dispatches from the Admiralty confirming that the Dutch squadron out of the Texel was escorting a convoy of around seventy merchantmen, bound for America, as far as the Orkneys. The squadron, led by Admiral Johan Zoutman, consisted of seven ships of the line and five frigates, a similar disposition of forces, in terms of guns if not in quality of ships, to the British fleet.

At around 4.00am on the morning of 5 August, whilst sailing off Dogger Bank, the Dutch squadron was sighted, roughly eighteen miles to leeward of the British and close to the Texel. Worried that the Dutch might turn back to port Parker did not, as expected, give the order to prepare for battle but instead ordered a general chase. Instead of preparing their ships for battle Parker's crews were now busy above deck, setting and working the extra sails. However, Zoutman did not turn back to the Texel as expected. At 5.00am he hoisted his colours and as his ships pulled away from the convoy they formed a line of battle on the larboard tack. At 5.30am Parker signalled *Tartar* to stay with the British convoy. Captain Sutton led the merchantmen off to the west and they soon disappeared from view. With his frigates about a mile off to windward Parker now ordered his remaining ships to form a line of battle. A signal was also sent by mistake for *Dolphin* and *Preston* to change stations in the line, this placing one of Parker's weakest ships opposite the strongest part of the enemy line. At 7.00am *Bienfaisant* was ordered to make more sail. Other signals were also sent to maintain the line. Then, at 7.55am, the order for battle was given.

Neither side fired until they were within half a musket shot of one another. At approximately 8.00am Parker and Zoutman raised their red battle flags and the fleets opened fire. Once it had begun the battle would last for over three and a half hours. The British van was led by *Berwick* with *Dolphin* and *Buffalo* following close behind. Whilst the Dutch van was the strongest part of their line, for the British, *Berwick* apart, it was their weakest. The next ship in the British line was the flagship *Fortitude*. By placing his ship opposite Zoutman's flagship, *Admiraal Ruijter*, Parker had extended his own line beyond the Dutch rear, rendering the last ship in the British line, *Bienfaisant*, useless for most of the battle. At 8.00am the signal for close action was made. *Buffalo* was then ordered to make more sail, which she was unable to do due to damage sustained to her rigging. By 9.45am *Berwick*'s attack

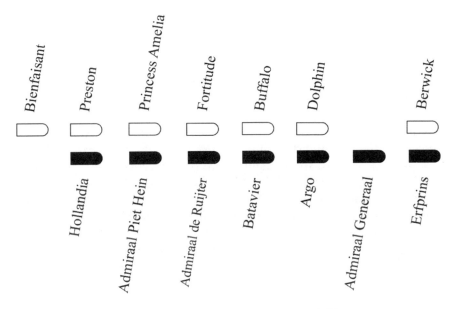

The Battle of Dogger Bank, 5 August 1781.

on the lead Dutch ship *Erfprins* had forced both vessels so far to leeward that Captain Ferguson's ship was hit in her larboard side by the next ship in the Dutch line, the 74-gun *Admiraal Generaal*. *Berwick* now had to make sail and tack to regain the line, consequently it was 11.00am before she could come to the assistance of *Dolphin*, now under attack from two Dutch ships. The signal to form the line once again flying from the flagship, *Fortitude* passed to the leeward of *Buffalo* and led the rest of the squadron past Captain Truscott's struggling ship. By 11.00am the Dutch rate of fire, *Admiraal de Ruijter* and *Admiraal Generaal* aside, had slackened. As *Fortitude* passed *Admiraal Generaal* there was a furious exchange of broadsides between the two vessels and Commodore Kingsbergen kept up the assault on each British ship that passed him in succession. At 11.35am, his ships crippled by enemy fire and the Dutch now dropping to leeward, Parker called a halt to the action.

For some time after the battle the two fleets remained close to one another but both sides had sustained serious damage and neither was in any state to restart the action. When Zoutman's fleet eventually turned and began escorting the Dutch convoy back to the Texel Parker's crippled squadron could not follow them. The following day a Dutch ship, believed to be *Hollandia*, was discovered sunk in twenty-two fathoms of water on the Dogger Bank sandbar with just her topgallant masts sticking out of the water. Her pendant was recovered by Captain Patton of the frigate *Belle Poule* and brought aboard the flagship.

Both sides had suffered greatly in the action. Dutch losses were counted at 142 killed and 403 wounded, although there were private accounts stating that their losses were much higher. Whatever the true number, the Dutch fleet did not put to sea again during the war. British losses were counted as 104 killed and 339 wounded. Captain Macartney was killed early in the engagement and First Lieutenant Hill took over the command of *Princess Amelia*. Captain Graeme had also lost an arm. Aboard the flagship there were twenty killed and sixty-seven wounded. *Fortitude*'s first lieutenant, Martin Waghorn, had been injured during the engagement but had refused to go below to have his wound seen to. Lieutenants Harrington and Hinkley were also wounded. Following the engagement Saumarez directed the repairs to the flagship's masts and rigging. *Fortitude*'s mainmast had been shot through three times, there was a great deal of damage to her standing rigging and the other masts had also lost shrouds, stays and backstays. Most of *Fortitude*'s running rigging, her braces, lifts and halliards had been shot away and the bowsprit had lost its jib boom and the mizzen its driver boom. All the boats were damaged as were two lower-deck and three main-deck guns. The hull had also been struck ten times just above the waterline.

In the promotions that followed the victory, Lieutenant Waghorn was made acting captain of the frigate *Artois*, replacing Captain McBride who had moved to *Princess Amelia*, and Saumarez was made acting captain of *Preston*, receiving his promotion on 5 August. Saumarez's new command had received damage to her masts and rigging, her boats had been shot to pieces and the hull had also been damaged. One lower bow port had been shot out and various hanging knees, carlings and pieces of spirketing, the complex timbers that made up the hull's construction, were in need of repair. On 23 August 1781, whilst still at sea, attempting to bring *Preston* home, Saumarez was appointed commander of *Tisiphone*, a new design of fireship then fitting out at Sheerness for employment in the Channel Fleet.

On 18 September the North Sea Fleet arrived at the Nore where George III was waiting to meet Parker's returning ships. Having dined together aboard the royal yacht Parker and the King then retired to *Fortitude*'s Great Cabin where the captains and officers of the squadron were waiting to be received. When Saumarez was introduced to the King he enquired whether James was related to the Saumarez who had sailed with Anson on his voyage round the world and his brother, the captain of *Antelope*. Parker replied 'Yes, please your Majesty, he is their nephew, and as brave and as good an officer as either of his uncles.'[2] Recording this conversation in his diary Saumarez noted: 'Not so good an officer as one of them, but better than the other-they were both brave officers.'[3] Protesting over the state of the ships he had been forced to fight in, Parker refused the offer of a knighthood and immediately resigned as commander of the North Sea Fleet.

In instructions dated 23 August 1781 Saumarez had been ordered to Sheerness to take command of *Tisiphone* from Lieutenant John Stone who had been overseeing the coppering and fitting out of the new ship following her launch on 9 May. Whilst *Tisiphone* was a brand-new design the idea of sending in a burning ship to disrupt an enemy fleet was as old as naval warfare itself. In previous centuries the Royal Navy had employed merchantmen in this role but as the technology developed by the late seventeenth century it began building vessels specially designed for the purpose. Whilst outwardly no different than any other sloop employed by the navy these ships featured the extensive use of deck gratings to create drafts throughout the vessel and downward-hinged gunports that would remain open after the tackle had been burned through. Below decks cofferdams protected the masts and prevented them from coming down too early and large sallyports allowed the crew to escape en masse at the last moment. At the start of the war Admiral Richard Kempenfelt had argued that the fireships employed by the navy were slow sailers that could not keep up with the fleets to which they were attached, reducing their usefulness. To address this issue a new class of fireships based on a captured French frigate, *Panthere*, was ordered in November 1779. *Tisiphone* was the first of nine ships built to this design.

Tisiphone's fitting-out completed, the ship sailed from Sheerness to the Nore, where Saumarez received more men from the guard-ship *Conquistador*, an old Spanish ship captured at Havana in 1762. Placed directly under the command of Captain Allen of the 64-gun *Sceptre* Saumarez was instructed to take, burn, sink or destroy any French, Spanish, Dutch or American ship 'he could cope with'[4] should he part company with *Sceptre* and fall in with the enemy.

Sailing from the Nore, *Tisiphone* arrived at Torbay on 17 September. Expecting to find the Channel Fleet at anchor Saumarez was frustrated to discover that Vice Admiral Darby had in fact departed two days earlier. Darby had, however, left instructions for Saumarez to spend a week cruising off the Lizard. At the Lizard Saumarez received further instructions to proceed to Plymouth upon the completion of his cruise. On 29 September, whilst still at sea, Saumarez wrote a report to the Navy Office detailing his first impressions of *Tisiphone*.

I judge it necessary to inform you that HMS under my command is so extremely crank as to require an additional Quantity of Ballast. In a moderate Topgallant breeze she has heeled so much as to require two Reefs in her topsails, and off the Lizard under close reef'd Topsails and Courses it was often requisite for the safety of the Ship to start all the sheets, her Main Deck ports being then entirely under water. She is notwithstanding a very fine ship and I am convinced must sail very well, but her being fitted as a Fireship occasions so much additional weight aloft and her Boats and Booms being necessarily so very high as must make her more tender than she otherwise would be. I flatter myself you will please in consequence of this representation to order twenty or at least 15 Tons of Iron Ballast to be delivered for her use.[5]

It was not unusual for a newly-launched ship to be incorrectly ballasted (by 'crank' Saumarez meant his ship was unstable). Because they were all essentially handmade it would be difficult to gauge how a ship would handle before she entered the water for the first time, even if she were of an existing design. Thankfully *Tisiphone*'s master would have known how much additional ballast would be needed and where to place it to get the ship sailing just as Saumarez would have liked.

From 27 September to 12 October *Tisiphone* was at anchor in Plymouth Sound. The crew were variously employed taking in stores, cleaning the ship, painting her sides and masts and making sails and covers for the ship's boats. Once a week they were employed in junk work, picking apart old pieces of rope to make oakum. On 9 October Saumarez received the fifteen tons of ballast he had earlier requested. Sailing the short distance from Plymouth Sound to Spithead on 12 October, *Tisiphone* dropped anchor again the following day. In mid-November Saumarez was granted a week's leave and he went to London. Visiting the Admiralty there was a chance meeting with Admiral George Rodney. Rodney was about to depart for the West Indies and told Saumarez that he would apply to have him under his command and would take the first opportunity to make him a post captain. Thrilled by this news Saumarez returned to Spithead where he was surprised to see *Royal George*, the flagship of Rear Admiral Kempenfelt (the Channel Fleet's third-in-command) now at anchor. The two men knew each other well; Kempenfelt had served as captain of the fleet aboard *Victory* under Hardy and, like Saumarez, was deeply religious, having several hymns published during late 1770s. On 22 November Saumarez was ordered to join Kempenfelt's squadron of twelve ships of the line that was preparing to sail from Spithead to counter a French threat to the Caribbean.

With Britain now at war against America, France, Spain and Holland and her navy stretched almost to breaking-point, the American War had presented France with an opportunity to regain the Caribbean islands of Grenada, Tobago and Dominica, lost to Britain during the Seven Years War. With their slave based sugar plantations these islands were a source of huge wealth for whatever nation owned them. In late 1781 the British government began receiving reports that a large fleet was assembling at Toulon for an attack on the Caribbean. Admiral de Guichen's fleet was estimated to consist of seventeen ships of the line and 200 transports bearing over 12,000 troops. The French were expected to join up with twelve Spanish ships off Cape St Vincent then proceed to Madeira. At Madeira seven of de Guichen's ships were to separate and sail with the Spanish ships and the bulk of the transports to the Caribbean; three were to head for the East Indies with 3,000 troops to reinforce Admiral de Grasse, whilst the remaining seven were to sail for Cadiz.

Repairs to two of his ships, *Courageux* and *Queen*, along with further weather delays prevented Kempenfelt's squadron from leaving Spithead until 2 December 1781. As they sailed out into the Channel the fast-sailing *Tisiphone* scouted ahead with the squadron's frigates, searching for de Guichen's fleet. At 8.00am on the morning of 12 December, whilst sailing off Ushant, *Tisiphone*'s lookouts spotted a dozen strange sails off to the south-east. These vessels were the French transports; de Guichen's fleet was further off to leeward, still hidden below the horizon. Saumarez signalled *Victory* and Kempenfelt ordered his two-decked ships and frigates to give chase. At 9.30 de Guichen's fleet came into view sailing ahead and to the leeward of their transports and an hour later it began forming a line of battle. Kempenfelt now crowded sail and headed for the gap between the two groups of ships. The French ship *Triomphante* had stayed with the convoy and as the British fleet approached she sailed out in front of the lead British ship *Edgar* and attempted to rake the 74 but Captain Elliot's ship luffed and fired a broadside into *Triomphante*'s stern. Kempenfelt now turned his attention to the unprotected convoy of transports. During the course of the day's action twenty-one transports with around 1,200 troops aboard were captured. Several more had in fact struck but Kempenfelt could not get prize crews aboard them as it was now evening and the weather had turned heavy and squally. Breaking off the action, Kempenfelt gave the order for his squadron, which had become dispersed, to form the order of sailing.

The following morning de Guichen's fleet was spotted off to leeward. Kempenfelt ordered his ships to form the line of battle but realising he was outnumbered he broke away and instead instructed *Agamemnon* and *La Prudente* to shadow the convoy of transports in order to pick off any stragglers and he ordered the fast-sailing *Tisiphone* to Barbados with dispatches for Admiral Hood. As a number of *Tisiphone*'s men had been sent to one of the captured transports to act as a prize crew Saumarez had to wait for men to be sent across from *Victory* before he could leave the fleet, weighing anchor on 15 December. On 25 December the ship hit squally weather and the crew were employed pumping eighteen inches of water from the hold. When *Tisiphone* arrived at Carlisle Bay, Barbados on 28 January 1782 there was no sign of Hood's fleet so Saumarez reported to Captain Stanhope aboard the frigate *Pegasus*. Stanhope instructed Saumarez to sail to St Kitts, advising him to keep well to windward of the French islands of Martinique and Guadeloupe.

At 4.00am on 30 January *Tisiphone*'s lookouts sighted two French ships off to the east. These were the 84-gun *Triomphante* and the 110-gun *Terrible*, detached by de Guichen from his fleet to sail for Martinique. Spotting *Tisiphone* they immediately gave chase but Saumarez's fireship was able to keep well ahead of the two enemy ships and at around 8.00am they broke off the chase and headed off northwards towards Martinique. However, the chase had put such a strain on *Tisiphone*'s masts and rigging that three hours later she lost her main topgallant and fore topmast. One of the midshipmen, Mr Robb, fell to the deck from his lookout position at the fore topmast head but he was thankfully uninjured. Saumarez hove to and *Tisiphone*'s people set about repairing the damaged masts.

Twice frustrated in his attempt to attack Barbados by foul weather and contrary winds, de Grasse had now turned his attention to St Kitts. Situated 360 miles to the north-west of Barbados it was far easier to reach with a prevailing easterly wind. Anchoring in Basseterre Bay on 11 January, de Grasse's 6,000 troops had quickly taken possession of most of the island, forcing General Frazer and his 1,200 men back to Brimstone Hill Fort. Embarking men and provisions at Antigua Hood had now sailed for St Kitts. Taking advantage of a change of the wind he was able to draw de Grasse out to sea and on 24 January drop anchor in his stead, a manoeuvre which Captain Manners of *Resolution* called 'the most masterly I ever saw'.[6]

At 2.00pm on the afternoon of 30 January *Tisiphone* arrived at English Harbour, Antigua and Saumarez went on shore to speak to Commissioner Laforey. Saumarez was told that Hood had arrived at St Kitts and that de Grasse was now cruising to the south of the island. To avoid the French fleet Saumarez would have to approach the island from the north-east, navigating a narrow passage between St Kitts and the smaller island of Nevis rarely attempted by any large ship. Advised to take a pilot on board Saumarez returned to his ship and at 6.30pm

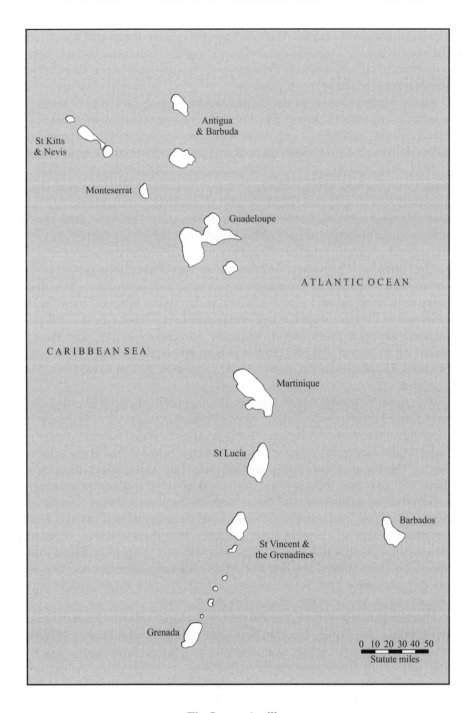

The Lesser Antilles.

Tisiphone weighed anchor. With the pilot to guide them and a man at the chains taking constant soundings *Tisiphone* safely negotiated her way through the dangerous channel and dropped anchor at Basseterre Road around midday on 31 January.

Having safely delivered the dispatches he had carried with him since leaving Kempenfelt's fleet in December, Saumarez was now informed by Hood that the intelligence was of such importance that it would also need to be delivered to Sir Peter Parker at Jamaica. With the French fleet cruising just five miles offshore Saumarez suggested that his new fireship might be of more use to Hood if she remained at St Kitts and that Kempenfelt's dispatches could be sent in another vessel. Hood agreed and *Tisiphone* remained at St Kitts. On 6 February *Tisiphone* made two unsuccessful attempts to cut enemy vessels out from Basseterre Road. In the second attempt, aimed at an enemy brig, her pinnace was lost.

On Thursday 7 February 1782 Saumarez was dining aboard *Ajax* with her captain, Nicholas Charrington, when he found that his presence had been requested aboard Hood's flagship. Excusing himself, Saumarez returned to his boat and, having been rowed across the bay to *Barfleur*, he soon found himself standing in the admiral's Great Cabin being informed by Hood that, due to the lack of any other suitable vessels in his fleet, *Tisiphone* would, that very day, be sailing with dispatches for England.

This time Saumarez could make no argument against leaving the fleet. Once Hood's clerks had finished producing copies of the admiral's dispatches Saumarez returned to his boat and, with 'a heavy heart',[7] ordered the bow man to push off. Just then a pinnace bearing Captain Henry Stanhope of the 74-gun *Russell* pulled up alongside Saumarez's boat. The two men had known one another since their time together commanding galleys in the Sakonnet Passage and when Stanhope discovered that Saumarez was being sent home he offered to exchange commands instead as his health had deteriorated and he was eager to return home. Saumarez accepted Stanhope's offer to speak to Hood and Stanhope went aboard the flagship. A few minutes later he reappeared on the gangway and told Saumarez that Hood's flag-captain had suggested he speak to the admiral in person.

Having listened to Saumarez's proposal Hood remained silent for a while before speaking. 'Captain Saumarez,' he said 'you know not how much I wish to serve you, Captain Stanhope shall go home as he desires and you shall have command of the *Russell*.'[8] Ten minutes earlier Saumarez had been preparing himself for a return home and an extended period 'on the beach', now he was the post captain of a Third Rate ship of the line.

Chapter 4

Russell and the Battle of the Saintes: February 1782 – September 1782

For much of the early eighteenth century British ship design had lagged behind that of her rivals on the Continent, France and Spain. Obstinacy and blind faith in outmoded ideas had doomed the Royal Navy to be equipped with poorly-designed ships. Ships such as the three-deckers of 80 guns that were unstable in all but the calmest of seas, forcing their lower-deck gun ports to remain shut, or the cramped two-decked 70s, so small that they could not carry guns of any decent size. But in August 1755, the old Surveyor of the Navy, Sir Joseph Allen went mad and was forced to step down. Within three weeks his replacement, Thomas Slade, had drawn up a new design based on a captured French prize that offered the best compromise between size and firepower, the two-decked 74-gun ship of the line, a class of ship that would become the bedrock of the navy. Over the years Slade modified his original design, *Dublin*, numerous times and in 1761 he introduced the Modified *Ramillies* class. Five ships were constructed to this design, *Russell* being the second. Built at the Royal Navy dockyard at Deptford her keel was laid down in June 1761 and she was launched in November 1764.

At 168ft 6in in length and with a burthen weight of 1,642 tons *Russell* was almost 60ft longer and over 1,200 tons heavier than Saumarez's previous command, *Tisiphone*. At a cost of around £32,800, including fitting out, she had also been over three times more expensive and had taken two years longer to build. Of course, what really set *Russell* apart from *Tisiphone* were the fifty-six 32-pounder and 18-pounder long guns arrayed along her upper and lower gundecks that, at 781 imperial pounds, gave *Russell* a broadside weight sixteen times more powerful than that of *Tisiphone*.

On 9 February an excited Saumarez had written home to his mother: 'It will give all my friends pleasure to hear that Sir Samuel Hood has appointed me to command the *Russell*. My most sanguine views could scarcely extend so far as getting at this time so fine a ship. This fortunate event goes far to compensate my absence from home … it will require a short time before I can be perfectly established, I will however venture to say the *Russell* will at all times do her part as far as far as depends on me.'[1] Although Saumarez had been disappointed not to have been mentioned in despatches following the Second Battle of Ushant he knew that Kempenfelt had sent a letter of recommendation to Hood and was certain this had contributed to his recent advancement. Two days previous he had been in charge of fifty-five men, now he was responsible for the safety, health and welfare of almost 550 men. Worryingly for Saumarez, when he took over command of *Russell* from Stanhope he found her crew in a near-mutinous state, with ominous reports of shot-rolling, crewmembers rolling shot along the decks in the dead of night as a menacing demonstration of their discontent towards their officers. Compared to some of his more brutal, less enlightened colleagues, Saumarez was remarkably sympathetic in his treatment of the ordinary sailor. He kept regular rest days and insisted that his officers treat the men with respect. Whenever possible he avoided flogging and would rather appeal to a sailor's sense of duty and responsibility than resort to violence. However, *Russell*'s crew would need careful handling and Saumarez would need all his experience to get the ship operating efficiently. Saumarez quickly asserted his authority over his new command, giving seamen Whittey and Barber twelve lashes each for theft on 11 February. Theft was considered to be one of the worst crimes aboard a ship as it bred mistrust amongst the crew.

On 12 February General Frazer, the besieged British army commander on St Kitts, finally surrendered. There no longer being any reason to remain at the island, Hood decided to quit St Kitts and deliver his fleet to Rodney who was sailing to Barbados with reinforcements from England. On the evening of 14 February Hood summoned all his captains aboard *Barfleur* and announced his intention of quitting the island that night. Hood's captains synchronized their watches and at 11.00pm the ships cut their cables and slipped out of the anchorage under the cover of darkness, evading de Grasse's Fleet. On 19 February Hood arrived at Antigua where the fleet took on provisions. On 25 February, whilst still off Antigua, he met Rodney who had sailed north from Barbados. The following day de Grasse sailed for Fort Royal, Martinique.

Having sailed south in an unsuccessful attempt to stop de Grasse from returning to Martinique, Rodney now took the fleet to St Lucia, so as to be in a position to defend both that island and Barbados from French attack. Arriving there on 1 March the ships took on water and provisions and the sick were landed. Soon after their arrival they were joined by three more ships from England, *Duke, Warrior* and *Valiant*. On 4 March, whilst anchored off Carenage in the north-west of the island, the weather turned squally and *Russell* struck a submerged rock, damaging her rudder and stern, the force of the impact throwing several seamen from their hammocks. Saumarez weighed anchor, moved further out to sea and signalled for assistance. The following day the ship was towed into port and her rudder was sent ashore to be repaired. Between *Russell* dropping anchor on 6 March and returning to sea on 11 March fifteen seamen deserted the ship.

On 18 March the fleet put to sea and cruised off Martinique in the hope of intercepting a convoy of transports that was expected to arrive from France. However, by sailing close to Guadalupe and Dominique the convoy escaped detection and reached Martinique unmolested. The fleet returned to St Lucia and Rodney went on shore. On the morning of 8 April the frigate *Andromache* signalled that the French were putting to sea. De Grasse eventually emerged from port with a fleet consisting of thirty-three ships of the line and a convoy of 123 transports carrying 9,000 troops. The French admiral was headed for St Domingo, where he planned to join up with twelve Spanish ships of the line and 15,000 troops for a joint French and Spanish assault on Jamaica. Rodney made the signal for all boats to return to the fleet and for his ships to weigh anchor. By late morning the British fleet had cleared Gros Islet Bay and Rodney gave the signal for a general chase. His fleet of thirty-six ships was divided into three sections; the Red Division, commanded by Hood, Rodney's White Division and the section in which *Russell* was sailing, Rear Admiral Drake's Blue Division. With the advantage of the Trade Wind de Grasse managed to say ahead of Rodney, during the night the lights of the French ships were clearly visible as they shepherded the convoy of troopships. By the morning of 9 April both fleets were to the north-west of Dominica. Around fifteen of de Grasse's ships had reached the waters between Dominica and a small group of islands south of Guadeloupe known as the Iles des Saintes whilst the remainder of his fleet and the transports were becalmed near St Rupert's Bay, Dominica. Rodney's fleet, off to the south, was also becalmed but around 7.30am the wind picked up and the British van, led by Hood, began to push northwards. Ahead of them were two French ships that had become detached from the rest of their fleet, the 80-gun *Auguste*, flagship of Admiral de Bougainville, and the 75-gun *Zele*. Rodney had not yet given the signal to engage the enemy and by picking up the same breeze as Hood's ships *Auguste* and *Zele* were able to rejoin their own fleet unmolested. At 8.30am de Grasse ordered his ships in the

Saintes channel to tack and head south towards Hood's division. After an initial encounter in which only long-range shots were fired, at 10.00am the French van, led by de Grasse's second-in-command, the Marquis de Vaudreuil, engaged Hood's division. *Barfleur* was heavily engaged and three other ships received severe damage to their rigging. Tacking and wearing round, Vaudreuil attacked the British van once more. During this latter engagement Rodney's centre moved up and engaged the enemy whilst the Drake's division remained becalmed and took no part in the action. At around 1.45pm the British rear finally got up at which point de Grasse disengaged and Rodney ordered a ceasefire. By the end of the action all the ships of Rodney's van and centre had been engaged with *Royal Oak*, *Montagu* and *Alfred* suffering the worst damage. *Alfred* had led the British line until the arrival of *Royal Oak* and her captain, William Bayne, had bled to death after his leg had been shot off. One French ship, *Caton*, was so badly damaged she had to leave the fleet and sail to Guadeloupe to be repaired.

During the night Rodney reversed the order of sailing so that his ships with the heaviest damage were in the rear of the line whilst the least damaged, *Russell* included, were in the van. Whilst Rodney spent the next day repairing the damage to his ships de Grasse was busy beating to windward in the Saintes channel. On the night of 10 April *Zele* collide with *Jason*. *Jason* had to sail to Guadeloupe for repair and *Zele*, now minus her fore topmast, began to drop astern of the other French ships. With Rodney's ships approaching his straggler from leeward late on 11 April de Grasse was forced to turn back and defend *Zele*. At 2.30am on 12 April, *Zele*, captained by the inexperienced Chevalier de Gras Preville, was involved in another collision, this time with *Ville de Paris*. Having lost her bowsprit and foremast *Zele* was forced to return to Guadeloupe under tow from the frigate *Astrée*. Hood now detached *Monarch*, *Valiant*, *Centaur* and *Belliqueux* to give chase to the two ships. Once again De Grasse had to take his fleet to leeward in order to defend *Zele*. Hemmed in, with Rodney's fleet one side and the Iles des Saintes the other, a fleet battle was inevitable.

Recalling his chasing ships at 7.00am, Rodney ordered his fleet to form line of battle one cable's length apart. At 7.38am the flagship signalled that *Russell* was out of position. Two minutes later Rodney signalled for the fleet to close in line of battle. Sailing past the French on the opposite tack the battle began at 7.45am when the lead British ship, *Arrogant*, engaged the ninth ship in the French line. The French followed their usual tactic of firing high into the British ships masts and rigging and as a result there were few casualties. At 7.50am *Russell* backed her mainsails and engaged several enemy ships in passing at close range.

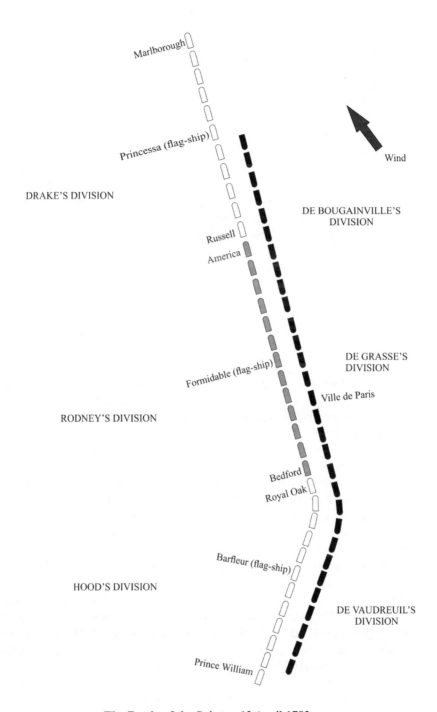

Marlborough

Princessa (flag-ship)

DRAKE'S DIVISION

DE BOUGAINVILLE'S
DIVISION

Russell

America

DE GRASSE'S
DIVISION

Formidable (flag-ship)

Ville de Paris

RODNEY'S DIVISION

Bedford

Royal Oak

Barfleur (flag-ship)

HOOD'S DIVISION

DE VAUDREUIL'S
DIVISION

Prince William

Wind

The Battle of the Saintes, 12 April 1782.

Around ten minutes later de Grasse ordered his leading ships to bear away from the variable winds off Dominica and this resulted in both fleets developing a dog-leg. De Grasse's fleet was also sailing in reverse order with de Bougainville's squadron in the van and the squadron led by de Vaudreuil (de Grasse's second-in-command) in the rear.

At 9.00 am, having passed the last ship in the French line, Saumarez's ship luffed up and he backed the main topsail. In the distance he could see the hulk of a French ship, totally dismasted, rolling on the swells. *Russell*'s mizzen mast was severely damaged, so her sails were unbent and her topgallant mast and yards were sent down onto the deck. The ship's rigging was patched up and *Russell*'s main and mizzen topsail yards were fished (a temporary repair using splints of wood). Powder was redistributed around the ship and by 9.30am the decks were once again cleared for action.

Sailing directly astern of *Russell*, Captain Thompson's 64-gun *America* now wore out of formation in order to sail back down the French line and engage the enemy to windward. The squadron's sailing order having been reversed, Saumarez was 'glad to have the experience of an old experienced officer'[2] to guide him and he quickly followed Drake's second-in-command out of the line, setting his ship's fore topsail to save his damaged main topsail yard from additional strain. Finding there was no signal from the flagship (it would be another hour before Drake gave the order to wear and tack), Thompson rejoined the squadron but *Russell*, now to the windward of the French, continued on down towards the centre of de Grasse's fleet. At around 11.30am the wind, which had been blowing from the north, changed direction and began blowing from the south. With the wind now against them, the French were thrown into confusion and a gap was created in de Grasse's line through which *Formidable*, *Namur*, *St Albans*, *Canada*, *Repulse* and *Ajax* all sailed. Having passed through this gap, Rodney was surprised to see one of Drake's ships already engaged with the enemy to windward. Other gaps in the line also appeared, Captain Gardner's *Duke* sailed through one unsupported and further south Hood and the remaining twelve ships of his division also broke through to windward. Attempting to regain some control over his ships at around 1.30pm de Grasse ordered his fleet to form a line on the port tack, but his signals were largely obscured by smoke and went unanswered. Their cohesion lost, the French now began to drift away in groups or individual ships to the south-west. At 2.20pm Saumarez saw Rodney signal *Royal Oak* to take the dismasted French ship he had spotted earlier under tow. *Russell* now beat to quarters. At 3.40pm she engaged three ships of de Bougainville's squadron sailing on the opposite tack in passing then headed off towards de Grasse's flagship. At around 6.00pm *Russell* ran under *Ville de Paris*'s stern, raking the French three-decker before firing a series of broadsides against her ornate but poorly-protected larboard quarter. *Russell* was soon joined by *Barfleur* and several other British ships. By 6.30pm *Ville de Paris* was surrounded by no less than nine British ships of the line with no means of escape. Her masts and rigging had been badly shot up, there was no rudder to steer her by and her powder was running so low it was now being handed out by teaspoon. At the sight of another British ship, *Formidable*, bearing down on her, de Grasse's flagship finally hauled down her colours and surrendered.

By the end of the battle five French ships were in British hands, *Ville de Paris*, *Glorieux*, attacked by *Formidable* and *Canada* as they passed through the enemy line, *Caesar*, dismasted and in flames (she blew up around midnight), *Hector*, also dismasted, and *Ardent*, taken by Rodney's centre. The British had lost 274 killed and 853 wounded. Two captains, William Bayne of *Alfred* and William Blair of *Anson*, were now dead and one, Robert Manners, captain of *Resolution*, would die later from his wounds. Saumarez reported ten men killed and twenty-nine injured aboard *Russell*. He would later decline an offer from *Russell*'s lieutenants and ward-room officers to be presented with a sword in recognition of his contribution to the battle. French losses were never given. However, along with six dead captains they were estimated to include 15,000 sailors and soldiers who had either been killed, wounded or taken prisoner, of these nearly 300 had been killed or wounded aboard *Ville de Paris*. The day following the battle was spent making repairs to *Russell*. Whilst the sailmakers prepared cots for the wounded, the crew washed down the bloodied decks and repaired the rigging, working alongside the carpenters who were busy fishing *Russell*'s wounded masts, repairing the boats and plugging the numerous shot holes in her hull.

Collecting his ships, Rodney sailed north in the hope of discovering whereabouts of the French fleet, now commanded by Vaudreuil. Off Guadeloupe the British were becalmed for three days, which allowed repairs to those ships worst damaged by the recent action to be effected. Arriving off St Domingo's southern coast on 26 April Rodney left Hood to cruise to the north of the island whilst he went with the fleet's most damaged ships to Jamaica. On 29 April Rodney arrived at Port Royal and went ashore suffering from ill health. It was now decided that Vice Admiral Sir Peter Parker, the commander of the Jamaica squadron, would take *Sandwich* (with de Grasse aboard) *Intrepid*, *Ajax*, *Lowestoffe* and *Pomona* and sail with the next convoy of merchant ships bound for England. *Russell* and *Shrewsbury* were too badly damaged to sail with this group of ships and would follow with the next convoy once they had been made safe for travel across the Atlantic. Parker sailed from Jamaica on 22 May but just three days out *Ajax* sprung a leak and had to return. *Russell* was ordered to take her place but Saumarez's ship was in no state for a quick return to sea. Her topmasts had been removed along with her shattered mizzen mast and she had barely any stores aboard. However, after three days of furious activity the crew had the ship repaired and ready to sail. Setting out from Barbados with 300 French prisoners in her hold, *Russell* eventually found Parker's squadron and took *Ajax*'s place alongside the other ships returning to England.

Russell arrived at the Downs on 29 July 1782. From there she sailed to Chatham where she was to be paid off. Saumarez received permission to go ashore but there was a near-mutiny when the crew, most of whom had spent almost three years away at sea, discovered they were being transferred to another ship bound for the East Indies. Saumarez returned to the ship and, after lengthy discussions, persuaded the men to return to duty. *Russell* was finally paid off on 24 September and Saumarez travelled to London to visit Earl Howe who confirmed his commission as a post captain. Now a captain without a ship to command Saumarez returned to his native Guernsey on half pay. He would not return to sea for another eleven years.

Chapter 5

Half-Pay in Guernsey:
September 1782 – March 1793

Now a post captain with an already distinguished service career, when Saumarez returned home in September 1782 he suddenly found himself somewhat of a local celebrity amongst the small island community, in demand for dinners, balls and other social gatherings. Saumarez was also an acquaintance of Prince William (later King William IV), a fellow officer in the Royal Navy, also adding to his standing amongst the elite of Guernsey. The prince visited the island twice, first in 1785 as a young lieutenant aboard *Hebe*, then two years later as captain of *Pegasus*. During this latter visit a dinner was held aboard *Pegasus* to which Saumarez and his brothers were invited. Later there was a grand ball in the recently-opened Assembly Rooms attended by some 200 guests.

Britain and France were now at peace, but how long this would last no one could say. Whilst Britain was blessed with deep-water ports and sheltered anchorages such as Falmouth, Plymouth and Portsmouth on her south coast, France had no such ports on her side of the Channel from which large fleets could operate. In 1776, just prior to her entry into the American War of Independence, work was begun on modernising the port of Cherbourg, situated across the Channel from Portsmouth. This work involved the sinking of two lines of massive 65-foot high cones to form a breakwater. The work continued through the 1780s and in June 1786 Louis XVI made his one and only trip away from Paris to see the sinking of one of these large stone-filled wooden cones. Eager to impress the English with this feat of Gallic engineering, a group of Royal Navy officers were invited to join Louis in his tour of Cherbourg. Saumarez, with his expert knowledge of French coastal waters and his fluent French, was an obvious choice to accompany Louis on his visit. Having watched the sinking of the cone and a subsequent naval review, Saumarez and his fellow officers accompanied

Louis and his ministers to Le Havre where they had a seat at the King's dinner table.

On his return to Guernsey Saumarez immersed himself in island affairs. An enthusiastic supporter of the Church, he was also beginning to be involved in charitable works. All this was interrupted by the Dutch Crisis of July 1787 when opponents of the House of Orange gained French support, threatening Britain's interests in the region. There was a sudden naval mobilisation and Lord Howe gave Saumarez command of the 32-gun frigate *Ambuscade*, then fitting out at Plymouth. However before *Ambuscade* was ready for sea the situation in Holland had resolved itself (the sudden mobilisation had caused France to back down) and Saumarez returned to Guernsey.

Following a lengthy courtship, on 8 October 1788 Saumarez married his first cousin, Martha Le Marchant, the pretty twenty-year-old daughter of William and Mary Le Marchant. Through his marriage Saumarez acquired Saumarez Park and became Seigneur of the Fief Saumarez. At the centre of the estate, one of the largest on the island, was a two storey granite building with single storey wings either side that was later enlarged by Saumarez's descendants. The fiefs were landholdings granted to the Sausmarez by the Dukes of Normandy in the eleventh century that had subsequently passed to the Le Marchants, a wealthy family of wool merchants. With tax paying tenants Saumarez now had the security of a small but regular income. A few days after his wedding Saumarez wrote to his brother, Richard. 'It is needless to attempt giving you any idea of my joy at this occasion. The abundant blessings which Providence is pleased to pour down on me, who am ever unworthy the least of its favours, makes my heart glow with boundless gratitude and love … to have the power of making her happy who has ever been the joy and delight of my soul, far surpasses all that I had ever formed of felicity in this world.'[1]

On 9 October 1789, almost exactly a year after their wedding, Martha gave birth to a baby boy, James. Saumarez had just settled into his new role as father when, in the spring of 1790, there was another international crisis, this time between Britain and Spain. The Nootka Sound Crisis or Spanish Armament, as it was also known, arose out of the seizure by the Spanish of a British fur-trading settlement in Nootka Sound, Vancouver Island, in May 1789. The government having decided to send a sizeable fleet to back up its claims in the region, the navy now began a mobilisation that would see twenty-nine ships of the line fitted out for service.

On 6 May Saumarez was placed in command of the 64-gun *Raisonnable*, fitting out at Chatham. During his absence from Martha the couple wrote to one another at least twice a week, sometimes every other day. Martha's letters to Saumarez were full of society gossip, family news and concerns over household management. Learning of a chance meeting in London between Saumarez and a Miss Pierce who had turned down an earlier offer of marriage from her husband, Martha declared, 'She claims a portion of my esteem & regard from her having once possessed so great a share as yours – I sincerely wish the new connection she has formed may be equal to her merit, though it can never equal, much less make amends for the happiness she rejected'.[2] In another letter Martha wrote to tell her husband she had, with some difficulty, found a servant with good references who was, unfortunately, rather ugly, a fact she though he would not mind. Saumarez wrote back, light-heartedly admonishing Martha for thinking him 'so indifferent to beauty in our servants'.[3]

With France in the grip of revolution Spain found herself unsupported in her territorial ambitions for North America. Alone, her navy did not have the resources to match the large fleet assembling at Portsmouth and in October 1790 the Spanish government backed down and her claims to territory in North America were abandoned. On 20 October *Raisonnable* was paid off and Saumarez returned home. Saumarez and Martha soon developed a pattern of spending the summers at Ryde on the Isle of Wight and winters in Bath. On 7 December 1792 Martha gave birth to a girl, Mary, at Princes Buildings, Bath. Two months later war was declared between Britain and France and by March 1793 Saumarez was back at sea.

Chapter 6

Crescent versus *Reunion*: March 1793 – November 1793

On 14 July 1789 the Paris mob had stormed the Bastille, executing the prison governor and parading his head on a spike through the city streets. A month later the newly-formed National Assembly issued the Declaration of the Rights of Man and of the Citizen. For several blood-drenched years France was engulfed in a violent revolution during which tens of thousands fell victim to the guillotine. Britain, with its constitutional monarchy, had broadly supported the revolution but when Louis XVI was executed on 21 January 1793 the government responded by expelling the French ambassador. Eleven days later France declared war against Holland and Britain. Britain, the Netherlands, Spain, Prussia and Austria now formed an alliance against France, the First Coalition.

At the outbreak of hostilities the recent 'Spanish Armament' mobilisation meant that the Royal Navy had twenty-six ships of the line and around thirty frigates in commission. Eighty-seven ships of the line were laid up 'in Ordinary' and there were a further 191 unrated vessels of various descriptions in service; sloops, brigs, schooners, fireships and bomb vessels. By the end of the year the number of ships of the line in commission would rise to eighty-five. Across the Channel the Marine Nationale possessed 246 vessels, which included eighty-six ships of the line and seventy-eight frigates divided between the fleets at Brest, Rochefort, Lorient and Toulon. In addition there were said to be a further thirty ships in the process of being built.

Once war had been declared the Channel Fleet was dispatched to blockade Brest and Lord Hood's Fleet was sent out into the Mediterranean to protect trade and to assist the Sardinians in any way possible. It was also known that there was serious opposition to the revolution in the south of France and there was a possibility of capturing Toulon, Marseilles or even Corsica.

On 24 January 1793 Saumarez was appointed captain of the 36-gun frigate *Crescent*, bringing to an end his extended period 'on the beach'. At the same time he received orders placing him under Commodore Hyde Parker, commander-in-chief of the Channel Fleet. For his first lieutenant Saumarez had requested the services of George Parker, the nephew of Admiral Sir Peter Parker. Beginning his book time aboard *Barfleur* aged just six, Parker, like Saumarez, had served throughout the American War. Joining Parker aboard *Crescent* were Lieutenants Charles Otter and Peter Rye. Little is known about Otter but Rye had first sailed aboard *Winchelsea* and had recently returned from a year-long voyage to New South Wales aboard the troopship *Gorgon*, delivering convicts to Britain's distant colony and returning with ten mutineers from Captain Bligh's *Bounty*. Rye's patron was Earl Spencer and the Rye's and the Le Marchant's were also acquaintances. (Rye's grandmother knew Saumarez's father-in-law and his parents, Robert and Hannah, were following Saumarez's career closely.)

Travelling from Bath to Portsmouth Saumarez called in on Rye's father to discuss his son's recent promotion and the shocking news coming out of France that Louis XVI had been executed. On 28 January Saumarez arrived in Portsmouth and he went aboard his new ship. Saumarez's commission was read out and he was introduced to his warrant officers. *Crescent*'s sailing master was William Warren, the boatswain, in charge of discipline aboard ship, was Peter Sadler and Saumarez's new surgeon was William Nepecker. His midshipmen were William Bamber, Thomas Falaise, William Lovick, Joseph Marrett and Thomas Mansell. Having received a host of applications from friends, family members and other acquaintances, Saumarez also had eight 'young gentlemen' aboard ship whose respectability he had to vouch for. These included his own cousin, Philip Dumaresq. The surgeon, Nepecker, had arrived on board ship on 16 March with his seventeen-year-old son, Frederick, in tow and he was entered in *Crescent*'s books as a surgeon's assistant. *Crescent*'s remaining standing officers, the gunner, Michael Alyward, and the ship's carpenter, Jonathan Rundell, were also employing their own children as assistants, the fourteen-year-old Jason Alyward and the two Rundell boys, Nicholas, aged thirteen and the eleven-year-old Jonathan. As standing officers, who remained with the ship whilst it was in Ordinary, it is highly likely that the gunner and carpenter's wives were amongst the several women who were aboard ship as well, although their names were not listed on *Crescent*'s muster.

Whilst there was a glut of officers in the navy, finding enough ratings to properly man a ship remained a problem. However, soon after the outbreak of war several towns had begun offering bounties to volunteers (three guineas for an able seaman, two guineas for an ordinary seaman, one guinea for a landsman) and on 24 February twenty-three volunteers from Exmouth were sent aboard *Crescent*. These men joined around eighty volunteers from Guernsey, including sixteen men who had arrived aboard *Tisiphone* on 28 January. The ship also received twelve seamen from *St George*, twenty men from *Drake* and nineteen seamen from *Edgar*. On 4 March a detachment of thirty-four marines from *Brunswick* led by Lieutenant Thomas Oldfield arrived aboard ship, helping to bring *Crescent* up to a compliment of 270 men. The large number of men volunteering from Guernsey is worthy of note as Channel Islanders traditionally had an aversion to the Royal Navy, preferring instead to serve aboard merchant ships or the more lucrative privateers that operated out of the island. It is hard to say what the men from Guernsey signing up to serve aboard *Crescent* were more attracted to, sailing with a fellow Guernseyman famed across the island for his heroics in the last war, or the share of the prize money that Saumarez's heavy frigate might earn capturing enemy vessels.

For nearly a century it had been the policy of the Navy Board to order the smallest vessels possible for each rate in order to keep construction and operating costs down. However, alarmed by the appearance of larger, more powerfully-armed French frigates during the American War, in October 1778 the Admiralty had requested that the Navy Board stop the construction of 32-gun frigates and instead build vessels of 36 or 38 guns with a main deck armament of twenty-eight 12-pounders (the same as carried aboard the larger French frigates). The Navy Board had clearly already given this idea some thought for they responded by suggesting that it would in fact be possible to construct frigates of 36 or 38 guns strong enough to mount 18-pounders. They also sent the Admiralty drafts for two such ships, a 36 designed by Sir John Williams and a 38 designed by Sir Edward Hunt, the joint Surveyors of the Navy. These vessels gave 50–60 per cent more broadside weight than the existing 32-gun frigates, and were also 170–240 tons heavier. With full lines and deep hulls, they were weatherly and manoeuvrable ships, if not particularly fast for frigates. The first 38 ordered by the Admiralty was named *Minerva* and the first 36 *Flora*. *Flora*'s sisters were *Thalia*, *Crescent* and *Romulus*. Both *Minerva* and *Flora* were built at Royal Dockyards to iron out any problems with their designs; subsequent vessels were built by private contractors. Ordered in August 1781, *Crescent* was built by John Nowlan and Thomas Calhoun at Bursledon dockyards, Southampton. Her keel was laid down in November 1781 and she was launched in October 1784. With ornate frieze paintings along her upperworks and intricate carvings around her bow and stern *Crescent* was an attractive-looking vessel, a last hurrah before the Admiralty ordered that both frieze paintings and carvings be phased out to keep costs down. For the next five years *Crescent* remained in Ordinary, finally being commissioned in May 1790 in response to the Nootka Sound Crisis,

On 1 March Saumarez reported *Crescent* ready for sea. Having received instructions to sail to the Channel Islands in company with the brig-sloop *Drake*, *Cockatrice* and three troopships, *Crescent* left Spithead on 9 March and anchored in St Peter Port the following day. Wind conditions prevented the troopships from continuing on to Jersey until 14 March when Saumarez was able to send them under the escort of the cutter *Liberty*. Receiving intelligence that a French brig had been seen to the north of Guernsey off the Casketts, *Crescent* and *Drake* got under way. Pushing through the Race of Alderney during the night, the brig was spotted the following morning off Cherbourg. Having taken the brig, a vessel of about 100 tons loaded with salt for Le Havre, Saumarez ordered *Cockatrice* to escort it back to England. Two more vessels, a brig and a galliot, were now spotted off to the north-west and Saumarez ordered *Drake* to give chase. Later that afternoon a cutter arrived with information from Governor Le Mesurier that the French intended to attack Alderney. Responding to Le Mesurier's request for assistance, *Crescent* cruised off the west coast of Alderney for several days until Saumarez was sure that the attack had been foiled. However, anchoring off St Peter Port on 18 March, Saumarez received more reports of intended French attacks on Jersey and Alderney and so *Crescent* remained at Guernsey for a further week. On 23 March five men deserted ship. Two days later *Crescent* sailed for Spithead where she had six 18-pounder carronades added to her quarterdeck and forecastle.

In April *Crescent* was ordered to escort a convoy of troop transports to Ireland and to return with two regiments for the garrison at Guernsey. *Crescent* sailed from Spithead on 13 April and arrived off Cork four days later. Whilst Saumarez waited for the transports to assemble he exercised his men at the long guns and with the small arms. He also took the opportunity to go ashore and purchase a cabinet for Martha. On 30 April *Crescent* departed Cork in company with four transports bearing the 26th and 27th Regiments of Foot and another vessel with 180 volunteers for the navy. On 1 May, whilst at anchor off Waterford, two of the transports got into difficulty and collided, one vessel losing her bowsprit, the other her mizzen mast. Once repairs had been made the convoy set off, arriving off the Lizard on 4 May. Saumarez now sent the vessel carrying the navy volunteers to Falmouth and continued on with the troopships to Guernsey. Returning from the Channel Islands in company with *Suffolk* and a convoy of twenty-five transports carrying French prisoners, on 17 May, *Crescent* subsequently dropped anchor at Spithead. On 22 May Saumarez was ordered to take the 28-gun *Hind*, Captain Cochrane, under his command and cruise off the south-west coast of Ireland for the protection of inbound and outbound trade. On 29 May *Crescent* and *Hind* were joined by the sloop *Spitfire* and on 4 June Saumarez's squadron captured the *Espoir*, a French privateer of 12 guns. Forty French seamen were taken aboard *Crescent* and the remaining eighty prisoners were sent to *Hind* and *Spitfire*. A petty officer and twelve seamen were sent across to the prize which was escorted back to Britain by *Hind*. On 22 June there was further success when *Crescent* captured a privateer of 10 guns out of Brest, *Le Club de Cherbourg*, that had been harassing British shipping, taking four vessels on her previous cruise. *Le Club de Cherbourg*'s crew of twenty-eight men were taken on board *Crescent* and a prize crew sent across to the privateer. On 25 June *Crescent* returned to St Peter Port where *Saumarez* found *Hind* and *Espoir* at anchor. Saumarez was able to grab a few precious hours ashore with his family before *Crescent* sailed for Spithead that same day.

On 4 July Saumarez was ordered to take a quantity of specie aboard *Crescent* and to sail to Plymouth. Arriving at Plymouth on 11 July Saumarez picked up a convoy of merchantmen which he escorted to the Downs. Following his recent successful cruises, on 18 July Saumarez was given the command of a squadron that included the frigates *Concorde*, Thomas Wells, and *Thames*, James Cotes and was ordered to sail 300 nautical miles to the west of the Scilly Isles from where he was to provide protection for the homeward-bound trade convoys from Jamaica and the Leeward Islands. Now in command of a powerful cruising squadron Saumarez was hopeful of capturing a clutch of prizes, or better still, that he might be involved in a similar action to that fought between a British and French frigate earlier in the year. The dramatic capture of *Cleopatre* by *Nymphe* off Brest on 17 June had caused a great deal of excitement within the service and had seen her captain, Edward Pellew, rewarded with a knighthood.

Crescent sailed from Spithead on 26 July but when Saumarez arrived on station he was disappointed to discover that the convoys which he had been sent to protect had already arrived safely in port. Having been ordered to remain at sea until 20 August, Saumarez continued to patrol the western approaches to the Channel, but on 17 August, just days before they were due to return home, the squadron was caught in a storm off the Scilly Isles during which *Concorde* parted company, *Thames* lost her bowsprit and *Crescent* split her main yard and lost her main topmast, damages that forced both ships to abandon their cruise and return to port. *Crescent* had not been out of the water since June 1790 and it was now decided to take the opportunity to give Saumarez's frigate a long overdue repair. On 25 August *Crescent* entered the dry dock at Portsmouth. Saumarez took an apartment at Ryde for the duration of the refit and sent for Martha and the children, James and Mary. It was during this period that the couple's next child, Martha, was conceived. *Crescent* spent seven weeks in dry dock. Her masts were repaired, her rigging renewed and replaced and her hull cleaned. With his ship finally ready for sea again on 5 October Saumarez found that she was now thirteen men short of her full compliment. Arguing that *Crescent*'s masts and yards were the same as for a 38-gun frigate he asked for more men but this request was turned down.

By late 1793 anger at the execution of Louis XVI had turned into a Royalist revolt in the staunchly Catholic Vendée region of western France. Following a failed attempt to take the city of Nantes on 17 October the Royalist army had marched north, then divided. Whilst part of the army blockaded Saint-Malo in Brittany, the remainder marched further west round the coast to Granville. On 18 October, *Crescent* was ordered to sail to the Channel Islands with dispatches for the local army commanders then to cruise off Saint-Malo to look in at the French port.

Before sailing Saumarez had heard reports of two French frigates operating out of Cherbourg, one of these ships, *Reunion*, was attacking British shipping under the cover of darkness before returning to port with her prizes the following morning. Eager to put to sea as soon as possible, *Crescent* weighed anchor on the evening of 19 October and by nightfall had cleared St Helens on the Isle of Wight. By early the next morning the ship had crossed the Channel and was roughly nine miles off the lighthouse at Cape Barfleur, sailing on the larboard tack. Shortly after dawn a lookout aboard *Crescent* spotted two vessels, *Reunion* accompanied by a cutter, approaching from seaward. The wind, which had been blowing from the west had now switched to the south, hampering *Reunion*'s efforts at returning to Cherbourg and allowing *Crescent* to gain the weather gauge and get between the French vessels and the coast. *Reunion* and the cutter approached to within two miles of *Crescent* before they discovered they had a British frigate to windward. They immediately crowded sail and tacked in an effort to escape. The cutter fled back to Cherbourg with sweeps and sails but *Crescent*, fresh out of port, her rigging taught and her hull scraped clean, quickly chased *Reunion* down and by 10.30am was within pistol-shot of the French frigate's larboard quarter.

When the action began the two ships were roughly five miles from the French coast where a large group of spectators had gathered to watch the early-morning spectacle of a ship to ship battle. Saumarez had ordered his men to fire at *Reunion*'s rudder whilst the French gun crews followed their training and aimed their fire at *Crescent*'s masts and rigging. *Reunion*'s rudder was soon disabled and she lost both her main topsail yard and her fore yard. However, *Reunion*'s broadsides had succeeded in bringing down *Crescent*'s fore topsail yard and fore topmast which both fell over the starboard side of the ship. Saumarez had been maintaining his ship's position by backing and filling his mizzen topsail but with her fore topsail gone *Crescent* was turned into the wind and came to, all her sails aback. In a display of superb ship-handling skills Saumarez now brailed up *Crescent*'s mizzen sail and backed his remaining square sails. *Crescent* quickly wore round on her heel and with the wind once again behind her slipped beneath *Reunion*'s stern and starboard quarter. In passing under *Reunion*'s stern it was noticed that her colours were no longer visible and Saumarez assumed that the French captain had struck. However, *Reunion*'s flag had merely been shot away and she fired another broadside at *Crescent* as Saumarez's ship came alongside. With *Crescent*'s larboard gun crews fresh into the action the battle was rejoined with increased British

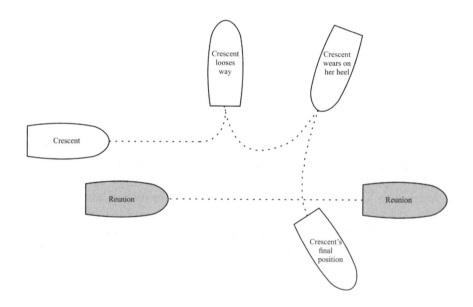

***Crescent* versus *Reunion*, 20 October 1793.**

vigour. Finally, at 12.30pm, *Reunion*'s officers began waving their hats in the air to indicate that their ship had struck.

By the end of the battle thirty-four of *Reunion*'s crew of 321 had been killed and a further eighty-four wounded. One shot had entered her starboard quarter and travelled the length of the gundeck, killing and maiming twenty-one men before exiting the ship through the larboard bow. *Reunion*'s stern was shattered and her rudder head and wheel had been shot away. According to a report published in *The Times* shortly after her arrival in port, '*Reunion*'s sails [were] so peppered, that they can be converted to nothing but paper … the ceilings of the wardroom, etc. entirely covered with blood, and the whole of the main-deck has the appearance of a slaughter-house shocking to look at.'[1]

Apart from the loss of her fore-topsail yard and fore topmast there had been no other damage of any note to *Crescent*. One shot had struck the forecastle apron, setting fire to the priming of the 9-pounder on the opposite side of the deck. The gun had discharged, firing at some gunboats coming out of Cherbourg. Remarkably there had been no deaths aboard Saumarez's ship and, apart from the broken leg one crewman received from the recoil of his gun during the first broadside, the only other injury was a wound to Lieutenant Rye's head.

Early in the battle a ship had appeared in the offing which Saumarez assumed to be the second frigate out of Cherbourg. (This frigate, *Semillante*, had attempted to leave port but had been baffled by contrary winds.) The captain of *Reunion*, Denain, must have assumed the same for he had delayed his surrender until the last possible moment. Thankfully the frigate turned out to be the British *Circe*, Joseph Yorke. Arriving four hours after the battle had ended Yorke took 160 prisoners from *Reunion* and continued on with the dispatches for Guernsey to fulfil Saumarez's original orders. *Crescent*'s First Lieutenant, Parker, was made commander of *Reunion* for her journey back to Spithead and Otter and Rye were made *Crescent*'s first and second lieutenants respectively. Midshipman French was promoted to lieutenant and filled the position vacated by Rye.

The day after the battle Saumarez wrote to his brother Richard. This was his first major battle since becoming a husband and a father and his thoughts naturally turned to his wife. 'It is unnecessary for me to observe, my dear Richard, the great happiness I derive from the consciousness that this event will afford you and all our friends particular satisfaction. My dear Martha too, – I scarcely know how I shall disclose the circumstances to her; it embarrasses me as much as if it were a mournful subject.'[2]

Detained by light winds, *Crescent* finally arrived off the Isle of Wight on 22 October and Lieutenant Otter was sent to Portsmouth in the ship's boat with Saumarez's dispatches. Dropping anchor at Spithead the following day, repairs to Saumarez's ship were begun and *Reunion* was surveyed to assess her value and her suitability for employment in the Royal Navy. Saumarez would be disappointed to learn that *Reunion*'s prize money would be based on her having a crew of 300 when he knew the true number was 321. (The French had thrown most of their dead sailors overboard during the battle and Captain Denain had probably given a lower number to save face.)

On 24 October, the First Lord of the Admiralty, the Earl of Chatham, wrote to congratulate Saumarez on his capture of *Reunion*. Saumarez's dispatches appeared in the *London Gazette* two days later. Thanking his officer's and men 'for their cool and steady behaviour during the action', Saumarez had also recommended 'to their lordships' notice the three lieutenants, Messrs. Parker, Otter and Rye: their conduct has afforded me the utmost satisfaction'.[3] Several days later Saumarez received a letter from Philip d'Auvergne, writing from Falmouth to applaud his friend's success. Whilst Martha's parents looked after their two children, Saumarez and Martha travelled to London, the couple staying with Saumarez's younger brother Richard, surgeon to the Magdalen Hospital, a home for penitent prostitutes in Southwark. On 5 November Saumarez was taken in a carriage to St James's Palace by the First Lord. Presented to the King by Chatham, he became Sir James Saumarez, Knight Batchelor. Having applied for an extension of his leave, Saumarez remained in London until 15 November when he and Lady Saumarez returned to Ryde. On his return home Saumarez learned from Martha's parents that their youngest, Mary, then only ten months old, had been ill during their absence though her health was now starting to improve. Saumarez also received two letters. The first was from the Committee for Encouraging the Capture of French Privateers, Armed Vessels &c. who had requested that Saumarez accept a piece of plate valued at 100 guineas, but the second letter, a bill of £103. 6s. 8d. for his recent knighthood, was much less welcome. Saumarez refused to pay this money, declaring that it was hard 'to pay so much for an honour which my services have been thought to deserve'.[4] However, fearing that it might be looked upon poorly, he nevertheless directed the sender of the bill to whoever had paid for Pellew's recent knighthood. After a few precious days spent at home Saumarez returned to his ship and on 22 November *Crescent* reported ready for sea.

Chapter 7

Channel Service and the Escape of *Crescent:* November 1793 – June 1795

Joining the Downs Command of Rear Admiral John McBride, Saumarez was given command of a cruising squadron consisting of the frigate *Druid*, Joseph Ellison, a popular and courageous officer who had lost his right arm above the elbow in the previous war, the brig *Liberty* and the cutter *Lion*. Saumarez's first duty involved escorting a convoy of troopships to Guernsey where he picked up some pilots for McBride's squadron. Despatching *Liberty* to look in at Saint-Malo *Crescent* returned to St Peter Port on 28 November 1793.

With orders to reconnoitre the French coast, on the night of 5 December *Crescent*, *Druid* and *Liberty* sailed from Guernsey Road. Struggling against the wind off Cape Frehel the following morning they observed a convoy of ships at anchor off the Ile de Brehat further along the coast. Spotting two large ships and a brig in one of the bays to the north of the islands Saumarez decided on an immediate attack, but the tide was against the British and they were prevented from reaching the bay before the enemy had weighed anchor and hid themselves amongst the rocks. Having now entered the bay in which the enemy had been anchored, Saumarez realised that he could not follow them further without endangering the ships under his command. The two pilots that had recently boarded *Crescent* pointed out a passage through the rocks that they assured Saumarez was perfectly safe. However, there were many half-submerged rocks that *Crescent* had great difficulty in clearing. *Druid*, following close behind, was less fortunate and Ellison's frigate was temporarily grounded, receiving enough damage to her hull to warrant an immediate return to port. Saumarez therefore ordered *Druid* to abandon the pursuit and proceed to Plymouth with the brig *Liberty* whilst he returned to Guernsey. At midnight *Crescent* narrowly avoided running aground on the Roches-Douvres, a dangerous reef seventeen miles north of the Ile de Brehat, the men at the wheel only warned of their perilous situation at the last moment by the sound of breakers.

On 1 December an expedition consisting of around 7,000 British troops and a corps of French émigrés commanded by the Earl of Moira and Admiral McBride sailed from Portsmouth in an attempt to support the Royalist uprising in Northern France. On the morning of 2 December the expedition arrived off the coast of Cherbourg where Moira expected to be given a signal from the shore to indicate that the landings could proceed. Moira remained off the coast waiting for the signal but by now the uprising had all but collapsed and none was ever made. In early January Moira finally abandoned the expedition and embarked aboard *Crescent* which had been cruising off the French coast in company with *Melampus*, *Vestal* and *Albion*. On 6 January Saumarez's squadron arrived in Cowes and Moira was reunited with his troops. The following day *Crescent* returned to the French coast in company with her sister ship, *Flora*, Sir John Borlase Warren, the 36-gun *Nymphe*, Edward Pellew, *Druid*, two sloops and a cutter. Encountering strong winds on 9 January *Nymphe* sprung her foremast and had to return to Spithead. The remaining ships now chased three armed brigs off Le Havre, decoying them at first by flying French colours. Mid-chase Warren detached *Crescent* and *Nymphe* to look in at Cherbourg. The following day, whilst sailing close to the spot where *Reunion* had been taken three months earlier, *Crescent* encountered another French frigate attempting to return to port. Saumarez had hoped to get between the enemy and the land but the wind suddenly changed direction allowing the French frigate to escape back to port using her sweeps. During their encounter the French frigate had repeatedly fired signal guns to alert the other ships in the bay, though none came to her assistance.

On 25 January 1794 *Crescent* anchored in Cowes Road, Isle of Wight. A severe storm blowing up and there being no chance of a return to sea, Saumarez asked for twenty-four hours leave to visit his family. McBride granted Saumarez an extended leave and Saumarez spent a week in Bath, returning to Cowes on 2 February. During his leave Saumarez learned that his name had been mentioned in the debates that had followed the King's opening of Parliament. On a much more disappointing note he also learned that during his recent cruise Warren had captured one of the armed brigs they had encountered off Le Havre. This should have been good news as it was customary for captains of cruising squadrons to share out any prize money from captured vessels as indeed Saumarez, Pellew and Warren had all agreed to this prior to their cruise. However, although Saumarez was certain he could have aided in the capture of the brig had he not been detached by Warren he now learned he was to be denied his share of the prize money.

On a happier note, following the capture of *Reunion* Saumarez had helped the artist Thomas Elliot in the creation of two oil paintings depicting the action, one the start of the engagement, the other its conclusion. In order to make the paintings as accurate as possible Elliot had visited both *Crescent* and *Reunion* and talked to Saumarez and his officers. Saumarez now wrote to his brother Richard and told him not to purchase any of the prints that were being published as he had already acquired fifteen sets for his family and friends.

The bad weather that had prevented *Crescent* putting to sea continued on and off throughout February and on the morning of 20 February Saumarez's ship lost her main topmast and sprung her fore-yard which necessitated a brief return to Spithead for repairs. Refit completed, on 1 March *Crescent* sailed for Cherbourg in company with McBride's flagship *Invincible, Flora, Arethusa, Nymphe* and *Druid*. Looking in on Cherbourg Road the squadron spotted six enemy frigates, fifteen brigs and fifteen sloops at anchor. Sailing through the Race of Alderney on 7 March, *Druid* fired at a French privateer headed for the French coast but was prevented from giving chase by a nearby fort which returned fire. Two days later *Crescent* captured a brig loaded with wheat for Cherbourg. Saumarez sent the ship's master across to *Invincible* to be interrogated by McBride and sent a petty officer with four men to take charge of the prize and sail her back to Britain. On 13 March the squadron returned to Spithead where Admiral Sir Peter Parker had now hoisted his flag aboard *Royal William*.

In mid-March the Governor of Jersey, Lord Balcarras, began receiving reports that the French were preparing for an invasion of the Channel Islands. At Saint-Malo an army of around 10,000 men were said to be preparing to march along the coast to Granville Bay where they would embark on transports. There were also rumoured to be six ships of the line and several heavy frigates at Cancale Bay waiting to cover the invasion. McBride now ordered *Crescent* and *Druid* to look in at Cancale and further along the coast at Granville. On the voyage out the wind dropped and on 27 March the ships put in at St Owen's Bay, Jersey. Saumarez and Ellison went ashore to meet with Lord Balcarras but thick fog in the evening prevented them returning to their ships until the following morning. Returning to St Owen's after a night ashore, Saumarez and Ellison were alarmed to discover that their ships were

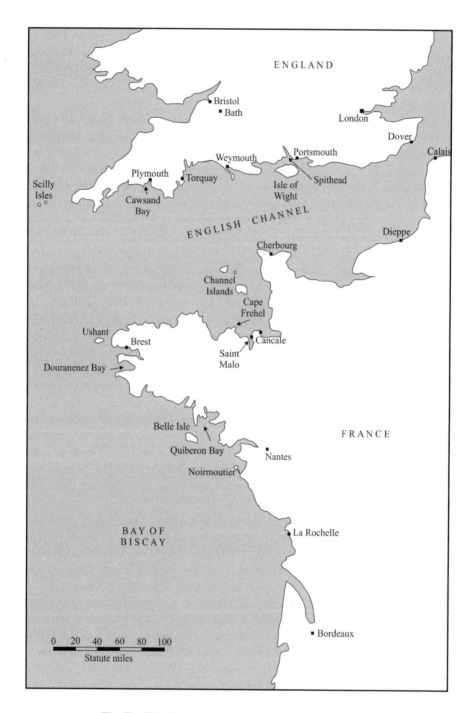

The English Channel and Atlantic Coast of France.

no longer anchored in the bay. However, *Crescent* and *Druid* soon hove into view and both captains had an uncomfortable row out to their respective ships in quite choppy seas. The wind, which had shifted to the south during the night, forcing the ships to change their anchorage, now prevented the squadron from looking in on the French coast so Saumarez detached a lugger with his third lieutenant aboard instead. Lieutenant French returned the following evening, 30 March, to inform Saumarez that there were eleven frigates in Cancale Bay, but that there were no sign of any ships of the line.

Crescent returned to Guernsey, anchoring in St Peter Port on 4 April. Over the course of the next week eight seamen were sent to hospital and two men were sent from the hospital to Saumarez's ship. Resuming her cruise, on 15 April *Crescent* fell in with two Danish vessels off Cape Barfleur and for several hours on 23 April the sound of gunfire could be heard in the distance. Watching the enemy activity along the coast and sending his French-speaking officers ashore to gain intelligence it soon became clear to Saumarez that the strength of the enemy forces at Cancale and Granville had been wildly over-exaggerated. With the threat of an invasion of the Channel Islands fast disappearing, on 28 April *Crescent* and *Druid* returned to Plymouth. The gunfire heard on 23 April turned out to have been an encounter between British and French squadrons off the Ile de Batz. Following an action lasting around three hours the frigates *Flora*, Borlase Warren, and *Arethusa*, Edward Pellew, had succeeded in capturing the French frigate *Pomone* and the corvette *Babet* for the loss of just four men.

Five weeks later, on 1 June, a much larger fleet action was fought between the twenty-five ships of Lord Howe's Channel Fleet and twenty-six ships of the line under Rear Admiral Villaret-Joyeuse, tasked with protecting a large grain convoy sailing from America to Brest to relieve the starving population of France. The battle, fought 400 miles off Ushant, was actually the culmination of five days of manoeuvring during which Howe was finally able to gain the weather gauge. Intending for his ships to cut through the enemy line and engage on the leeward side, Howe had prepared a special set of signals but in the event his captains either did not see, did not understand, or were simply unable to act on these signals. Regardless of the confusion, by the end of the battle six French ships had been taken (one of which sank shortly after the battle). For the British the Glorious First of June was seen as a resounding success. However, the vital grain convoy was able to reach Brest unmolested, saving the Revolution.

Having spent ten days cruising off the Lizard *Crescent* returned to Plymouth on 4 June, bringing to an end the six month agreement between Saumarez, Pellew and Warren to share out prize money gained on their cruises. As was often the case in such matters, squabbles over the prize money led to a falling out between Saumarez and Pellew. Pellew was perhaps the greatest, most courageous frigate captain of his age but there was something in his character that seemed to upset many of his fellow officers. The final meeting between Pellew and Saumarez ended in an undignified argument and it was twenty-eight years before the two men spoke to one another again.

On 6 June McBride ordered Saumarez to take the frigates *Druid* and *Eurydice* under his command and escort a convoy of three luggers and a cutter to Jersey. Sailing from Plymouth on 7 June at 3.30am the following morning the squadron were about thirty miles north of Guernsey sailing on the larboard tack when five ships were spotted off to the east and a further two more to the south-east. *Crescent* fired a signal gun and the closest group of ships all raised Swedish colours. However, when Saumarez made the private signal for the day but it was not returned, so he dispatched the lugger *Valiant* to investigate further. As *Valiant* approached the Swedish ships they hauled down their colours, raised French flags in their place and opened fire on Lieutenant Baker's vessel. Saumarez now found he was opposed by a much more powerful French squadron to windward; two 50-gun heavy frigates, two 32-gun ships and a 14-gun-brig-corvette. Saumarez ordered the slow sailing *Eurydice* to head south-west towards the Hanois whilst *Crescent* and *Druid* covered her retreat and the merchantmen turned back towards Plymouth. As the French began to overhaul Saumarez's squadron the two ships at the head of their line opened fire, but at too great a range to do any damage. Saumarez waited until *Eurydice* was close to shore and out of harm's way then turned south-west and made sail for the Hanois in company with *Druid*. However, Saumarez quickly realised that he would not outrun the French so in order to protect *Druid* he turned to face the enemy. Backing *Crescent*'s mizzen sail, Saumarez engaged each enemy ship as they came up. Once *Druid* was safely out of range Saumarez turned to the south-west to attempt an escape but found that particular course blocked by the enemy. Outnumbered, it seemed inevitable that *Crescent* would be overwhelmed and forced to haul down her flag, but these were Saumarez's waters. As a Channel Islander he had an intimate knowledge of Guernsey's shoreline, and he also had aboard an old and experienced pilot, John Breton, who, like Saumarez, happened to live close to where the action was taking place. Ordering a press of sail he turned towards the shore as if he intended to run his ship on the rocks to avoid capture. Coming under fire from the shore batteries the French

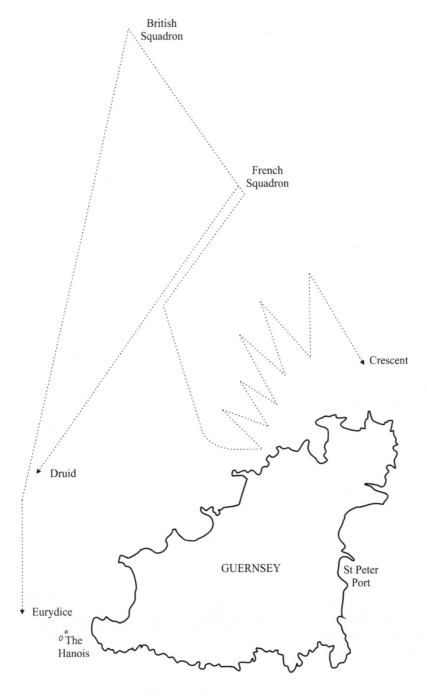

Escape of *Crescent*, 8 June 1794.

did not follow but fired some long-range shots at the fast-disappearing British frigate. Of course Saumarez had no intention of running his ship ashore, instead he ordered his helmsman to head for a narrow channel between two reefs that had never before been attempted by a ship the size of *Crescent*. As his ship carefully made her way down through the channel Saumarez asked Breton if he knew where they were and the old pilot pointed out both his and Saumarez's houses. Clearing the channel *Crescent* remained close to the shore, tacking against a north-east wind round the north of the island she reached St Peter Port shortly after noon. Coming in from the opposite direction *Druid* and *Eurydice* arrived safely in port shortly after.

The following day the lieutenant-governor of Guernsey, John Small, wrote Saumarez a public letter of congratulation which he forwarded to the Admiralty 'to do justice to merit and exertions far indeed above my praise'.[1] Saumarez's commander-in-chief, McBride, also passed on his commendations to the Admiralty. Early on in the action the luggers had become separated from the rest of Saumarez's squadron and had headed back to Plymouth. When *Cockchafer*'s commander, Lieutenant Hall, had gone aboard *Echo* to inform McBride that they had encountered a French squadron and that Saumarez's ships had been taken, McBride had demanded to know if Hall had seen them strike. The lieutenant replied that he had not but was sure that they could not have escaped from their predicament. Perfectly satisfied that Saumarez would not have surrendered, McBride, who was suffering from gout, threatened to throw his crutch at Hall before angrily dismissing him. He immediately wrote to Saumarez asking for a report of his situation and the conduct of the small vessels under his command. At the same time he also took the opportunity to inform Saumarez of the arrival of the Channel Fleet's *Phaeton*, Sir Roger Curtis, who had brought news of the recent fleet action between Howe and Villaret-Joyeuse.

Having sent McBride a report praising the efforts of Ellison and Cole on 14 June Saumarez sailed for Plymouth. That same day *Crescent* fell in with *Valiant*. On hearing the news of Howe's victory Saumarez admitted to being 'savage enough to wish a few more had been sunk or taken'.[2] The following day Saumarez wrote to his brother Richard, an author of several medical theses, and asked why he could not turn his hand to poetry or music and compose something similar to the 'The Famous Ninety-Two', a song written in celebration of a British naval victory over the French in 1692 that was still being sung more than a century later.

Sailing from Plymouth on 20 June *Crescent* arrived at St Peter Port on 2 July in company with *Druid*, *Thalia* and *Hebe*. For the next six weeks

Saumarez's squadron cruised off the Channel Islands, occasionally returning to Plymouth, and Admiral McBride declared that 'their defence could not be in better hands'.[3]

On 9 July Martha wrote to her husband from Stonehouse, Plymouth. After much discussion within the family a middle name had been chosen for their youngest child, Martha Harriet Saumarez. She was clearly a healthy baby. 'I never saw a child grow as much in the course of a month as she has done. If she continues she will soon be as fat as Mary.' Meanwhile young James was clearly missing his father. 'The dear boy returned to my room but he slept in his little bed which has been placed by mine ... The first words he spoke on waking were "I have been dreaming of my own papa".'[4]

Frustrated by their lengthy separation, on 22 August Martha vented her fury at McBride for keeping her husband from her side. 'It will be a long time before I forget the inconsistent conduct of your Commander on this occasion. Does he deign to assign any reason for changing his mind so often for if he has a spark of reflection he must be sensible of it? ... When I consider how many days in thy company I have lost by the fickleness of this capricious man I indeed then feel the disappointment.'[5] Her husband was a fine frigate captain and McBride, as Saumarez's commanding officer, could claim his share of any prize money, so he clearly had every reason for keeping *Crescent* at sea for as long as possible. Saumarez, it seems, was not the only officer to suffer the vagaries of McBride's command. Newly promoted to post in April 1794, Captain Graham Moore had waited several weeks to exchange command of his sloop, *Bonetta*, with Captain Charles Wemyss. However, discovering that Wemyss was due to arrive in port, McBride had suddenly ordered *Bonetta* back out to sea. Moore suspected, with some justification, that McBride wanted him to quit his ship so that he could give temporary command of *Bonetta* to one of his favourites.

On 19 August *Crescent* sailed from Plymouth for Weymouth, her arrival off the seaside resort coinciding with the George's annual visit to take the air. As *Crescent* dropped anchor on 23 August the men manned the yards to give the King three cheers and this was followed by a 21-gun salute. *Crescent* remained at Weymouth until 29 August, either riding at single anchor or sailing in company with *Southampton* (in use by the King during his visit). However, in a change from his usual routine, on 25 August George decided not to spend the day on the water at Weymouth. As his services were not required, Saumarez was able to travel to nearby Dorchester to see his sisters, Charlotte and Cartaret, both of whom appeared well, Charlotte having recovered from a recent illness. Saumarez was, however, required to return that evening to dine with the Prince of Wales aboard *Minotaur*. Upon hearing this news Martha hurried up from Plymouth to Dorchester in the hope of seeing her husband only to discover upon her arrival that his squadron had already put to sea. 'I will not tell thee how ardently I sigh for thy return,' she wrote 'but I will check all my murmuring. I endeavour to seek comfort in the hope of thy being soon returned.'[6]

Following a short cruise off Cherbourg Saumarez's squadron returned to Weymouth on the evening of 14 September. In the gathering dusk the three frigates, *Druid*, *Thalia* and *Hebe*, sailing in advance of *Crescent*, failed to spot that the guard-ship *Trusty* had made the private signal of the day it and it was not returned. *Trusty* immediately proceeded to Weymouth Road, making the signal for having sighted the enemy at sea. At Weymouth the troops were hurriedly ordered to their stations, the shore batteries manned and the royal carriages made ready. As *Crescent* approached Weymouth Road *Trusty* fired a signal gun and prepared to fire her first broadside. Alerted to the danger, Saumarez made the night signal just in time. Saumarez described what happened next in a letter to his brother Richard. 'I immediately went on shore, and found the royal family at the rooms, not without apprehension of the enemy's landing. The King desired to see me, and very heartily laughed at the circumstance. I remained near an hour in conference with their Majesties in the tea-room; a very distinguished honour, I assure you, as even the lords in waiting are scarcely ever admitted during meals: I was highly flattered at the very gracious and flattering reception I met with.'[7] The following morning found the King back on the water aboard *Southampton*.

In early October there were bad storms all along the south coast and Martha was relieved to hear from her husband that he was safe. Her only disappointment was that Saumarez had sought shelter in distant Torbay, not Plymouth. 'My Saumarez we must endeavour to console ourselves with the expectation that your next cruise will not be long & then I trust we shall meet – oh that I could come to say part no more!'[8] For some time now Martha's father had been looking for a suitable property in Bath for her and the family and in late October he finally found a house in Gay Street facing George Street with a rent of 4½ guineas a week.

Following a brief stop off at Guernsey on 23 October *Crescent* proceeded to cruise off The Lizard. On the 29th she returned to Cawsand Bay. Having not been re-coppered since January 1785, on 8 November *Crescent* was taken in to dry dock at Portsmouth. Martha had hoped *Crescent*'s refit would allow her to see more of her husband but this was not to be. The couple had managed to spend the day together on 5 November but then Saumarez had to return to his ship. Travelling with her family to their new home in Bath Martha just had time to pen an ink-splattered letter to her husband during one of their stop-overs 'I was disappointed at not seeing Thee after our chaise drove off, as I was in hopes to have had one last look as you put in our sweet girls, but their dilatoriness depriv'd me of this satisfaction.'[9] Stopping off at Exeter, then Taunton, Martha finally arrived at Bath around 5.00pm on 6 November. She soon settled into her new home at no 3 Gay Street. The three-storey building with its freshly wallpapered, ample-sized rooms was comfortable, if a little cold.

Coppering completed, *Crescent* was finally ready for sea on 15 January. On 17 January she sailed from Plymouth and three days later dropped anchor at Spithead. Sailing to join the main Channel Fleet of Earl Howe on 29 January, Saumarez found that his duties had now changed. He was no longer to seek out and attack enemy vessels (in fact he had orders to avoid such action if at all possible). Stationed with the other frigates of the inshore squadron between Ushant and the dangerous Black Rocks off Brest, he was to keep an eye on the port and report back any movements of the French fleet to Earl Howe's blockading ships further out to sea. Denying the enemy navy and her merchant ships access to the sea was perhaps the most important work carried out by the navy during the war but most seamen hated it. With little chance of capturing enemy prizes it was unremittingly tedious and, especially in the cold winter months, extremely arduous. Blockade work was also very dangerous as ships could easily be driven onto the rocks close to shore. Saumarez found his position in the fleet 'certainly more desirable than a less conspicuous one … Lord Howe is remarkably gracious, and has overwhelmed me with compliments in his opinion of my merits.'[10] Following his recent successes Saumarez had now set his sights on the command of a ship of the line but was well aware that he had 'more to accomplish in order to show myself deserving of it'.[11] Nevertheless, he had already put in a request to the Admiralty but had been informed by Chatham that the First Lord could find no suitable vessel.

In July 1794 the Whig opposition split and the moderates, led by the Duke of Portland, joined the government. The Secretary of War, Henry Dundas, was replaced by Portland and in December the Whig peer, Earl Spencer, replaced Chatham at the Admiralty. Saumarez, like so many other officers in the service, saw the possibility of advancing his career and within days of Spencer's appointment was writing to the new First Lord to request a ship of the line.

Again a lack of suitable ships meant that Spencer could not comply with Saumarez's request, however he was eager to help 'an officer of so much acknowledged merit'[12] and informed Saumarez that he would be promoted at the first opportunity.

On 21 January Martha had written to her husband to tell him she had spent the evening with a new acquaintance, Fanny Nelson. 'She is a cheerful, pleasant woman and I passed a cheerful, pleasant evening.'[13] Fanny's husband, Captain Horatio Nelson, was the navy's rising star. Eighteen months younger than Saumarez, he had not yet been in any major fleet action but with important family connections (his uncle was Comptroller of the Navy) he had made post in June 1779, almost three years before Saumarez was given command of *Russell*. Sailing with Lord Hood's Mediterranean Fleet as captain of the 64-gun *Agamemnon*, Nelson had been given command of the naval forces ashore during the sieges of Bastia and Calvi in early to mid-1794, losing the sight of his right eye during the latter siege when he was hit in the face by gravel thrown up by shot.

The Channel Fleet remained off Brest until 1 March 1795 when it returned to Spithead. Whilst at sea Saumarez had heard that the 74-gun *Orion* would soon be available as her captain, Thomas Duckworth, had been appointed to *Leviathan*. On his return to port Saumarez immediately wrote to Spencer asking that he be given command of *Orion* and for *Crescent*'s officers and men be turned over to her. Saumarez did not have to wait long for Spencer's decision. On 4 March he wrote to the First Lord to thank him for his appointment to *Orion*, once again requesting that he be allowed to take *Crescent*'s crew with him to his new command. The Admiralty refused his request but he was, however, allowed to take Lieutenants Otter and Rye along with his most trusted warrant and petty officers to *Orion*, then fitting out at Portsmouth. These included Boatswain Peter Sadler, Gunner Michael Alyward, Carpenter Jonathan Rundell and the Surgeon William Nepecker. Saumarez was also able to retain Midshipmen Lovick, Mansell and Marrett. Admiralty regulations stated that Third Rates such as *Orion*, which had a design compliment of 550 men, required five lieutenants, so Otter and Rye were joined (in order of seniority) by Lieutenants Charles Mason, Jonathan Luce and James Barker.

Orion was the second ship of the Modified *Canada* class, a revival of a 1760 design by the Surveyor of the Navy, William Bately, for a 74-gun ship of the line. Built by William Barnard at Deptford Dockyard, *Orion*'s keel was laid down in February 1783 and the ship was launched in June 1787. Assigned to Howe's fleet she had taken part in the Glorious First of June during which action five of her crew had been killed and a further twenty-four wounded. *Orion* was similar in appearance to

Russell, the first 74 Saumarez had commanded – she was just two feet longer but with roughly the same overall displacement. The main difference was in her armament: the extra length allowing her to have two extra 18-pounders on the upper gun deck. Her quarterdeck armament had also been uprated: eight 32-pounder and six 9-pounder carronades compared to *Russell*'s fourteen 9-pounders.

As it would be some time before *Orion* would be available, on 15 April Saumarez was temporarily appointed to the 74-gun *Marlborough*. Sailing from Spithead in company with *Minotaur, Invincible, Excellent* and *Blonde, Marlborough* spent six weeks cruising between Ushant and Cape Finisterre. On 8 June Saumarez returned to Portsmouth to take command of *Orion* which was now ready for sea. Saumarez's appointment to a ship of the line had been perfectly timed for within weeks *Orion* would be involved in a large fleet battle off the coast of north-west France.

Chapter 8

Orion and the Battle of Ile de Groix: June 1795 – April 1796

In June 1794 a small army of Catholic Chouans had begun fighting against the forces of the Convention in Brittany, northern France. Unlike the Vendeans, who had attempted to fight as regular soldiers, the Chouans, led by Georges Cadoudal, had adopted much more successful guerrilla tactics, ambushing Republican military detachments, executing informers and attacking poorly-defended Republican towns. At first Britain supported the Chouans by supplying them with arms and setting up an intelligence system, based in Jersey and run by Saumarez's old friend, Philip D'Auverne, who now styled himself the Duc de Bouillon. English frigates operated along the coast of northern France, dropping off and picking up spies several times a week and D'Auverne soon began receiving reports that the French were having difficulties supplying the islands off the coast of Brittany, Belle Isle and the smaller Isle de Yeu. If the British could capture these islands they would make a good base to launch an attack on the mainland.

Encouraged into action by the French émigré population, by the spring of 1795 the government had devised a plan whereby a small army of French Royalists and regular British troops would be landed on the coast of Brittany with enough arms to supply the local counter-revolutionary forces. The place chosen for the landings was the site of an earlier naval battle, Quiberon Bay. The naval force would be led by Captain John Borlase Warren and consisted of the frigates *Anson, Artois, Galatea, Arethusa, Concorde* and Warren's 44-gun *Pomone*. Warren was ordered to take under his command three ships of the line, *Robust, Thunderer* and *Standard*, along with the fifty-five transports and land the troops either at Quiberon, Bourgneuf, or the Isle de Yeu. As the expedition approached Brest it was to be joined by Bridport's Channel Fleet which would provide support during the landings. The cantankerous and widely-disliked Bridport was already upset at not having been confirmed as commander-in-chief of the Channel Fleet whilst Howe remained ashore in poor health. Discovering that command of a major naval expedition had been given to a junior officer did little to improve his humour. Over the coming months what assistance he gave to Warren he gave grudgingly.

On 12 June *Orion* weighed anchor and sailed with Bridport's Channel Fleet from Spithead. Warren's expedition departed Portsmouth the following day and headed out into the Channel. After several days of thick fog contact was finally made with Bridport's fleet on 16 June. The two fleets now turned south-east towards Quiberon Bay with Warren's squadron sailing in advance of the Channel Fleet to act as a screen. On 19 June, as the British expedition approached Belle Isle, the frigates, *Arethusa* and *Galatea* sighted fifteen ships of the line to the south-west and signalled Warren. This was Vice Admiral Villaret-Joyeuse's Brest Fleet which had sailed from port on 12 June but was now headed for shelter at Belle Isle having been blown off course by a gale on 18 June. Warren ordered the transports to tack away from the French and he dispatched *Thunderer* and a lugger to try and find Bridport. Once he had been made aware that the French fleet was at sea Bridport sailed back towards the coast in an attempt to put himself between the expedition and Villaret-Joyeuse.

At dawn on 22 June the Channel Fleet was sailing on the larboard tack, roughly fifty miles from Isle de Groix, when the frigates *Nymphe* and *Astrea* made the signal for having sighted the enemy. By his manoeuvres Bridport soon realised that Villaret-Joyeuse had no intention of engaging him in battle and at 6.30am made the signal for his best-sailing ships, *Sans Pareil, Orion, Russell* and *Colossus*, to give chase. Fifteen minutes later he ordered the rest of his fleet to follow. With little wind the chase continued for the rest of the day and through the night.

During the night *Sans Pareil, Orion, Russell* and *Colossus* had been joined by *Irresistible* and *Queen Charlotte*. By early next morning these six British ships had caught up with the stern most ships of Villaret-Joyeuse's fleet which had crowded sail and was heading back to Lorient. At around 6.00am the slow-sailing *Alexandre*, now under tow by the frigate *Régénérée*, had begun firing her stern chasers at the closest British ships, *Orion* and *Irresistible*. Grindall returned fire with his bow chasers and, having manoeuvred his ship to windward of the French 74, Saumarez directed his larboard guns at *Alexandre*'s stern. *Régénérée* now abandoned the tow and left *Alexandre* to her fate. At 6.15am the next ship in the French line, *Formidable*, received a devastating broadside from *Queen Charlotte*, *Sans Pareil* fired a broadside in passing and a fire was soon observed on the French ship's poop deck. Eventually her

61

mizzenmast fell over the side, and she bore up and struck. By 7.15am *Queen Charlotte*'s sails and rigging had been badly cut up by enemy fire and she was proving unmanageable. Falling back, she soon came under fire from *Alexandre* but a broadside from the British three-decker was enough to compel this smaller ship, already heavily damaged by *Orion*'s superior gunnery, to surrender. Following a joint attack by both *Queen Charlotte* and *London, Tigre* also hauled down her colours. At this point *Royal George* now came up and joined the action, Bridport's flagship firing into the larboard bow of *Tigre*, not realising she had already surrendered. The French fleet were now within three miles of the coast, close to the protection of the shore batteries. At around 8.15am Bridport ordered his ships to cease firing and he wore his fleet away from the shore and the enemy. After several tacks Villaret-Joyeuse anchored his fleet secure from attack between Isle de Groix and the entrance to Lorient.

Total losses for the French fleet were never given but aboard the prizes they amounted to 670 killed and wounded. By the end of the battle British losses amounted to thirty-one killed and 131 wounded. The worst casualties were aboard *Queen Charlotte* which had four killed and thirty-two wounded, *Colossus*, five killed, thirty wounded, *Russell*, three killed and ten wounded and *Orion*, Saumarez's ship, having six killed and eighteen wounded. In the usual promotions that followed a battle Lieutenant Otter was made master and commander. Bridport gave orders for *Alexandre, Formidable* and *Tigre* to be taken under tow by *Prince, Barfleur* and *Prince George* and on 10 June the prizes departed for England. *Orion* had received a great deal of damage to her masts and rigging and her foremast and bowsprit needed replacing so she was ordered back to Portsmouth. She left the fleet on 9 July in company with the hospital ship *Charon* which she escorted to Weymouth. Two of the seamen injured aboard *Orion* during the recent action had subsequently died from their wounds but almost all the other wounded men had recovered. Following the battle there had been an outbreak of yellow fever aboard ship followed by another of smallpox. These gave Saumarez a great deal of concern but, by transferring those worst affected to the hospital ship, he was able to contain both outbreaks, although two seamen died aboard *Charon*. *Orion* arrived at Spithead on 15 July and went into dry dock. She required extensive repairs and did not report ready for sea until 18 August. Following an appeal from his second lieutenant, in early August Saumarez travelled to London to see Admiral Gambier at the Admiralty and enquire as to whether Rye could be made *Orion*'s first lieutenant following the recent battle. However, Saumarez was informed that this was against Admiralty rules. He subsequently met with Rye's patron, Spencer, who was willing but unable to help. Returning to his ship Saumarez advised Rye to write directly to Spencer. On 20 August Martha arrived in Ryde which allowed Saumarez a few precious days with his wife before returning to sea.

In mid-July the government had decided to send additional troops to Warren's besieged forces in Quiberon Bay. The expedition, led by Major General Doyle, would be made up of elements of the British Army; 4,000 men together with a further 1,500 Royalists commanded by the Earl of Moira. The fleet of 126 vessels – troopships, ordnance ships, victuallers and other vessels – would be protected by a squadron commanded by Admiral Sir Henry Harvey consisting of *Prince of Wales*, *Queen Charlotte*, *Prince*, *Russell*, *Arethusa*, *Jason* and *Orion*. Having lost their foothold in Quiberon Bay it had been decided to land men on the island of Noirmoutier, situated off the mouth of the Loire in Bourgneuf Bay. But first the Isle d'Yeu, situated twenty miles further south, would have to be taken. With a small harbour that could handle around forty transports, the Isle d'Yeu might prove a suitable alternative base for operations should the assault on Noirmoutier fail.

The expedition sailed from Spithead on 26 August but was beset by bad weather and did not arrive in Quiberon Bay until 10 September. Harvey and Warren now decided to take the fleet to Bourgneuf Bay. Whilst the two men began planning for the assault on Noirmoutier word came through from the commander of the Royalist troops, Charette, that he no longer had enough men to fight his way to the coast, let alone hold on to Noirmoutier once it had been taken. Warren now turned his attention to the Isle d'Yeu. The island was taken without opposition and by 12 October the troops had disembarked and set up camp. Unfortunately the island proved to have less shelter for the troopships as initially thought and the British would therefore have to return to Quiberon Bay. *Orion* spent the following month blockading the coast between Rochefort and Lorient. On 26 October Saumarez wrote to his brother, Richard. 'We experienced hitherto remarkable fine weather, which I hope will continue; but nothing can equal our unvaried scene, fixed to this confounded spot, without the least prospect of anything falling in our way. We have not even the advantage of hearing from England ... In short, my dear friend, I am heartily tired of so inactive a situation and shall very sincerely rejoice to be relieved of it.'[1]

By now it was clear that the landings in Quiberon Bay had been a total failure. The expedition was abandoned and Warren was recalled but not before he had been instructed to land any Royalist troops that wished to join Charette and his army on the mainland. The weather had now deteriorated and in the face of harsh winter storms Harvey could not get to the Isle d'Yeu to re-embark the troops and there they remained, slowly running out of provisions. On 24 November *Orion* attempted to land food, ammunition and money for the Royalists but was beaten by the bad weather. Another attempt the following day was equally unsuccessful. Finally, on 13 December, a break in the weather allowed several ships to anchor at the island and embark all the troops and their arms. Sailing from Quiberon Bay on 14 December the expedition arrived at Spithead on 30 December. Having sprung her lower masts in the November gales, *Orion* had to be taken into dock for repairs. Several ships had been badly damaged by the recent bad weather and the dockyards were now seriously overworked. *Orion* would not be ready for sea again until 25 April 1796.

Chapter 9

The Mediterranean Fleet and the Battle of Cape St Vincent: April 1796 – April 1797

In December 1795 the commander of the Mediterranean Fleet, Lord Hood, had demanded that the new First Lord provide additional ships for his fleet. Spencer's response was to dismiss Hood from both his Mediterranean command and the Admiralty Board. Hood's replacement as commander of the Mediterranean Fleet was Vice Admiral William Hotham. In two encounters with the Toulon fleet in March and July 1795 the overly-cautious Hotham failed to make the most of his opportunities. Thankfully, both for Hotham's increasingly strained nerves and for British naval strategy in the Mediterranean, in December 1795 command of the fleet passed to Admiral Sir John Jervis, a much more energetic and capable officer than his predecessor.

Soon after assuming his new command, Jervis, who was known throughout the navy as a strict disciplinarian, began to send his fleet on frequent manoeuvres, watching from his flagship to make sure his captains remained on their quarterdecks and did not return to their cabins as, under previous commanding officers, they had been prone to do. Jervis also understood that, apart from being well led, the effectiveness of the fleet also relied on the welfare of its men. Hammocks and bedding had to be cleaned once a week and decks regularly scrubbed. Sick bays were also moved from the lowest deck to the upper deck where there was better ventilation. By these measures Jervis rapidly turned the Mediterranean Fleet into the most effective fighting unit in the navy.

Her re-fit complete, on 20 April *Orion* sailed from Portsmouth to Spithead where *Royal William* and *Queen Charlotte*, the flagships of

Admirals Peter Parker and Roger Curtis, were at anchor. On 17 May *Orion* sailed for Cape Finisterre as part of a squadron consisting of Admiral Harvey's flagship *Prince of Wales, Juste, Hector, Theseus, Trident* and the frigates *Pallas, Phaeton* and *Latona*. On 12 June Saumarez was detached to Fayal in the Azores to obtain provisions for the rest of the squadron. *Orion* remained off Fayal for a week before rejoining Harvey's squadron which was now cruising some thirty miles to the west of the Azores. Travelling down to Cape Trafalgar and back up to Cape Finisterre, the squadron returned to Spithead on 17 August. A month later Saumarez received orders to join Alan Gardner's Channel Fleet Squadron off Brest.

By late 1796 the war was going badly for Britain. In April the commander of the French Army of Italy, Napoleon Bonaparte, had defeated the Austrians at Millesimo, and Nice and Savoy were soon ceded to the French Republic. The Austrians were again defeated at Lodi in May and by the end of the month the French were in control of Milan. On 25 June Napoleon's army entered Leghorn, an important Royal Navy base. The British were able to maintain a close blockade of the port from Porto Ferrajo but their hold over the Mediterranean was growing precarious. In September 1796 Britain's ally Spain swapped sides, forming an alliance with France and declaring war on Britain and Portugal. At a stroke France had at its disposal 132 ships of the line compared to Britain's 123. However, Britain had been in coalition with Spain long enough prior to the breach to realise that her navy's ships were both poorly maintained and manned. The Spanish economy was in ruins and there was no money to pay for the navy, now led by General Cordoba y Ramos, a man with no experience of senior naval command who had been chosen purely for his inability to say no to the Spanish Prime Minister, Manuel Godoy.

A week before the Spanish declaration of war against Britain Admiral Langara had sailed from Cadiz with a fleet of nineteen ships of the line and ten frigates. On 1 October he encountered a division under the command of Admiral Man returning to the Mediterranean from Gibraltar. Alarmed by his encounter with the Spanish fleet Man turned round and headed for England, depriving Jervis of seven much-needed ships of the line. For this failure Man never served at sea again. With a fleet numbering just fifteen ships Jervis was forced to relocate from Toulon to Gibraltar and Nelson was sent to Elba to organise the withdrawal of the British garrison from the island. There was a further relocation of Jervis's fleet to Lisbon to assist Britain's ally, Portugal. On 10 December *Courageux* was wrecked in a storm and several days later *Bombay Castle* was lost on a sandbank in the Tagus. Damage to other ships further reduced Jervis's fleet to just ten ships of the line; *Victory, Britannia, Barfleur, Captain, Blenheim, Goliath, Excellent, Egmont, Culloden* and *Diadem.*

On 10 October the Channel Fleet returned to Torbay. From there *Orion* sailed to Spithead to refit and to water. Whilst in Spithead Saumarez learned that Martha had given birth to a baby girl, Carteret. On 24 December *Orion* dropped down to St Helens to rejoin the Channel Fleet, now commanded by Bridport aboard his flagship *Royal George.* The fleet returned to Ushant on 3 January 1797. However, on 19 January Saumarez was instructed to join a squadron commanded by Admiral William Parker that had been ordered to Cape St Vincent to reinforce the Mediterranean Fleet. The squadron consisted of Parker's flagship, *Prince George, Namur, Irresistible, Orion, Colossus* and the frigate *Thalia.* The junction with Mediterranean Fleet took place on 6 February 1797 and brought Jervis's command up to fifteen ships of the line.

On the morning of 13 February *Minerve*, flying the broad pendant of Commodore Nelson, arrived back at the fleet from Gibraltar. Sailing from the Rock on 12 February Nelson's ship had been chased by two Spanish ships of the line and whilst still in the Straits a large Spanish fleet had been spotted at sea. Nelson went aboard *Victory* to report to Jervis and by sunset the flagship had signalled for the fleet to prepare for battle and to keep close order. During the night the signal guns of the Spanish ships could be distinctly heard in the distance.

The Spanish ships had left Cartagena on 1 February bound first for Cadiz and then Brest where they were to link up with the French fleet of Admiral Morard de Galles. The fleet, commanded by Admiral Don Jose de Cordoba, was made up of twenty-seven ships of the line, twelve frigates and four merchant ships, which were to be escorted as far as Cadiz. It was only a small convoy of merchantmen but they were carrying a precious cargo of mercury, vital for processing silver into coin. Having successfully passed through the straits of Gibraltar and out into the Atlantic the Spanish ships were then caught by strong easterly gales which blew them off course. By the time the winds eased the fleet was spread out and hundreds of miles from Cadiz. Cordoba could have continued on further north towards his final destination but instead decided to turn his fleet round and head back to Cadiz.

Visibility on the morning of 14 February 1797 was poor. Once the early morning mist started to clear the outlying British frigates began to report that they had spotted sails to the south. As Jervis stood next to his flag-captain, Robert Calder, and his other senior officers on *Victory*'s quarterdeck, first eight, then twenty, then twenty-five Spanish ships appeared out of the fog ahead of them. The Spanish now began forming a line of battle but their crews were poorly trained and it was all rather untidy. Cordoba's flagship fired off one signal after another in an attempt to organise the fleet and they just about managed to form into two loose groups to the south of the British. The larger, more westerly group consisted of twenty ships whilst a little way to the east the remaining seven ships made up the smaller group. There was no sign of the frigates as they were still off escorting the merchant ships. From his flagship in the centre of the British line Jervis now ordered his fleet into line of battle. Thomas Troubridge was leading the line in *Culloden*, his ship badly damaged from a collision with the 74-gun *Colossus* two days earlier. *Orion* was third in line behind *Prince George*. Nelson had shifted his flag back to *Captain* and his ship was third from the rear. At around noon the British, heading roughly south-west, forced their way between the two Spanish formations and as the larger Spanish formation started to turn towards the north-east, the smaller group of ships made a move towards it by sailing north-west. The British ran up their colours and *Culloden* led the fleet towards the large Spanish formation, Troubridge's ship heading straight for a massive three-decker. At the last moment the Spanish ship bore away and *Culloden* fired two broadsides in quick succession as she swept past her. Behind her the other British ships came into action one by one.

The two formations were now sailing in opposite directions in lines roughly parallel to one another at a distance of about 400 yards. Seeing Jervis suddenly covered in blood, his flag-captain, George Grey, rushed across to see if he was all right but it was not the admiral's blood, but that of a sailor stood nearby who had been killed. As the British fleet proceeded down the Spanish line Jervis now ordered his ships to tack; he wanted to turn his fleet round so that they could continue to attack the larger formation by sailing back up the Spanish line. Troubridge had anticipated Jervis's signal and *Culloden* had started to tack almost before the order was given. The fleet now tacked in succession, *Blenheim* followed by *Prince George*, *Orion* and *Colossus*. Murray's ship had just begun her manoeuvre when her foreyard and fore topsail yard were both shot away, preventing her from tacking. Forced to wear instead *Colossus* received a raking broadside from a nearby Spanish three-decker. Seeing the danger Murray's ship was in Saumarez backed his topsail to come to *Colossus*'s assistance, *Orion* providing covering fire whilst Murray completed his manoeuvre before resuming her position in the line.

Troubridge had done well to anticipate Jervis's order but it would still take some time for the whole fleet to finish tacking. By the time the British van were sailing back in a north-east direction, the rear of the British line would still be sailing in the opposite direction, which would

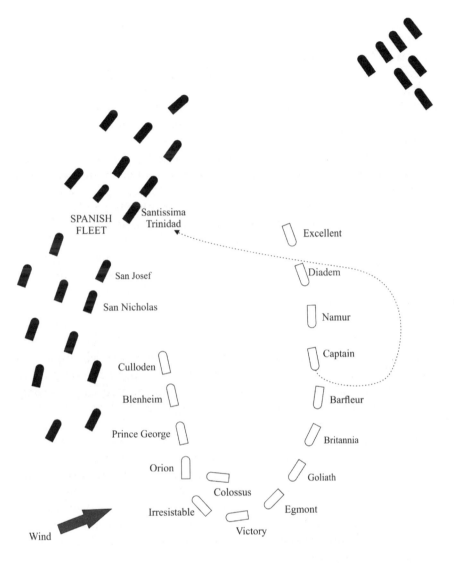

The Battle of Cape St Vincent, 14 February 1797.

give the two Spanish groups an opportunity to pass behind the rear of the British and link up with one another. Nelson, in his position towards the rear of the line, immediately saw the danger and ordered his flag-captain, Miller to wear out of formation, *Captain* was a nimble ship and was able to cross in front of the last ship in the British formation, *Excellent*, before she headed off to intercept the massive 120-gun *Santísima Trinidad*, one of the most powerful ships then afloat.

Jervis saw *Captain* wear out of formation, immediately understood what Nelson was attempting, and ordered 'each ship to take suitable station and engage as arriving up in succession'. This was the order for a general melee: the ships closest to Nelson were now those at the front and the rear of the British line which had now doubled back on itself. *Culloden* and Collingwood's *Excellent* made for *Captain*, which by now was being fired upon by *Santísima Trinidad* and four or five other Spanish ships.

Captain divided her fire between the 112-gun *San José* and the 80-gun *San Nicolás*. Troubridge's ship soon became disabled and fell away but her place was soon taken by *Excellent*, Collingwood placing his ship between *Captain* and the Spanish ships and opening fire on *San Nicolás*. *Blenheim*, *Prince George* and *Orion* now joined the action. After an hour-long battle against *Salvador del Mundo* the Spanish three-decker finally surrendered to Saumarez's ship and *Orion*'s last remaining boat was lowered from her stern, Lieutenant Luce taking possession of the prize as *Orion* made sail for the other ships, following closely behind Parker's flagship, *Prince George*.

By 3.00pm *Captain* was severely damaged. She had lost her foremast and most of her rigging, her sails were shot through, her wheel was also gone and she was losing steerage way. The two Spanish ships were also disabled. After *San José*'s mizzenmast was brought down by a shot from *Captain* she crashed into *San Nicolás* and the two ships became locked together. With the last bit of steerage way Nelson ordered his ship to be put alongside *San Nicolás*, he then ordered his boarders away. Nelson's first lieutenant, Edward Berry, leaped across to the Spanish ship, Nelson following close behind with several other members of the crew. By the time Nelson reached the quarterdeck Berry was already on the poop, hauling down the Spanish ensign. Finding themselves coming under fire from the admiral's stern gallery of *San José* the boarding party then quickly moved onto the second Spanish ship which offered no resistance. At 4.15pm the English colours were hoisted on both ships.

Following the capture of *Salvador del Mundo*, *Orion* had, for some time, been engaged with Cordoba's flagship, the massive four-decker *Santísima Trinidad*, the largest ship then afloat. Briefly assisted by *Excellent* and *Blenheim*, superior British gunnery had eventually succeeded in bringing down the Spanish ship's fore and mizzen masts and just before 5.00pm she ran up a white flag. Thinking this only indicated a truce, Saumarez had continued firing until *Santísima Trinidad* hoisted the Union Jack over the Spanish flag to indicate she had indeed surrendered. However, Saumarez could not yet take her as a prize as he had no more boats, or indeed crew, to spare. Those Spanish ships that had not yet been in action were now forming a line to windward of the British and Jervis made the signal for his fleet to wear and come to the support of the damaged *Captain* and *Colossus*. Forced to abandon his prize by what he called Jervis's 'ill timed, but doubtless necessary manoeuvre'[1] there was little Saumarez could do but watch *Santísima Trinidad* re-hoist her colours and sail off towards the rest of her fleet. At 4.50pm Jervis signalled for the fleet to form the line behind *Victory*. Within ten minutes firing on both sides had ceased.

The worst casualties suffered by the British fleet during the battle had been aboard *Captain*, *Culloden* and *Blenheim*. *Captain* had lost twenty-four men killed and fifty-six wounded whilst *Culloden* had ten dead and forty-seven wounded. Nelson had been injured during the battle when a large splinter from one of *Captain's* rigging blocks struck him in the side. *Blenheim's* casualties numbered twelve dead and forty-nine wounded. Thankfully, aboard *Orion* there had been no deaths and only eight wounded. Casualties among the rest of the fleet were also light, there were very few deaths and the maximum number of wounded was fourteen aboard *Irresistible*. The Spanish losses of around 250 killed and 550 wounded were by comparison much greater. Stepping aboard *Salvador del Mundo* Lieutenant Luce noted that there were more than fifty Spanish seamen lying on the decks with wounds that needed amputation. Those that had been amputated were bleeding to death. *Orion's* prize crew eventually found the Spanish doctor mid-butchery and with great difficulty refrained from throwing him over the side.

After the battle there appeared to be some doubt as to whether *Santísima Trinidad* had in fact surrendered to *Orion* as Saumarez had insisted. In a subsequent meeting between Nelson and Saumarez aboard the flagship Nelson declared 'it was true, Saumarez, that the *Santísima Trinidad* struck to you; the Spanish officers have acknowledged it.'[2] However it had been meant, Saumarez took this as a slight against his character; his account did not need corroboration, especially not from the enemy. 'Who ever doubted it sir?' He replied testily 'I hope there is no need for such evidence to establish the truth of the report of a British officer.'[3]

The morning following the battle saw the British fleet sailing slowly east towards Lagos Bay, twenty miles east of Cape St Vincent, towing the four captured Spanish ships (*Orion* had *San José* under tow) along with *Captain*. Both *Culloden* and *Colossus*, the two ships that had collided prior to the battle, were now handling so badly that they were barely able to stay with the line. The Spanish fleet, still visible in the distance was still more or less intact and could have easily re-started the action

71

if Cordoba had wanted to, indeed at one point during the afternoon it appeared as if they might, but in the end the Spanish fleet turned and sailed back to Cadiz.

Jervis did not single out any particular officer for individual praise in his official despatches, though in a private letter to Lord Spencer he praised both Troubridge and Hallowell. Nelson was quick to send his own version of events back to Britain on the frigate *Lively*. His despatches caused a sensation in a country tired of war and starved of good news, his account of the capture of *San Nicolás* and *San José*, what he called his 'Patent Bridge for Boarding First Rates' in particular capturing the public's imagination.

The Spanish prisoners, estimated by Saumarez to be around 3,000 men, were landed at Lagos Bay and the fleet proceeded to Lisbon, anchoring in the Tagus on 1 March. On 6 March Jervis detached *Irresistible*, now bearing Nelson's broad pendant, *Leander* and *Orion* to intercept two convoys, one from San Sebastian that was expected to join the outbound trade to the West Indies assembling at Cadiz and another from Buenos Ayres consisting of several treasure ships bound for Spain. The three-week cruise proved unsuccessful as the Spanish treasure ships could not be located and on 28 March the squadron returned to Lisbon and Nelson transferred back to *Captain*.

Reinforcements, including the 110-gun *Ville de Paris*, had now arrived from Britain and on 2 April Jervis, now Earl St Vincent, resumed his blockade of Cadiz. Hoping to tempt the Spanish out of port he began a loose blockade with Nelson, now a rear admiral, in command of the advanced squadron (*Captain*, *Orion*, *Zealous*, *Culloden*, *Irresistible*, *Colossus* and *Romulus*) cruising between Cape St Vincent and Cape St Mary. On 10 April Saumarez wrote to Martha of his situation. 'It is pleasanter than remaining in the constant order of sailing, more especially to me, who thou knowest to be so great an enemy to all order. These two days past we have had blowing weather which has prevented our taking a view of our friends in Cadiz ... I shall not have the patience to remain much longer without dying of the vapours.'[4]

On 13 April Nelson was dispatched into the Mediterranean with *Captain*, *Colossus* and *Leander* to escort the convoy of 3,400 troops being evacuated from Elba to Gibraltar. This now left Saumarez in charge of the inshore squadron. On the morning of 26 April his ships were cruising off the Spanish coast when two enemy vessels were spotted to the south-east. Saumarez immediately ordered the 74-gun *Irresistible*, George Martin, and the frigate *Emerald*, Velterers Cornewall Berkeley, to give chase. Realising they had been spotted, the Spanish frigates *Santa Elena* and *Ninfa* made for the safety of Conil Bay, north of Cape Trafalgar where they dropped anchor. Successfully rounding the Laja de Cape Rocha, a dangerous rock formation to the north of Conil Bay, *Irresistible* and *Emerald* engaged the Spanish ships and, after an action lasting an hour and a half *Santa Elena* and *Ninfa* hauled down their colours. Having cut their anchor cable the crew of *Santa Elena* let their ship drift onto the rocks before escaping ashore. She was towed off the rocks but sank shortly after. The Spanish had lost eighteen killed and thirty wounded in the encounter, while the British had one dead and one wounded aboard *Irresistible*. Prior to the battle both Spanish ships had been carrying a large quantity of specie but they had successfully loaded the treasure onto a Spanish fishing vessel which then passed through the British fleet unmolested. Aboard *Ninfa* the British discovered three boxes containing dissected birds and plants intended for the Spanish Royal Family. Saumarez forwarded these to the Spanish admiral, Massaredo, under a flag of truce.

With peace expected between both sides at any time the British and Spanish at Cadiz were eager to maintain cordial relationships. Massaredo had kept St Vincent's blockading ships informed of news from Britain and there was also an exchange of personal messages. Saumarez now entered into a correspondence with Massaredo concerning the exchange of prisoners. On 29 April Massaredo wrote to Saumarez. 'You will imagine sir, much better than I can express, the sense of gratitude which I feel in hearing of the kind assistance and attention which you show to the brave men who were wounded and of the good accommodation which the officers and men in general have met with. Together with my gratitude on this account, do me the honour, sir, to receive the real estimation and respect with which I offer myself to your services. God guard you, sir, many years!'[5] Saumarez was rapidly proving himself a skilled diplomat and on 11 May St Vincent wrote. 'You approve yourself so able in the diplomatique, that you need no assistance from me: in truth, a better despatch could not have been penn'd than yours of yesterday to Don Joseph De Mazarrado.'[6]

In late April the government had sent St Vincent a proposal to attack Cadiz in order to capture or burn the ships in port and the arsenal. St Vincent was given permission to use the troops and artillery recently evacuated from Elba together with 1,000 troops from Gibraltar commanded by General O'Hara. When Saumarez heard of the plan he told St Vincent 'that if possession was taken of Fort St Mary, it would in a great degree leave us as masters of the entrance of Cadiz, and enable us to drive all the outward ships up the harbour, and possibly destroy some of them'.[7] Cadiz, was however, stoutly defended. The harbour wall bristled with guns and there were around 4,000 soldiers in the port. St Vincent eventually shelved his plans for a full-blown assault on Cadiz and began organising a series of small scale attacks instead.

Spanish gunboats operating in the waters off Cadiz remained a nuisance, frequently attacking the ships of the inshore squadron and St Vincent now ordered Saumarez to lead an expedition to cut out several of these vessels which had been observed at anchor at Cadiz. However, from his position close to shore Saumarez was better able to observe these vessels and smelled a trap. Thinking the mission close to suicidal he refused to take any married men with him. Having voiced his disappointment at his name being omitted from the mission list posted in the ward room, Captain John Savage soon found himself stood before Saumarez in the admiral's Great Cabin. Saumarez assured the captain of the marines that neither his zeal nor his intrepidity were in question but told him: 'This is a desperate enterprise, many will fall; and if you should be one, who is to support your wife and family? The case is different with me: I am ordered and my duty is to obey. Perhaps if Lord St Vincent knew what I do, he would not send us.'[8] Saumarez would hear no further arguments from Savage. The expedition set of but had not gone far when a severe storm blew up. Struggling against strong headwinds the boats were forced to return to their ships. As Saumarez had suspected, it was later discovered that the Spanish gunboats were unmanned and had been moored permanently in position with chains to lure the British within range of the shore batteries.

Chapter 10

Mutiny and Blockade:
April 1797 – April 1798

Since the commencement of the war with France the navy had been forced to rely on impressment, an authority from the state to draft seamen between the ages of eighteen and fifty-five for military service. However, the supply of pressed men could not keep pace with demand and in 1795 Parliament passed the Quota Act, from then on each county and large port had to provide a set number of men for the navy every year. More often than not these men were petty criminals offered an alternative to a life behind bars.

By early 1797 high levels of inflation caused by the war had begun to seriously affect seamen's wages, unchanged since 1658. At the same time ships were spending longer at sea and the sudden influx of Quota Men, unused to life aboard ship and often intent on causing mischief, had seriously affected the morale amongst crews.

In April the growing discontent over years of poor pay and increasingly bad working conditions finally resulted in a full-scale mutiny at Spithead, all sixteen ships of Bridport's Channel Fleet refusing to weigh anchor when they were ordered back to sea. Having ignored all the warning signs, the Admiralty was now forced to enter into negotiations with the mutineers, whose demands were, in fact, quite reasonable. They included improved pay, more fresh vegetables while in port, proper care of the sick and an end to the custom where the purser was able to keep two ounces in every pound. After several weeks of negotiations the mutineers and the Admiralty finally came to an agreement. The sailors' demands were met and, following the issue of a royal pardon, on 17 May the fleet finally put to sea. The following day Martha wrote to her husband, happy to report a satisfactory conclusion to the mutiny: 'With heartfelt pleasure I acquaint Thee that Disciple & Order are once more restor'd. This Mutiny while it stands recorded as the most serious that has ever threatened this Country must at the same time excite the astonishment of the World at the regularity with which these men conducted themselves who at other times, when left to their own conduct ... are the most Disorderly Beings upon the Earth!'[1]

With St Vincent's fleet having recently been reinforced by ships from England there was a very real possibility that the mutiny might now spread to his own fleet. *Theseus* was a particularly troublesome vessel and was 'in a most deplorable state of licentiousness and disorder'.[2] Her captain, John Alymer, an officer whom St Vincent thought 'not fit to command',[3] had been keeping a continuous armed guard aboard ship, fearing her mutinous crew would sail to Cadiz given half a chance. On 24 May Nelson, now a rear admiral, returned to the fleet from Gibraltar. Two days later Aylmer was transferred to *Captain* and Nelson, Miller, his six lieutenants and about forty of his men moved to *Theseus*. After a couple of weeks a note was found on *Theseus*'s deck stating that thanks to Nelson, Miller and the officers from *Captain* the ship's company was now 'happy and comfortable' and would 'shed the last drop'[4] of their blood to fight the French and support Nelson.

In order to keep up the pressure on the Spanish and to keep his own men occupied and distracted from mutinous thoughts, St Vincent now ordered Nelson to carry out a night assault on Cadiz. On the night of 3 July a bomb vessel with Nelson aboard was towed into position by eight ships' boats, including *Orion*'s launch commanded by Acting Lieutenant John Tancock, an officer who had first served under Saumarez as a master's mate aboard *Crescent*, a route frequently taken by passed midshipmen still waiting to be promoted. The operation quickly ran into difficulties for when the bomb vessel's crew tried to fire the mortar it failed go off. By now the alarm had been raised and the Spanish had sent gunboats to investigate. Nelson got into his barge and went off in pursuit of the gunboats with Miller following close behind in his launch. Shots were fired as Nelson and his crew attempted to board the largest Spanish vessel and there was desperate hand-to-hand fighting with swords and cutlasses. Twice Nelson was nearly killed but each time his life was saved by his coxswain John Sykes, who at one point used his arm to deflect a cutlass blow aimed at Nelson's head. Miller and his crew soon boarded the vessel and joined in the fighting. The Spanish were eventually overpowered and the boat taken. With the arrival of the other British boats the remaining Spanish gunboats withdrew. The operation was largely a failure and although Nelson had shown great personal courage it had been poorly planned and executed. The lieutenants in charge of the ships' boats were inexperienced and had been poorly briefed by Nelson, the bomb vessel had been abandoned in the fight against the gunboats and it was with some difficulty that Miller had managed to recover it.

Discipline remained a problem aboard the blockading British ships and St Vincent was kept busy trying to maintain order. He had already threatened to fire on *Marlborough* when her crew refused to hang one mutineer. *St George* was a particularly troublesome ship and in order to maintain discipline several men were removed to other ships, *Orion* included. On 8 July St Vincent had two of *St George*'s crew arrested for mutinous behaviour and court-martialled. On Sunday 9 July, barely twenty-four hours after their sentence had been passed, the men were hanged from the yardarm of *St George*, watched by two boatloads of crew from every ship in the fleet. Nelson approved of St Vincent's actions but when Vice Admiral Sir Charles Thompson complained publicly over the use of a religious day for executions St Vincent dismissed him from the fleet. One can easily imagine what Saumarez, a devout Christian who detested flogging, thought over the affair but he appears to have kept his own counsel.

According to Saumarez's biographer, Ross, three days before the hangings a mutinous sailor, due to be hanged himself, had arrived from *St George* aboard *Orion*. On the morning of 9 July Saumarez sent for this man. Reminding the sailor, a carpenter's mate, of his duties and responsibilities and of the seriousness of his crimes, Saumarez then surprised the sailor by informing him that he was not sending him back to *St George* to watch the execution of his fellow sailors. Overcome, the sailor was said to have broken down and promised to serve Saumarez loyally from then on.

During a night raid in April one of St Vincent's best young officers, Captain Richard Bowen of the frigate *Terpsichore*, had cut out a Spanish vessel worth £30,000 from the port of Santa Cruz in Tenerife, a stopping-off point for treasure ships on their way back from the Americas to Spain. St Vincent now agreed to a plan devised by Nelson and Troubridge to attack the port and cut out the treasure ships. Arriving at Tenerife on 20 July the first two British assaults achieved little and were quickly beaten off by the Spanish. Exasperated by these failures Nelson decided he would lead the next attack, a frontal assault on the town, personally. As he stepped out of his boat, sword in hand, he was hit above the right elbow by a musket ball. Nelson was taken back to his ship and his shattered arm was amputated. By early morning only half of the landing force had made it ashore, their ammunition soaked through. Negotiations were begun with the local Spanish governor, a truce was agreed to and the British were allowed to march back through the town with drums beating and colours flying.

The raid, which was of no strategic importance, had been a complete disaster, with 153 men dead and 173 wounded. Nelson might have lost an arm but the navy had lost some of its best young officers including Bowen. On 16 August, three weeks after they had left Tenerife the squadron finally reached the British fleet stationed off Cadiz and a dejected Nelson reported to St Vincent aboard his flagship *Ville de Paris*. St Vincent arranged for Nelson to return home along with all the other men wounded in the battle and on 20 August *Seahorse* left its station off Cadiz bound for Spithead.

During Nelson's absence command of the inshore squadron had once again devolved to Saumarez. On 12 August St Vincent bet him £100 that a peace deal would be signed between Britain and Spain within a month. Following their wager *Orion* escorted a convoy to Gibraltar where she remained to be re-provisioned before returning to blockade duty off Cadiz. On 8 September Saumarez made a note in his diary: 'Received from the Earl of St Vincent 444 dollars and a half'.[5]

On 15 November Sir William Parker took over command of the inshore squadron to allow *Orion* to sail to Lisbon with the bulk of St Vincent's fleet for a refit. *Orion* entered the Tagus on 25 November and returned to Cadiz a month later. Saumarez continued his exchange of letters with the Spanish, for which he continued to receive the approval of his commander-in-chief. There was also news from home. In October 1797 Napoleon had been made commander of the Army of England and with an army of 50,000 men camped outside the Channel ports and talk of a fantastical 'floating machine' a quarter of a mile long. Martha wrote of the invasion scare that had gripped the country. 'All descriptions of People have caught the generous flame … it is truly delightful to see Patriotism surmounting avarice & all other selfish passions.' The sailors of the recently-mutinous Channel Fleet had subscribed a month's pay to the defence of their country and Martha was confident that 'all the corps in the country will follow this noble example'.[6] Napoleon eventually concluded that any invasion of England would end in disaster and so turned his attention elsewhere, proposing that French forces invade Egypt.

On 7 February 1798 the Cadiz Fleet put to sea. Hoping to engage the Spanish St Vincent left the Tagus and sailed to Cape St Vincent. In the meantime Massaredo had been forced to return to port. His crews were all inexperienced, (before sailing he had stripped all the fishing boats at Cadiz of their crews), several ships had run aground and others had got into difficulty. Disappointed to have missed the Spanish, St Vincent returned to the Tagus. *Orion* remained with the fleet until 28 April when she was ordered to Gibraltar for a refit.

Chapter 11

Chasing the French:
April 1798 – August 1798

On 1 April 1798 the British government had received a letter from the Austrians requesting that the Royal Navy return to the Mediterranean. The British were desperate for Austria's support in the war against France but Austria, a co-signatory of the Treaty of Campo Formio, would not form a new alliance with Britain unless she promised to protect Austria's southern flank. On 6 April the government agreed to send a part of St Vincent's fleet back into the Mediterranean. By then they had become aware of a massive build-up of men and equipment at Toulon as well as the northern Italian ports of Genoa, Civitavecchia and Bastia. A large French fleet was about to set sail, but no one quite knew where it was headed, though most in the Cabinet believed that Cadiz was the most likely destination. This changed on 1 May when the government received intelligence that the types of transports gathering at Toulon and the Italian ports would be unsuitable for use in the Atlantic: this meant that the most likely destination for the French fleet was somewhere in the Mediterranean, one or two in the government even suggesting Egypt as a possibility. It was known however, that Napoleon was touring the Channel ports and the threat of an invasion of either England or Ireland had not yet diminished. Later that day the Cabinet decided to send a further ten ships of the line to St Vincent at Cadiz and on 2 May he was ordered to send 'a squadron under the command of some discreet flag officer into the Mediterranean with instructions to him to proceed in the quest of the said armament, and on falling in with it ... to take and destroy it'.[1]

On the morning of 30 April Nelson returned to the fleet aboard his new flagship, *Vanguard*. St Vincent had already decided to dispatch a force to hunt for the French fleet, pre-empting his instructions from the Admiralty, and Nelson was immediately ordered to sail to Gibraltar where he would be joined by two more 74s, Saumarez's *Orion* and

Alexander, Alexander Ball, along with two frigates and a sloop. Nelson was to scout along the southern coast of France past Toulon and on towards Genoa in an attempt to discover whether the enemy fleet had yet sailed, then return to Gibraltar.

Having come to the conclusion that a substantial force would have to be sent to find and destroy the French fleet that was now at large, the Admiralty had instructed Rear Admiral Roger Curtis, who was cruising off the coast of Ireland with a squadron of eight ships, to sail south and join up with St Vincent's fleet off Cadiz. *Vanguard* and the frigate *Emerald* reached Gibraltar on 4 May, where Nelson rendezvoused with *Orion, Alexander*, the frigate *Terpsichore* and the sloop *Bonne Citoyenne*. *Orion* had been at Gibraltar for a week, enough time for the ship to be watered and provisioned and for a gang of workmen from the dockyard to caulk the hull. *Alexander* had arrived at Gibraltar on 2 May, just two days before Nelson who brought with him a letter from Saumarez's eight-year-old son, James: 'Sir Horatio Nelson being on his return to Lisbon, I am very happy to send a few lines by him. The Figs and Plums arrived last night and we are very thankful to you for them. Mary says she would rather see you than all the Plums and I think so too. We had a party the other day and all found me like you and I am very glad of it. Cartarette is a very pretty little girl and I wish you could come and see her.'[2]

Having reached the last friendly port in the region *Vanguard* took on the stores that would require for the long voyage ahead. Nelson's flag-captain, Edward Berry also cleared some deck space by removing several spare topmasts, a decision he would soon come to regret. At 6.00pm on 8 May Nelson hoisted the signal to weigh anchor. Light winds meant that the ships had to be slowly warped out of the harbour and it was daylight before the squadron finally headed out into the Mediterranean. Nelson had been expecting to be joined by two more frigates, *Flora* and *Caroline*, but neither vessel showed up at the rendezvous. On 17 May *Terpsichore* captured the French privateer *Pierre* whilst seventy miles south of Toulon and Nelson learned that Napoleon had arrived at Toulon ten days earlier and that the French fleet, twelve ships of the line commanded by Admiral Brueys aboard his flagship *L'Orient*, were almost ready to put to sea. *Pierre*'s crew did not know, or would not say, where they were headed. Nelson sent an update of the situation to St Vincent and positioned his squadron so that he could watch the French fleet from a safe distance as it sailed out of port.

By 17 May Nelson's small squadron were positioned roughly seventy-five miles south of Toulon, reporting back to St Vincent on the preparations of the French fleet. The wind, which had been moderate for most of the passage eastwards, now began to build and by the evening on 20 May the ships were all close-hauled and making preparations for the bad weather that was about to hit them. The largest sails, the courses, were taken down and the topsails were reefed to prevent them from tearing apart in the gale. The rain grew stronger and the winds continued to build until finally around midnight the ships found themselves in the middle of a raging storm. At 3.00am *Orion's* main topsail was shredded to ribbons and blew overboard. Saumarez now ordered extra breech ropes to be fitted to the long guns to prevent them breaking free and crashing about the decks as the ship began rolling heavily in the swells.

Dawn revealed the sad spectacle of Nelson's flagship minus her foremast, main and mizzen topmasts. The squadron had been dispersed and there was no sign of either *Terpsichore* or *Bonne Citoyenne*. Now sitting under bare poles, a virtually unmanageable *Vanguard* was in danger of being wrecked on the nearby coast of Corsica. All was not lost, however: the small, rarely-used spritsail beneath her damaged bowsprit was unfurled and the ship slowly began to wear round until she was finally pointing away from danger. With some difficulty *Orion*, *Alexander* and *Emerald* managed to keep company with *Vanguard* as the storm raged on into the evening. However, during the night the remaining frigate, *Emerald*, parted company with the squadron.

Throughout the early hours of the morning the storm finally began to ease off. Saumarez was hailed by Nelson and informed that he intended to head for Orestano Bay, on the western side of Sardinia. Land was sighted around midday but it soon became clear that the crippled *Vanguard* would not be able to make it to their intended destination. Nelson decided therefore to head for the sheltered anchorage at San Pietro, a small island off the south-west coast of Sardinia. At 3.00pm *Vanguard* hoisted a signal requesting *Alexander* to take her under tow. This was a difficult manoeuvre and it took several attempts before Ball was finally able to get a line across to Nelson's flagship. The worst was not yet over, however, as now that the two ships were joined together there was a very real danger of them crashing into one another in the heaving waves.

At around 6.00pm the wind dropped and the two ships began to drift towards the shore. *Alexander* and *Orion* both set their studding sails to catch what little wind there was and an hour later San Pietro was sighted eleven miles distant. By midnight they were so close to the island that, through the darkness, they could just make out the line of surf as it crashed onto the rocks. Nelson and Ball spoke to one another through their ships' loudhailers. Nelson told Ball that he should release the tow to save his own ship but Ball stubbornly refused. In the early hours of the morning of 23 May the ships were finally saved by a breeze that sprang up from the north-west and *Orion* scouted on ahead to look for a safe passage into the bay. By noon *Alexander* and *Vanguard* had managed to limp into the shallow, calm anchorage of Carloforte where they were greeted by the port captain who informed Nelson that, owing to an alliance between France and Sardinia, Royal Navy ships were not allowed to anchor in his port. Nelson responded by informing the officer that he would send someone ashore to speak to the governor.

With the two ships lashed together, repairs were begun. Whilst *Orion* cruised offshore, carpenters from all three ships set about repairing *Vanguard*'s broken poles using spare masts, yards and every other scrap of wood they could lay their hands on. The shattered foremast was lifted out and replaced by *Alexander*'s spare fore topmast, the bowsprit was fished and the mizzen topmast was replaced by a converted spar from *Orion*. On 24 May Nelson wrote 'the exertions of Sir James Saumarez in the *Orion*, and Captain A. Ball, in the *Alexander*, have been wonderful; if the ship had been in England, months would have been taken to send her to sea: here, my operations will not be delayed four days.'[3]

After several days' furious activity, repairs to Nelson's small squadron were finally completed and by 25 May *Vanguard* and *Alexander* were sitting at anchor alongside one another, ready to put to sea again. That morning Saumarez had gone ashore to speak to the governor of San Pietro, Francesco Maria de Nobili, who agreed to provide the British with as many oxen, sheep and poultry as could be sourced within the next twenty-four hours. Whilst Saumarez was ashore meeting with the governor a ship was spotted off the island and *Orion* was ordered to investigate. Saumarez returned to his ship but was disappointed to discover that it was not the enemy but a neutral vessel from Cagliari. Two days later another vessel was spotted and again *Orion* gave chase. This time the vessel proved to be a Spanish brig laden with wheat. Rather than burn the ship Saumarez decided to allow the crew on shore to raise money for a ransom. Having received several slaughtered oxen, two bullocks and some vegetables from de Nobili, *Vanguard* and *Alexander* weighed anchor and left San Pietro early on 28 May, the governor giving the British squadron a nine-gun salute on its departure, an act for which he received an official reprimand from the King of Sardinia.

The winds were now light and progress slow as Nelson's squadron sailed towards Toulon. The brig captured by *Orion* had been sent to Gibraltar with Nelson's dispatches but Saumarez was still worried news of the gale might reach Martha before she learned that they were all

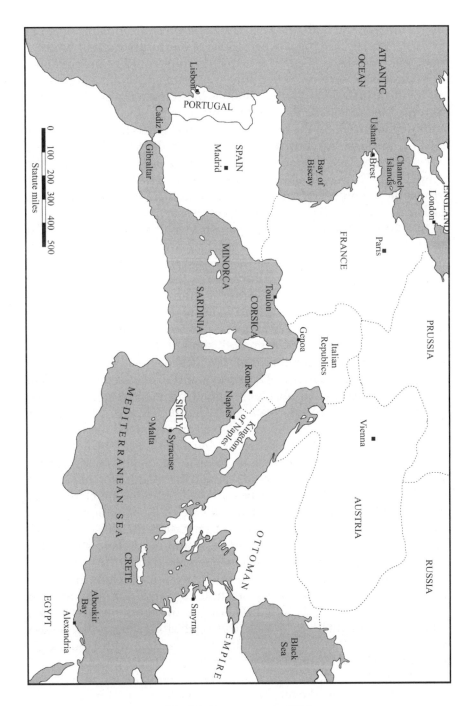

The Mediterranean in 1798.

83

safe. Saumarez and Ball dined aboard *Vanguard* and Saumarez noted in his diary 'We all form great expectations of our future success, which, I trust, will be realised. Certain it is that no ships could be ordered on a more promising service.'[4] On 5 June *Vanguard*'s lookouts spotted the sails of the British sloop *Mutine*, Thomas Masterman Hardy, dispatched from the Mediterranean Fleet with news from St Vincent. Rather than simply report back on the movements of the French fleet, Nelson was now to find, 'take, sink, burn or destroy' it.[5] In order to do this St Vincent was sending Nelson a detachment of eleven of his best ships under the command of Thomas Troubridge. Nelson decided that when Troubridge arrived they should first sail for Corsica and then, if need be, carry on further down the Italian coast to Naples to search for the French.

On 7 June *Orion* captured a Spanish vessel out of Genoa whilst *Alexander* gave chase to a second vessel. Saumarez did not have enough men to put aboard his prize so he decided to ransom her for 10,000 dollars. Aboard the vessel were thirty-six ex-Jesuit priests and a number of Swiss recruits for the Italian army, eight of whom agreed to serve aboard *Orion* with the marines. During the night *Orion* lost contact with *Vanguard*. With *Alexander* now almost out of sight Saumarez feared that he might become separated from both ships. The following afternoon however, Saumarez was relieved of 'the most acute anxiety'[6] when he fell in with *Leander*, Thomas Thompson, and discovered that Nelson had been joined by Troubridge's squadron (*Culloden*, *Bellerophon*, *Minotaur*, *Defence*, *Zealous*, *Audacious*, *Goliath*, *Theseus*, *Majestic* and *Swiftsure*). On 9 June *Orion* fell in with Nelson's enlarged squadron and the following day they were joined by *Alexander*.

Nelson now had a dilemma as to who to make his second-in-command. Saumarez was the senior captain in the squadron but Nelson would have preferred to give the position to Troubridge, his close friend of over twenty years. St Vincent was aware of the situation – he too favoured Troubridge and had given permission for Nelson to send Saumarez home but Nelson realised he would need every ship at his disposal to fight the French and so *Orion* remained part of his squadron. In the end Nelson dodged the problem by not officially having a number two. This was clearly a snub to Samaurez, but he and Troubridge were friends and he kept his thoughts on the matter, whatever they might be, to himself. During the following weeks Nelson would meet, weather and sea conditions permitting, with Troubridge, Saumarez, Ball and his most senior captains as often as possible aboard *Vanguard* to discuss their tactics once they eventually fell in with the French. They examined every possibility, every eventuality, including night actions and attacks on ships at harbour. Doubling the line was also discussed. This entailed sailing down either side of the enemy line to attack it. It was a particularly risky manoeuvre as it ran the risk of ships accidentally firing on one another and Saumarez had openly voiced his concerns when it was suggested. As well as being dangerous he also thought it unnecessary, owing to the superior gunnery of the British crews.

The fourteen British ships of the line now set sail for Corsica. The weather throughout the week was changeable, light airs one minute, heavy thunderstorms the next, during one brief squall *Bellerophon* lost her fore topmast and a studding sail. By 12 June the squadron had reached the northern tip of Corsica. The squadron turned south and late in the evening they reached Elba. Having sailed along the coastline of Corsica with no sign of the French fleet Nelson decided to dispatch Hardy in *Mutine* to the port of Civitavecchia, fifty miles north of Rome, in order to seek out more intelligence. The squadron sailed down along the eastern coast of Corsica, past the harbour at Bastia, They then passed through the narrow straits that separate the island of Elba and the small, low lying island of Pianosa before heading off along the Italian coast. *Mutine* returned from Civitavecchia on 14 June, having gained no new information and so Nelson decided to sail for Naples to see if the British ambassador, Sir William Hamilton, might have some idea of the whereabouts of the French fleet, or better still, some definite information from home.

On 15 June Saumarez dined with Nelson aboard *Vanguard*. A day earlier the squadron had fallen in with a Tunisian vessel which had signalled that the French were now at Syracuse. Although the accuracy of this information could not be confirmed it did nothing to dispel Nelson's growing suspicions regarding the ultimate destination of the French fleet. Nelson discussed with Saumarez the possibility that the French were headed for Alexandria with the intention of linking up with Tipu Sahib in order to drive the British out of India. Saumarez hoped they would frustrate French plans by attacking the enemy 'before they reach the place of their destination; and, as we know them to have a great number of troops embarked in their men-of-war, they will become an easier prey to us.'[7]

On the night of 15 June Midshipman Hill was spotted entering the cabin of *Orion*'s Fourth Lieutenant, Francis Cateby Roberts, under suspicious circumstances. His fellow officers agreed that the 'dreadful crime of s——y'[8] had not occurred but *Orion*'s fourth lieutenant was still expelled from the wardroom. Saumarez asked Nelson to convene a court martial to try Roberts for 'infamous and scandalous actions unbecoming the character of an officer and a gentleman, in derogations of God's honour and corruption of good manners'[9] (the thirty-second Article of War) and Nelson agreed to try Roberts at the first available opportunity.

Early on the morning of 17 June the British squadron sailed into the Bay of Naples, dropping anchor several miles offshore. Nelson sent Troubridge ashore to meet with Hamilton and by 8.00am *Culloden*'s captain was back aboard the flagship reporting to Nelson. The French had been seen off Malta on 8 June, preparing to attack the island, but Hamilton could not say for certain where they would be headed for next. Nelson had asked for ships to help search for the French fleet but as a neutral the Kingdom of the Two Sicilies was not in a position to provide Nelson with his desperately-needed frigates. However, the Queen of Naples, Maria Carolina, sister to the murdered Marie Antoinette, would do whatever she could to support Nelson; all the ports in the Kingdom of Naples would be open to the British and although Nelson could not have any extra ships, he could have whatever other supplies he needed.

Troubridge and Hardy returned to their ships and the squadron weighed anchor. There was little wind to speed their passage and it was the evening of 19 June before they reached Calabria at the toe of Italy's boot, from where they had a clear view across to the volcanic island of Stromboli. The next day Sicily and the Straits of Messina could be seen in the distance. *Orion* took on a local pilot, an old man who reminded Saumarez of Charon, the ferryman of Hades. Passing close to the remains of the Faro of Messina, an ancient lighthouse that once guarded the entrance to the straits, the ships slowly and carefully made their way through the dangerous waters. As they entered the straits several small boats from Messina came out to greet them. The British consul, James Tough, went aboard *Vanguard* and informed Nelson that Napoleon had captured Malta, and that the French were now at anchor off the island of Gozo to the north of Malta. Pushed along both by the wind and the tide the ships sped on through the straits, cheered on their way by people lining the shores. As they emerged out of the straits into the Ionian Sea, the local pilots left the ships, and, with a fresh wind from the north-west, the British squadron pressed on for Malta.

At daybreak on 22 June Nelson's squadron was roughly thirty-five nautical miles south-east of Cape Passero in Sicily when lookouts from *Defence*, John Peyton, spotted the sails of four ships in the distance, *Leander* was immediately sent off to investigate. Later that morning *Mutine* spotted another vessel, which turned out to be a Genoese brig out of Malta. After an exchange of signals Hardy learned that the brig had passed through the French fleet which had left Malta four days earlier. Ordering his ships to shorten sail, Nelson requested a meeting with his senior captains, Saumarez, Troubridge, Darby and Ball. Nelson began the meeting by explaining the general situation as he understood it; the French had taken Malta six days previous, left a garrison on the island then departed. Having asked if any of his senior captains could say for certain that the French were headed for Sicily, he then suggested an alternative destination for the enemy fleet, Egypt. The assembled captains all agreed that they should push for Alexandria. However, sailing upon the 'merest conjecture only, and not on any positive information', Saumarez was glad that the final decision rested with Nelson and not with him as he feared 'it would be more than my too irritable nerves would bear. They have already been put to trial in two or three instances this voyage.'[10] The meeting had just broken up when *Leander* signalled that the four ships she had been sent to investigate were all frigates. Nelson did not want to waste any more time, so he recalled *Leander* and at 9.00am the British squadron turned, and headed off for Alexandria. The four ships that *Defence* had spotted that morning were in fact Bruey's outlying frigates. The previous night, as the French fleet sailed east, several officers had reported that they had heard the sounds of signal guns in the distance. Passing within several miles of each other during the night, the French and British had narrowly avoided a meeting that would almost certainly have changed the future course of the war.

Nelson's squadron travelled the 600 nautical miles to Alexandria in six days, aided by favourable north-westerly winds. The lack of fast-sailing frigates was crippling Nelson's efforts to find the French but he nevertheless kept his squadron sailing in close order. Nelson's starboard column consisted of *Culloden*, *Theseus*, *Alexander*, *Vanguard*, *Minotaur*, *Swiftsure* and *Audacious*. The larboard column, under the command of Saumarez, was made up of *Defence*, *Zealous*, *Orion*, *Goliath*, *Majestic* and *Bellerophon*. On 28 June the squadron arrived off Alexandria and looked into the harbour, but to their great disappointment all they could see was four frigates, some merchantmen and a solitary Turkish line of battle ship which was offloading its main guns. As the ships sailed on towards the remains of the mighty Pharos lighthouse, Nelson sent *Mutine* into the port to see if the British consul any more information. Saumarez suggested they remain in Alexandria for a little while, pointing out how quickly the squadron had just sailed the 600 miles from to Sicily to Egypt. The final decision of course lay with Nelson and at 11.00am the next morning the squadron left Alexandria heading north towards Turkey. Saumarez breakfasted with Nelson and spent the rest of the day aboard *Vanguard*. The ships now had to beat, with all sails, against the strong breeze that was blowing from the west. By 4 July the squadron was within fifty nautical miles of Cape Chelidonia in western Turkey. The ships were all running desperately low on food and water and, with the French still nowhere in sight, the decision was finally taken for the squadron to turn and head back to the nearest friendly port, Syracuse in Sicily.

The British reached Syracuse on 18 July. The entrance to the harbour was narrow but the winds were light and all the ships made it through without mishap and were at anchor by 3.00pm. Beyond its narrow entrance Syracuse opens out into a large, almost landlocked semi-circular harbour. This was the first opportunity that *Vanguard*, *Alexander* and *Orion* had had since leaving Gibraltar nearly two months earlier to replenish their supplies of water, which were almost exhausted. The situation aboard the other ships was not much better. The officers having been allowed ashore, Lieutenant Roberts made the most of the opportunity and fled *Orion* before his court martial could be held. Saumarez later wrote that he had found it necessary to send the unfortunate officer away. In his place he promoted Midshipman Dumaresq who, though he now received the pay of a lieutenant, could not be confirmed in that position, having not yet served six years as a midshipman.

Having received reports from several neutral vessels entering the harbour regarding the whereabouts of the French Nelson was now convinced that he was correct in his original assumption that they had sailed to Alexandria. However, rather than sail to Egypt direct, Nelson decided to sail via Greece in the hope of picking up some definite intelligence first. Re-provisioned, the squadron sailed from Syracuse on 26 July. At first the wind was so light that the ships had to be towed out of the harbour using the ships' boats, though it soon increased in strength. By 28 July the squadron had reached the southern coast of Greece and *Culloden* was despatched into the Gulf of Coron. Meeting with the Turkish governor Troubridge was informed that the French fleet had been seen about four weeks earlier off the coast of Crete, sailing south-east. *Culloden* rejoined the rest of the squadron towing a French brig loaded with wine behind her, a gift from the governor.

Troubridge reported back to Nelson and around 5.00pm *Vanguard* signalled to the other ships and they prepared to sail back to Alexandria. With the assistance of a fresh breeze the squadron covered the 800 nautical miles from Syracuse to Alexandria in four days. On 31 July all fourteen of Nelson's captains were summoned aboard *Vanguard* to receive their final instructions. That evening *Alexander* and *Swiftsure*, Benjamin Hallowell, were sent to scout ahead of the rest of the squadron which by now was spread out over several miles, with *Culloden*, towing its captured brig still laden with wine well to the rear. Early the next day the lookouts on *Alexander* spotted the Egyptian coast and by 10.00am the towers and the Pharos of Alexandria had come into view. The tricolour was flying from a number of the city's buildings and the previously empty port was now crowded with vessels including several hundred French transports, but there was still no sign of the French fleet, *Alexander*'s lookouts could only see two Turkish ships of the line and six French frigates. Ball signalled *Vanguard*. Saumarez wrote 'despondency nearly took possession of my mind, and I do not recollect ever to have felt so utterly hopeless or out of spirits as when we sat down to dinner.'[11] A fresh signal from the flagship ordered *Alexander* and *Swiftsure* to continue on further eastwards. The French fleet were nowhere to be seen but a despairing Nelson had no choice but to sail on, he was almost out of options. The ships pressed on and *Zealous*, Samuel Hood, and *Goliath*, Thomas Foley, now took the lead as they sailed along the Egyptian shoreline. At 2.30pm *Zealous* signalled that she had spotted a fleet at anchor. Fifteen minutes later she sent another signal: 'Sixteen sail of the line at anchor bearing east by south.' Cheering broke out on all the ships as the news quickly spread around the squadron. After a twelve-week, 1,800-mile chase the French fleet had finally been found.

Chapter 12

The Battle of the Nile: August 1798 – January 1799

Upon hearing that the French had been spotted, dinner was abandoned aboard *Orion* and, having quickly drunk a toast to their success, Saumarez and his senior officers raced onto the quarterdeck. The distance between the British and French ships was now roughly nine miles, Nelson's squadron had become stretched out with *Goliath* and *Zealous* racing ahead of the other ships. *Culloden*, still towing her French prize, was several miles to the rear and both *Alexander* and *Swiftsure* were even further away to the west. With only a light wind blowing into the bay from the north it would be dusk by the time the British finally engaged the French. With no accurate charts of the bay Nelson would either have to risk a dangerous night action in uncertain waters or postpone the attack until the next morning, but to wait meant losing the element of surprise along with the favourable wind. Nelson therefore decided on an immediate attack and at 3.00pm the signal 'Haul on the wind on the larboard tack' was sent up *Vanguard*'s halyards. The ships nearest to *Vanguard* quickly and smartly formed up in line whilst Troubridge immediately cast off the French brig and attempted to catch up with the rest of the squadron.

Just before 4.00pm *Goliath* and *Zealous* rounded the shoals of Aboukir Island. In front of them, in a line roughly three miles distant, lay thirteen French ships of the line. Bruey's ships were anchored in shallow water near to the shore in a line nearly two miles long, bows facing north-west. The lead ship *Guerrier* was close, though not as close as she should have been, to a line of shoals that ran out across the bay from Aboukir Point to a small, fortified, island. The van consisted of four 74-gun ships, *Guerrier*, *Conquerant*, *Spartiate* and *Aquilon*. Then came the larger ships: Admiral Blanquet's 80-gun *Franklin* was positioned ahead of the 120-gun *L'Orient* whilst another 80-gun ship, *Tonnant*, was positioned astern of Bruey's flagship. The rear of the French line, under the command of

Admiral Villeneuve consisted of three 74-gun ships, *Heureuse, Timoleon, Mercure*, Villeneuve's 80-gun flagship *Guillaume Tell* and the 74-gun *Genereux*.

The British ships continued to turn to larboard, until they were sailing almost parallel to the French fleet. Around 4.20pm two signals appeared on *Vanguard*'s halyards: the first was the order to 'clear for action'; the second was to prepare to anchor at the stern. Nelson's next two signals, hoisted together around 5.00pm, were orders to attack the enemy's van and centre. Nelson's plan was to sail down the enemy line and attack the van in force, overwhelming it. He would ignore the rear of the French line which, with the wind against them, would be unable to come to the aid of the other French ships. Nelson's final signal was one that was to remain flying throughout the battle: 'Engage the enemy more closely.'

Like most of the ships in the British squadron there were several women aboard Saumarez's ship, the wives of both seamen and officers. Ann Hopping, the wife of *Orion*'s second gunner, who was earning extra money as a seamstress, had just begun mending one of Saumarez's shirts when she heard the drum beating the men to quarters. As *Orion*'s crew raced to their stations to prepared the ship for battle Anne made her way down to the grand magazine in the bowels of the ship and was soon helping her husband Edward Hopping who was busy serving out the powder.

As *Goliath* drew closer to the French line Foley noticed that Bruey's ships were not using springs on their cables and had been left free to swing round into the shallows if the wind changed direction. If there was enough water in the shallows for a ship the size of *L'Orient* then there would clearly be enough for the smaller British ships. Foley's luck continued to hold for, when *Goliath* reached the lead French ship, he discovered that there was enough room to slip between its bow and the shoals to the north. Now *Goliath* would be able to turn and sail back down between the French fleet and the shore, doubling the line. Foley was confident that the French would not be anticipating such a manoeuvre and that the larboard sides of their ships would be completely unprepared for action. At 6.45pm, with darkness descending across the bay, *Goliath* turned, entered the shallows, and sailed down the inside of the French line, unleashing her first thunderous broadside on the lead French ship *Guerrier*.

As *Goliath* drew alongside *Guerrier* it became clear that the larboard guns of the leading French ship had indeed not been run out. Foley's ship dropped anchor but she was still running too much sail and by the time she finally came to a halt she found herself not alongside *Guerrier*

91

but the second ship in the French line, *Conquérant*. *Zealous* managed to successfully anchor alongside *Guerrier*, and, at a distance of around twenty-five yards, opened fire. After five minutes the French ship's foremast came crashing down across her bow and within twelve minutes she was completely dismasted.

By the time *Audacious*, Davidge Gould, dropped anchor opposite *Conquérant* Captain Dalbarade's ship had already been battered into submission by *Goliath*. *Conquérant* was a tired old ship, the rotten wood of her hull less capable of withstanding enemy fire than the other ships in her fleet and her smaller 18-pounders able to put up less of a fight. As the wounded Dalbarade was carried below he instructed his second-in-command to carry on fighting, but with the men refusing to stand by their guns the first lieutenant was soon forced to surrender to *Audacious*.

The next two British ships into action were *Orion* and *Theseus*. As she rounded the line Saumarez's ship fired a well-directed broadside into the heavily-engaged *Guerrier* but as she sailed past *Goliath* she was surprised by a broadside fired from a frigate stationed inshore of the main French fleet which injured two of *Orion*'s men. It was an unwritten rule of naval warfare that frigates and ships of the line did not fire on one another as it would be a very unequal contest. Shocked by this unexpected turn of events, Lieutenants Barker and Wells wanted to return fire immediately but Samaurez knew better, saying 'Let her alone, she will get courage and come nearer'.[1] Having shortened sail *Orion* lost way and as *Serieuse* caught up Saumarez ordered his helmsman to yaw the ship and for his starboard guns to fire. As expected, a single withering broadside at close range from *Orion*'s double-shotted guns completely dismasted the smaller ship. She veered away, and with her rudder now jammed, ran aground, half submerged in the shallows. Leaving *Serieuse* to her fate, the helm was put hard to starboard and *Orion* continued down the line of French ships. Saumarez had originally intended to anchor opposite *Aquilon* but, distracted by *Serieuse*, his ship was now too far to the east and could only give her original quarry a larboard broadside in passing. Anchoring at the bow not the stern as Nelson had ordered, *Orion* came to a halt in a position where she was able to fire on the starboard bows of *Peuple Souverain* and the starboard quarter of *Franklin*. Soon after *Orion* had dropped anchor a fire-raft was observed dropping down towards her. Fire, as events would later prove, was the greatest danger to any ship. The boat hanging over *Orion*'s stern had been shot through and the others were not ready so booms were therefore prepared to keep the raft away from *Orion*. Thankfully they were not needed as the current quickly swept the vessel past Saumarez's ship.

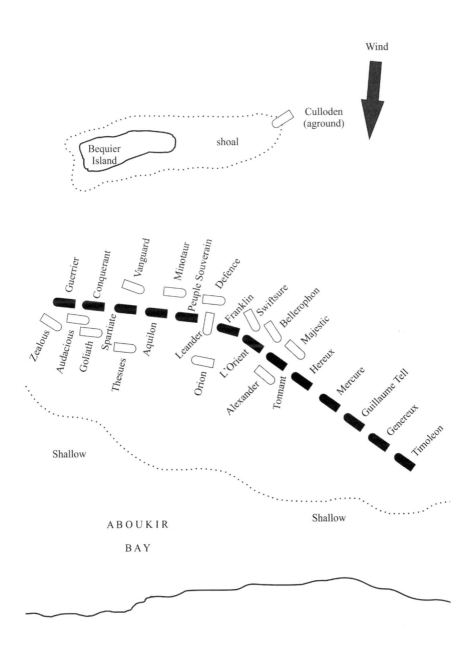

The Battle of the Nile, 1 August 1798.

93

The bay was now almost in complete darkness. Apart from their blue signal lights the only illumination came from the constant, sometimes simultaneous, flashes of gunfire that lit up the ships. With the inside of the French line crowded with British ships Nelson led the remainder of his squadron down the outside of it. Sailing past the shattered, mastless hulks of *Guerrier* and *Conquerant*, *Vanguard* dropped anchor close to *Spartiate*, firing her first broadside at the French ship just a few minutes after *Theseus* had taken up position on her opposite side. For a while *Vanguard* was exposed to fire from both *Spartiate* and the next ship in the French line, *Aquilon* but the pressure was relieved when *Minotaur* anchored alongside *Aquilon*, diverting some of her attention away from Nelson's flagship. The next British ship into action was *Bellerophon*.

Darby had originally intended to anchor his ship alongside *Franklin* but not for the first time that evening British anchor drill failed and by the time *Bellerophon* finally came to a halt she was stationed directly alongside the French flagship, the massive *L'Orient*, which now unleashed a devastating, double-shotted broadside at the smaller British ship. Once into action *Bellerophon*'s gun crews returned fire with a series of rapid broadsides. Almost immediately Darby was struck by in the head by a round fired by a French marine and he fell to the deck unconscious. *Bellerophon*'s first, second and fourth lieutenants were soon injured and with the fifth lieutenant now dead, Third Lieutenant Robert Cathcart assumed command of the ship. *Bellerophon* and *L'Orient* continued to trade blows for the next hour, *Bellerophon*'s masts becoming more and more precarious as her rigging continued to be shot through. Finally, around 8.00pm the mizzen mast gave way and fell down over the stern of the ship, shortly after this the mainmast crashed down over the starboard side of the forecastle.

Majestic also had trouble with her anchor drill and before she could be brought to she collided with *Hereux*, where she remained stuck for the next hour, only able to bring a few of her guns to bear. The British ship now came under sustained attack from *L'Orient* and Captain Westcott was soon killed by French musket fire. As his body was carried below his first lieutenant, Robert Cuthbert, took over command of the ship. It was only when *Majestic*'s jib boom broke that she was able to move clear of *Hereux*, anchoring across from the starboard bow of *Mercure*, the next ship in the French line.

Having abandoned her prize, *Culloden* was racing to catch up with the rest of the British ships. However, rounding the shoals that ran out from Aboukir Point, a man at the chains taking soundings, Troubridge's ship suddenly ran aground. *Culloden* immediately hoisted a warning to *Alexander* and *Swiftsure* and Ball and Hallowell both managed to alter course in time. Passing between *L'Orient* and *Tonnant*, Ball anchored his ship in a position where he could direct his fire at the French flagship's vulnerable stern. Very soon a fire was observed in the admiral's cabin which rapidly spread to the poop deck.

Seeing the fire taking hold of *L'Orient* and realising the danger his own ship, still anchored close to the French First Rate, was in, Third Lieutenant Cathcart ordered his ship's anchor cable to be cut. As *Bellerophon* drifted away from *L'Orient* her weakened foremast, her last remaining pole, came crashing down over the bows. Having narrowly avoided running aground *Swiftsure* was closing in on the French line when *Bellerophon*, dismasted and without any recognition lights, appeared in front of her out of the darkness. Thankfully Hallowell held his fire and as *Bellerophon*'s crippled hulk disappeared into the night *Swiftsure* continued towards the French line, positioning herself between *Franklin* and the bows of *L'Orient*.

Peuple Souverain had lost both her fore and main masts in her battle with *Orion* and *Defence* and her captain, Pierre-Paul Raccord, had been badly injured. Samaurez had also been injured, struck in the thigh by a large splinter of wood from one of *Orion*'s spare topmasts. He had been lucky; the same splinter had killed his clerk, Mr Baird and badly injured Midshipman Charles Miells, a favourite of his aboard ship. The force of the impact knocked Saumarez off his feet and he was dragged beneath the half deck by Captain Savage. Saumarez refused to go below with Miells to have his wound seen to and returned to the quarterdeck, though now limping badly. By now Nelson had also been wounded, struck above his right eye by a piece of shrapnel whilst examining a map of the bay. Convinced he had been mortally wounded and with blood pouring down his face, Nelson was helped down to the cockpit to see the ship's surgeon, but once there he insisted on waiting his turn with the other injured men.

Peuple Souverain's anchor cable having been shot through, the French ship drifted out of position and her place was now taken by *Leander*. As Thompson's ship approached out of the darkness many aboard *Orion* were convinced she was an enemy vessel and urged Saumarez to turn his guns on her. Thankfully *Leander*'s true identity was discovered before any damage was done. Thompson now anchored his 50-gun ship in a position of relative safety from where he could fire at the bows of *Franklin* and also direct raking fire at the larboard side of the massive ship anchored beyond her, *L'Orient*.

Having noticed that the fire aboard *L'Orient* was rapidly spreading across her poop deck towards the mizzen mast, Captain Hallowell ordered all of *Swiftsure*'s available guns to redirect their fire to the rear of the French flagship. As roundshot from *Swiftsure* tore into the French flagship, Admiral Brueys was struck and killed by a shot which almost split him in half. With the flames spreading uncontrollably across both the poop and quarterdeck, men began jumping into the sea; those that were not immediately shot to pieces swam to the nearest British ships where they were pulled, half naked, out of the water through the lower gunports. *Swiftsure* rescued fourteen men including one officer who was naked save for his hat, *Alexander* rescued twenty-eight men and *Orion's* men pulled another fourteen sailors from the water.

It was now obvious that the fire raging aboard *L'Orient* was totally out of control and it was only a matter of time before it reached the magazine and the French flagship blew up. Preparations were therefore made aboard *Orion* to secure the ship. The sails were furled and Saumarez ordered his gun crews to cease firing. All gun ports and hatchways were closed; the ship's magazine was shut and all the men were ordered below and given wet swabs and buckets of water. Whilst Saumarez and Ball both cut their anchor cables to put some distance between their ships and *L'Orient*, Hallowell remained where he was, confident that the explosion would pass over his ship. The captains of the French ships *Tonnant*, *Hereux* and *Mercure* also cut their cables. This manoeuvre caused so much confusion amongst the ships in the French rear that they began firing on one another in the darkness.

At 9.37pm *L'Orient* finally blew up. The massive explosion lit up the entire bay, briefly turning night into day. The force of the explosion was felt by all the ships in the bay and the thunderous, deafening roar could be heard as far away as Alexandria. As the last echoes of the explosion died away the bay fell deathly quiet, both British and French gunners stunned by the awesome spectacle of *L'Orient's* destruction. Then, after several minutes of utter silence, burning wreckage began tumbling from the sky, splashing into the water around the ships and thudding onto their decks. As Hallowell had anticipated, the explosion had passed right over *Swiftsure*, although two large pieces of wreckage did fall into her main and foretops. *Alexander* was also struck by the flaming debris and several of her sails along with a substantial amount of rigging caught fire. A few fragments fell aboard *Orion* but were quickly extinguished.

Admiral Blanquet's flagship *Franklin* was the first ship to resume firing after the battle's momentary pause, as if spurred back into action by the shattered pieces of timber, rope and red-hot pitch from *L'Orient* raining down onto her decks. However, two-thirds of the ship's crew were either dead or wounded and she was now surrounded by British ships. Less than twenty minutes after re-commencing the action

Blanquet's flagship only had three guns left and was forced to strike her colours, a lieutenant from *Defence* accepting her surrender moments before another lieutenant from *Swiftsure* stepped aboard.

By now Nelson, head bandaged and suffering from mild concussion, had returned to the quarterdeck of *Vanguard*. The French van having surrendered it was Nelson's intention to attack the remaining French ships. He therefore sent Lieutenant Thomas Bladen Capel in a boat across to the other ships to request that they re-anchor further down the French line. This would be a difficult manoeuvre as the battle had damaged each ship's rigging and, even though the winds were only light, too much strain would bring weakened masts crashing down. The only other ships that were able to move further down the French line were *Goliath*, *Theseus*, *Zealous* and *Leander*. Saumarez had given the order to run down the French line but was advised against it by his sailing master, Peter Bruff, who informed Saumarez that the moment they came broadside to the wind they would lose their badly-damaged fore and mizzen masts.

By 6.00am *Guillaume Tell*, *Genereux*, *Timoleon* and *Tonnant* had been engaged with *Alexander*, *Majestic*, *Goliath* and *Theseus* for just under an hour. The officer in command of the French rear, Admiral Pierre-Charles Villeneuve, had spent most of the battle stuck aboard his flagship *Guillaume Tell*, the wind against him, unable to help the ships in the French van. Indeed, he would later remark that he thought the battle had been lost the moment *Goliath* led the British down the inside of the French line. He had three options, he could stay put, he could move up to help, or he could lead his ships out of the bay. If he stayed put his ships faced the same fate as the rest of the French fleet. The wind was blowing from the north and in order to move up to help his ships would have to slowly beat their way forwards. Also, he had not, in fact, received any orders to assist the French van. Therefore, the safest, though most ignoble, solution was to flee from the carnage around him. Around midday Nelson spotted *Guillaume Tell*, *Genereux* and the frigates *Diane* and *Justice* trying to slip away and ordered Hood aboard *Zealous* to try and cut them off. Hood was too far away from the French ships to stop them but he did manage to reach *Bellerophon*, her flag now flying from the stump of her mizzen mast, in time to prevent her coming under attack from a French frigate which beat a hasty retreat as soon as she saw *Zealous* bearing down on her.

By the early hours of 3 August, the only French ships left in the bay that had neither surrendered, escaped or been destroyed were *Tonnant* and *Timoleon*. *Timoleon* had been run aground on the shoals and *Tonnant*, her decks crowded with survivors from the other French ships, was

97

now little more than a floating hulk. She finally surrendered when she saw *Theseus* and *Leander*, closely followed by *Swiftsure*, approaching. Rather than surrender their ship, the crew of *Timoleon* set her alight before escaping ashore. She blew up around midday, her destruction finally ending the battle.

This first major foray by a British detachment in enemy waters in over a year had resulted in a crushing victory. Not since the battle of Barfleur and La Hogue in 1692 – 'The Famous Ninety-Two' – had a French fleet been so decisively beaten. Attacking at night, and taking his ships into uncharted waters to do so, Nelson had almost completely destroyed the French Mediterranean Fleet, as a result of which Napoleon and his army were now stranded in Egypt. One of the mightiest ships then in existence had been sent to the bottom of the sea, whilst seven other French ships had been completely disabled. The French admiral, Brueys, and two of his captains, Dupetit Thouars of *Tonnant* and Thevenard of *Aquilon*, were dead, and Rear Admiral Blanquet and six more captains were injured. An estimated 5,225 French had been killed or wounded during the battle.

British losses, recorded at 218 dead and 678 wounded, were a fraction of those inflicted on the French. The heaviest casualties had been suffered aboard *Bellerophon*, following her battle with the much larger *L'Orient*, and *Majestic*, anchored alongside *Tonnant*, whose crew had fought bravely to the last. *Bellerophon* incurred losses of forty-nine killed and 148 wounded, whilst *Majestic* had similar losses – fifty men killed and 143 wounded. Other ships with high casualty rates included Nelson's flagship *Vanguard* and *Minotaur*. *Vanguard* had thirty killed and seventy-six wounded whilst *Minotaur* had twenty-three dead and a further sixty-four injured. *Orion* had lost thirteen killed and twenty-nine wounded. After the battle Nepecker operated on Midshipman Meills to amputate his arm. During the operation Miells was said not to have uttered a sound. When it was over he turned to Anne Hopping who had been assisting the surgeon and asked 'Have I not borne it like a man?'[2] Saumarez was greatly relieved to hear that Meills had survived the operation. However, soon after the young midshipman suffered a coughing fit and died.

On 2 August Nelson wrote a memorandum congratulating the men of his squadron and thanking them for their 'gallant behaviour in this glorious battle'.[3] Declaring his intention to hold a service of thanksgiving aboard *Vanguard* that afternoon, he requested that the other captains do the same as soon as was convenient. Saumarez, of course, needed little encouragement to give thanks to the Almighty and his ship was the first to hoist the Church Pennant at her mizzen peak.

Later that day Nelson's captains met aboard *Orion*. Saumarez declared that it was 'the most glorious and complete victory ever yet obtain'd'[4] and Ball noted that, as second-in-command, Saumarez 'would, unquestionably, receive some mark of distinction on the occasion'.[5] Uttering words that would soon come back to haunt him, Saumarez replied 'We all did our duty – there was no second-in-command!'[6] He proposed that they set up an Egyptian Club, in celebration of the victory and each captain agreed to pay £50 towards a specially-designed sword, which they intended to present to Nelson. Any surplus would go towards the widows and orphans of those who had fallen in battle.

Captain Westcott had been buried at sea following a twenty-gun salute on 2 August. Burials for the other British dead would continue for several weeks after the battle. Most were buried at sea, although some were interred on Aboukir Island, captured by the British on 3 August. Repairs to the British ships and their prizes were also begun. The mutinous carpenter's mate from *St George* saved from the short drop by Saumarez had already proved his worth in battle: now he assisted in the repair of *Peuple Souverain*, hanging over the side of the battered French ship in a cradle to repair the numerous shot holes in her hull.

It was 3 August before Saumarez was sufficiently recovered from his wound to meet with Nelson. Several of his fellow captains were also aboard *Vanguard* and had been discussing the action and their regret at the escape of the two French ships. Saumarez still disagreed with the decision to double the line, a tactic which had undoubtedly resulted in British guns killing British sailors, and had argued that it might have been better if they had all anchored on the same side of the French. When Nelson emerged from his cabin, head bandaged, Saumarez began to say: 'It was unfortunate we did not …'[7] but before he could complete his sentence Nelson suddenly declared 'Thank God there was no order.'[8] He then turned, entered his cabin and called for Ball. Still suffering from his recent wound Nelson was in no mood to get into an argument with his most senior captain over tactics. It would not be the last snub Saumarez received from Nelson that morning. Returning from his meeting, Ball announced to the captains assembled on *Vanguard*'s quarterdeck, 'Nelson says there is to be no second-in-command; we are all to be alike in his dispatches.'[9]

On 3 August Berry transferred to *Leander* and three days later Thompson's ship sailed for Cadiz with Nelson's dispatches. On the evening of 13 August the elusive frigates *Emerald* and *Alcmène* finally made their appearance in Aboukir Bay. Nelson was now able to dispatch Lieutenant Capel aboard *Mutine* with a second set of dispatches for the Admiralty. Repairs to all the ships having been completed, it was time for Nelson to split his squadron up. On 14 August a detachment under the command of Saumarez consisting of *Orion, Majestic, Bellerophon, Minotaur, Defence, Audacious, Theseus* and the captured French ships *Franklin, Tonnant, Aquilon, Conquerant, Spartiate* and *Peuple Souverain* slowly made their way out of the bay, headed for Gibraltar. They were followed five days later by *Vanguard, Culloden* and *Alexander*. This left Hood in command of the three most serviceable ships, *Zealous, Goliath* and *Swiftsure*, along with the newly-arrived frigates, all of which were to stay and blockade Alexandria. *Hereux, Guerrier* and *Mercure* were all beyond repair and were set on fire after they had been stripped of all useful supplies.

Saumarez's squadron departed from Aboukir Bay each ship with a French prize under tow. (The badly damaged *Majestic* and *Bellerophon* shared the towing of *Spartiate* between them.) *Orion*'s Lieutenant Barker was now in command of their prize *Peuple Souverain* and his place as first lieutenant aboard *Orion* had been taken by Wells. Following a recommendation from Saumarez, Mansell had been promoted acting lieutenant by Nelson and placed aboard *Aquilon*. Saumarez was pleased with the prizes and the money they would bring his officers and men but he knew the squadron's real achievement was not so much what they had taken but what they had left behind. 'We have left France only two sail of the line in the Mediterranean, except a few bad Venetian ships and some frigates. A squadron of five sail leaves us masters of these seas … These are the real fruits of our victory',[10] he wrote.

Slowed down by their prizes and their own damage Saumarez's ships had barely reached the entrance to the bay before the wind completely died away and they were forced to lay at anchor for the night. The next morning, before setting off again they received the first mail from home for many weeks. Saumarez pounced on the mail, eagerly sorting through the letters until he found all those addressed to him personally, around twenty in all. Four letters from Martha were read with great excitement. 'Before I had finished a page of one I flew to another, and so on for nearly an hour, till at last I found their date, and endeavoured to read them regularly.'[11]

As they sailed towards Gibraltar, labouring under the light winds, Saumarez regularly dined with the captains of his ships and with the two French officers from *Tonnant* who were now living in *Orion*'s wardroom. The exertions of being under sail once again together with the excessive heat had unfortunately slowed Saumarez's recovery. On 21 August he wrote, 'I am now, thank God, as well as ever.' 'My situation', he added 'is exactly as I could wish, the command of respectable squadron escorting the trophies of our victory.'[12] Lieutenant

Barker was as 'happy as a prince'[13] to be in command of *Peuple Souverain* and all of *Orion*'s officers were 'in rapture at the share the ship had in the action, except her captain, who is never satisfied'.[14] Five days later the squadron was overtaken by Nelson's ships. Saumarez spent half an hour aboard *Vanguard* and was happy to find Nelson in seemingly perfect health. 'He will ever retain the mark on his forehead which he has so honourably acquired; mine is in not so distinguished a place.'[15] Although he was taken off *Vanguard*'s sick list on 1 September Nelson still complained of splitting headaches for some time after.

The two British squadrons went their separate ways, but having to tow battle-damaged and jury-rigged ships in light winds meant that the progress of Saumarez's squadron remained slow. Saumarez busied himself as best he could by tidying his cabin to have it fit for Martha and the children upon his return to England. Arriving off Rhodes on 28 August the wind changed direction preventing *Orion* from sailing further north. Forced south, Saumarez carefully navigated his way through a passage between the islands of Kasos and Karpathos, assisted by Lieutenant Tancock who acted as a lookout at the mast head, with the rest of the squadron following *Orion*'s lead. On 2 September *Bonne Citoyenne* arrived with dispatches from Nelson who had arrived at Naples. Nelson's ships were in such a poor condition that he felt it necessary for Saumarez to send him *Minotaur* and *Audacious* once Saumarez was safely between Sardinia and Minorca.

The squadron spent three days in sight of Sicily, attempting to beat round Cape Passero on the southern tip of the island. However, the wind was blowing so strongly from the west that Saumarez was eventually obliged to head for Syracuse. At Syracuse the same wind was blowing directly out of the harbour so Saumarez was forced to sail further north. Whilst off Augusta the poorly-handling prize *Spartiate* ran aground close to the lighthouse but was refloated with no damage to her hull. Dropping anchor at Augusta on 15 September Saumarez received news from a vessel that had left Malta six days earlier that the Maltese were in revolt against the French, occupiers of the island since the arrival of Brueys' fleet in June 1798.

Watered and provisioned, the squadron sailed from Augusta on 21 September. In passing Syracuse several boats came out and Saumarez was able to send a letter to Martha, enclosed in another to Nelson at Naples. By the last week of September the wind had died to such an extent that Saumarez was forced to put in at Malta. As the British approached the island they spotted de Niza's blockading squadron of six Portuguese ships at anchor. In the Grand Harbour they also discovered the French ship *Guillaume Tell* and the two frigates that had fled from Aboukir Bay, but there was no sign of the other ship of the line, *Généreux*, although there were several unconfirmed reports that she had foundered. On 25 September Saumarez met a delegation of Maltese aboard *Orion* who persuaded him that the arrival of a substantial British squadron might induce the French garrison to surrender. After a brief discussion with de Niza, Saumarez sent a letter along with a flag of truce to the French commander, General Vaubois, demanding the surrender of the French forces on the island. Vaubois was an experienced commander, a veteran of the siege of Mantua, and his reply, when it eventually came after a three hour wait, was brief and dismissive. 'You have clearly forgotten that it is Frenchmen who hold Malta. The future of its inhabitants is a matter that does not concern you.'[16] Other than supplying the Maltese with around 1,200 muskets and ammunition from the captured French ships, there was little else that Saumarez could do to help and by then the breeze had finally picked up again and it was time to leave Malta and sail on towards Gibraltar.

On 28 September Saumarez's squadron fell in with the frigate *Terpsichore* which had been sent by Nelson to look for a convoy of store-ships bound for Naples. The men from *Audacious* and *Minotaur* having returned from the prize ships, Captains Louis and Gould now departed for their rendezvous with Nelson. As September turned to October Saumarez hoped that the month of his marriage to Martha would look more kindly on him and speed his return home. On 10 October, as his squadron neared Gibraltar, they met the British frigate *Espoir* and Saumarez learned that *Leander* had not yet arrived at the Rock. St Vincent, who had shifted his flag ashore due to ill health, hoped that Berry's ship had simply been dismasted and was sheltering in one of the Greek islands but Saumarez found the news far more disturbing.

The squadron, delayed by light winds, finally reached Gibraltar on the evening of 18 October. The whole garrison had come out to greet the ships and Saumarez found the whole occasion, especially the lavish praise from St Vincent, of whom he had grown wary, almost too much. 'The solicitous attention he shows to me almost overwhelms me,' he wrote 'and I wish to keep clear of laying myself under obligation, except as far as concerns the promotion of my officers.'[17] St Vincent informed Saumarez that once the sick were offloaded, *Orion, Defence* and *Theseus* would accompany the six prizes to Lisbon whilst *Bellerophon* and *Majestic* would remain at Gibraltar to be remasted. This news shocked Darby, who had anticipated an immediate return to England, his ship having so many holes in it that 'a post-chaise could be driven through her sides'.[18] A ball held in honour of Saumarez and the other captains was followed over the next few days by a round of dinner parties.

Whilst at Gibraltar Saumarez received two letters from Nelson approving of his action regarding Malta and his putting in to Augusta. There was also a letter from Ball, writing from Malta where he had now taken over the blockade of the island. Ball had sent Saumarez 'a case containing six fan-mounts, two boxes of perfume, four large and two small of Naples soap, amounting to eighteen Spanish dollars and a half'.[19] There was also news of *Leander*. She had been captured by the *Généreux* and carried into Corfu. 'Of course all our letters by her are destroyed, and our friends will suffer much anxiety until the arrival of Capel.'[20]

Orion and *Theseus* spent a week at Gibraltar then prepared to depart for Lisbon with the prizes. However, *Peuple Souverain* was too badly damaged to venture out into the Atlantic and it was decided that she should remain at Gibraltar as a guardship. Just before they left the Rock the brig *Transfer* arrived with news of *Leander*'s capture. Having already received Ball's letter, Saumarez had 'long before given her over for lost'.[21] He took some comfort, however, in the crew's brave defence of their ship.

On 24 October, whilst off Cadiz, Saumarez caught sight of the Mediterranean Fleet, with one ship, *Hector*, just a few miles distant. The following day *Orion* fell in with *Barfleur* and *Northumberland* and Saumarez learned that Capel had arrived in London with Nelson's dispatches. Later that day *Orion* and *Theseus* captured two vessels out of Genoa laden with expensive goods from Italian merchants. On 28 October *Orion*, *Theseus* and the prize ships arrived safely in the Tagus where Saumarez found various people waiting for passage back to Britain. Room was found aboard *Orion* for the Duc D'Havre, an exiled French Royalist and the Marquis de Montemart, but Saumarez regretted not being able to find space for General Trigge, his wife and their companion, Miss Raikes, with whom Captain Thompson had lately reached 'an understanding'.

Orion and *Theseus* finally arrived at Spithead on 25 November and Saumarez dispatched Lieutenant Dumaresq to fetch his son James who was staying in Newport. Frustratingly, Saumarez now discovered that *Orion* was being held in quarantine following her return from Egypt. To add to his ill humour while he waited, bad weather set in, preventing further communication with the shore. James arrived aboard *Orion* on 27 November and Saumarez learned that Martha was at the Fountain Inn in Portsmouth. Two days later *Orion* was finally released from her quarantine and Saumarez was free to go on shore. He remained at Portsmouth until 15 December when *Orion* sailed for Plymouth. On 6 January 1799 *Orion* was paid off and Saumarez and Martha travelled to London.

Chapter 13

Admiral Bruix's Cruise and the Blockade of Brest: January 1799 – January 1801

Following the capture of *Leander* Thompson, Berry and the ship's officers had been placed in a small French vessel with only two gallons of port, some salt meat and a bag of breadcrumbs for a journey to Trieste that would last a whole month. Upon their arrival at the Italian port the two captains travelled to Cuxhaven where they caught the Harwich packet, arriving back in Britain on 25 November 1799, the very same day that *Orion* was dropping anchor at Spithead.

Reunited back in London, Saumarez, Thompson and Berry now set about designing the sword that would be presented to Nelson. The ormolu hilt was in the form of a crocodile and the blade was engraved with different motifs. 'I hope that it will soon be finished and we shall all have the happiness soon to meet in the Egyptian Hall,'[1] Saumarez wrote to Ball. Another matter exercising their minds was the granting of prize-money. Nelson's letter explaining that *Guerrier*, *Heureux* and *Mercure* had been so badly damaged after the battle that they had to be burned was lost aboard *Leander* and he had not provided Capel with a duplicate. Saumarez, Berry and Thompson now wrote a joint letter to Nelson's prize agent, Alexander Davidson, explaining that Berry was 'in full possession of the sentiments of Lord Nelson'[2] and requesting that the government pay a fair price for these ships. This was eventually agreed to though Saumarez told Ball he thought the three ships had been undervalued.

On 6 January *Orion* was paid off and Saumarez quit London and returned to Bath. Two days after his arrival at Bath Earl Spencer wrote to inform him that he intended to give him the command of the 80-gun

Caesar as soon as that ship became available. Saumarez was offered the temporary command of a Third Rate but he turned this ship down. On 15 January Saumarez wrote to Spencer asking for as many of *Orion*'s crew as possible to be transferred to *Caesar*, 'having experienced their uniform good conduct for so many years'.[3] Spencer wrote to explain that he could not agree to this request as the reserving of a ship's company was a practice 'attended with so much inconvenience to the public service that it has of late been necessarily discontinued'.[4] This was in fact a rather short-sighted view of the matter: sailors were far more loyal to their captains and their officers than the Admiralty gave them credit and it was not for the navy that they fought but for their crewmates. Nelson would himself remark that 'the disgust of the seamen to the navy is all owing to the infernal plan of turning them over from ship to ship, so that men cannot be attached to their officers, or the officers care two-pence about them'.[5]

On 14 February, the second anniversary of the Battle of Cape St Vincent, Saumarez was given a vacant Colonelcy of Marine and was also appointed to *Caesar*, then fitting out at Hamoaze, Plymouth. From Malta Ball sent his congratulations. 'Be assured that your appointment to the Marines and the command of the *Caesar*, which are given to you as a mark of the high estimation in which you are regarded by the Admiralty and the public, has given me more joy than I should have received from the appointment of any other person on the list, because I have had the satisfaction of witnessing your bravery, zeal, and ardour in the service.'[6]

Saumarez went aboard his new ship on 26 February and his commission was read out to the assembled crew. Designed by the Surveyor of the Navy Edward Hunt and launched in November 1793 at Plymouth Dockyards *Caesar*, with her thirty 32-pounders on the lower deck, thirty-two 24-pounders on the upper deck and eighteen 9-pounders on the quarterdeck and forecastle, was the first 80-gun two-decker built for the Royal Navy since the 1690s. On 19 March *Caesar* proceeded to Cawsand Bay, where she remained at anchor, riding out a severe storm on 30 March. The following day the ship sailed for France in company with *Magnificent* and *Impetueux*, joining the Channel Fleet off Brest on 3 April. During the winter Bridport had maintained a loose blockade of Brest, his fleet reduced in numbers and commanded by a succession of junior flag officers whilst he remained ashore. On 16 April Bridport resumed his command, arriving off Brest aboard the 100-gun *Royal George* with five more ships, bringing the total number of ships in his fleet up to fifteen. On 20 April the fleet experienced a heavy gale but emerged from it unscathed. Bridport now sent *Anson*, Captain Durham, to reconnoitre Brest Roads. Durham reported that fourteen ships of the line had bent their sails and were preparing to put to sea. Bridport positioned his fleet twelve miles to the south-west of Ushant, ready to intercept the French when they came out. Four ships, including *Caesar*, acted as an advanced squadron, sailing closer to the shore. Looking into Brest Water at around 5.00pm on 24 April, Saumarez saw that the French fleet, twenty-five ships of the line and ten smaller vessels, were partly under way in Camaret Bay and Brest Water. Signals were made and by 10.00pm Bridport had been alerted. However, under the cover of fog Bruix turned south and slipped through the Raz de Sein, a dangerous channel through the rocks that lay off the headland. On the morning of 26 April the French fleet was spotted clearing the Raz de Sein by the frigate *Nymphe*. Captain Fraser tailed the French fleet for a short distance but then had to break off contact in order to speak to Bridport, now forty miles distant. Bridport had been caught out like this once before in 1796 when the Brest fleet had evaded his blockade and sailed for Ireland, only to be wrecked during a storm at Bantry Bay. When the French cutter *Rebecca* was captured bearing false dispatches for Ireland, Bridport's initial suspicions seemed to have been confirmed. Having first sent messages to St Vincent at Gibraltar and Lord Keith at Cadiz, Bridport headed off northwards in pursuit of the French.

As the fleet sailed to Ireland Saumarez sat down to dinner on 1 May with his senior officers and celebrated his wife's birthday by opening a bottle of his best wine. Following a gale lasting three days on 5 May the fleet arrived off Cape Clear where Bridport was disappointed to discover there had been no sign of the French fleet. The Admiralty had, in fact, already become suspicious of the dispatches discovered aboard *Rebecca* and had delayed the sailing of reinforcements. On 8 May *Caesar* spoke with *Anson* and Saumarez learned that the French fleet had been spotted a week earlier steering to the south. On 17 May Admiral Gardner finally arrived with the reinforcements from Plymouth that included *Royal Sovereign*, *Atlas*, *Triumph*, *Formidable* and *Canada*. Having received letters from Martha, who had been alarmed at false reports of an action between the British and French fleets, Saumarez advised his wife to 'follow the example of Lady Howe, who neither reads newspapers nor listens to rumours. I know not who are most to blame, those who invent them, or you who believe them.'[7]

On 24 May *Caesar* and *Achille* collided as the fleet entered Bantry Bay. *Caesar* emerged from the incident unscathed and Captain Murray's ship only received slight damage. There was still no sign of the French Fleet and Saumarez was convinced that his 'conjectures of the enemy being gone to Portugal, or the Mediterranean, and not destined for this country, are too surely founded'.[8] The Admiralty had also come to the same conclusion and had decided to send part of the Channel Fleet to the Mediterranean to reinforce St Vincent. On 26 May Rear Admiral Collingwood arrived aboard the frigate *Sirius* and transferred his flag to *Triumph*. It had not yet been decided which ships would be detached from the fleet but Saumarez had been aboard the flagship, *Royal George*, several times and had not heard his ship mentioned. A week later he learned that several ships were being sent to Cape Finisterre under Admiral Gardner. On 8 June *Caesar* and another sixteen ships separated from the fleet and steered for the Mediterranean. Falling in with a Danish vessel Saumarez learned that the French fleet had been spotted passing through the Straits with St Vincent in pursuit. In attempting to get down to *Royal Sovereign* to pass this information to Gardner, *Caesar* lost her fore topmast. When he finally reached Gardner's flagship Saumarez was surprised to find her now sailing in company with just *Magnificent* and *Russell*, the rest of the squadron having departed for the Mediterranean under the joint command of Admirals Cotton and Collingwood, leaving Gardner's small detachment to sail for Lisbon where they were to collect the five Nile prizes.

Bruix had sailed from Brest with orders to cooperate with the Spanish and to relieve Malta and Corfu. Continuing south, by 3 May he had arrived off Cadiz where Lord Keith's fleet were hanging onto their station in the face of a north-west gale. Keith formed a line of battle but could not attack the French fleet as it would mean abandoning his blockade and letting the Spanish out. Bruix was therefore allowed to continue onwards, passing Gibraltar on 5 May, Having watched the French fleet pass through the Straits, St Vincent, who was ashore and in ill health, immediately sent for Keith. On 12 May the sixteen ships of the Mediterranean Fleet sailed out into the Mediterranean. Now that the door to Cadiz had been left open the Spanish fleet were able to put to sea and they passed through the Straits five days later.

Keith now set off for Minorca where Duckworth was stationed with four ships of the line. Meanwhile Bruix had sailed for Toulon for repairs to his fleet. There he received new instructions to sail to Genoa with supplies for Massena's besieged army. Bruix was pursued up the Ligurian coast by Keith who got within sight of the French fleet before being forced to abandon the chase by contrary winds. Having abandoned his plan to supply Massena, Bruix now sailed to Cadiz where the Spanish ships brought his fleet up to forty-three ships of the line. The Combined Fleet then headed for Brest, arriving safely back in port twenty-four hours before the arrival of Keith. Bruix had successfully evaded the British but his fifteen-week cruise had been a failure. The French army in Egypt was still isolated, with no further possibility of relief, Malta was still besieged and Minorca remained under British control.

On 18 June *Royal Sovereign*, *Russell*, *Magnificent* and *Caesar* left the Tagus in company with the Lisbon convoy and the five Nile prizes, *Tonnant*, *Canopus*, *Spartiate*, *Aboukir* and *Conquerant*, all now refitted and bearing the British flag. After a three week journey Gardner's squadron and the prizes entered Cawsand Bay on 13 July, leaving *Magnificent* to take the merchantmen to Spithead. Four days later the prizes were escorted into Plymouth Sound. It was a rainy morning but a large crowd had turned out to welcome the ships home. The bands of the Marine Corps, the Royal Cornwall and the First Wilts had been posted on the headland and played 'Rule Britannia', 'God Save the King' and 'Britons Strike Home'. As each ship passed the headland their crews returned the hearty cheers from the crowd onshore and from the other ships in the Sound.

On 11 August Gardner's squadron sailed to Torbay where it remained until 2 September, putting to sea again to cruise off Ushant. Over the course of the next three months it put back three times. On 8 December *Caesar* dropped anchor at Torbay. The Admiralty were keen to discover whether the harbour at Torbay could provide a safe anchorage for the fleet during the winter and so *Caesar*, in company with the 98-gun *London*, John Purvis, remained at anchor there until 7 February 1800. During a particularly heavy gale *London* parted her cables and narrowly avoided being driven onshore.

In April Bridport, aged seventy-three and in poor health, finally resigned as commander-in-chief of the Channel Fleet. No one at the Admiralty was sad to see him go and Spencer already knew who he wanted as his replacement. Within days St Vincent, sixty-five years old and gout-ridden, was persuaded to return to sea. Hoisting his flag aboard the *Ville de Paris*, he took command of an enlarged fleet now numbering forty ships of the line. The captains under his command had been used to the lax discipline of Bridport, remaining in their cabins during fleet manoeuvres and taking leave ashore as and when it suited them. Learning that St Vincent was taking over command of the fleet these captains now proposed the toast 'God forbid the Mediterranean discipline should ever be introduced into the Channel Fleet'.[9] Apparently their new commander-in-chief had been no more popular during his time ashore. Earlier that month Martha had written to her husband: 'Lord St Vincent seems to be the terror of the Ladies … none that I have yet seen are glad at his coming.'[10] Saumarez was, of course, well used to the strict regime of the Channel Fleet's new commander-in-chief. Sailing from Torbay on 6 February *Caesar* cruised off Ushant for seven weeks before returning to Cawsand Bay on 24 March in company with *Royal Sovereign, Formidable, St George, Bellona* and *Triumph*. On 19 April *Caesar* rejoined the Channel Fleet, now at anchor at Torbay.

Sailing from Torbay on 24 April St Vincent now began a close blockade of Brest, An advanced squadron of five ships was anchored off the notorious Black Rocks, situated at the head of the Iroise, and a squadron of frigates operated between the Black Rocks and the Goulet. Three more ships of the line cruised off Ushant in support of the advanced squadron whilst other ships guarded the Raz de Sein. The remainder of the fleet lay further out to sea, within twenty miles of Brest. Under St Vincent ships now remained on station for up to five months at a time, fed and watered by convoys of victuallers sailing to and from the fleet, but regularly suffering shortages. This was extremely arduous and hazardous cruising and it soon became clear to St Vincent that many of his captains were not up to the job.

On 16 May the fleet was caught in a ferocious storm, the high seas laying several ships on their beam ends. The cutter *Lady Jane* and the sloops *Trompeuse* and *Railleur* foundered with the loss of all those aboard, *Montagu* lost all her masts and *Ville de Paris* her main topmast. The flagship's stern windows having been smashed in by a wave, St Vincent sat on a chair lashed to the quarterdeck giving orders. Saumarez's ship rolled so heavily in the mountainous seas that her lower yardarms were briefly under water. The carpenters were ordered onto the main deck where they stood by with their axes, ready to cut *Caesar*'s masts down if the ship did not right herself. The danger eventually passed but several gun-ports had been stove in and there was so much water on the main deck that the carpenters had to cut holes in the deck to let it out. The storm eventually blew itself out and the fleet returned to Torbay for repairs, with *Caesar* following several days behind.

Repairs completed, on 28 May *Caesar* returned to her station. Cruising off Ushant a month later Saumarez wrote to Martha: 'I am as well situated as possible. I enjoy the satisfaction of having a very quiet and well-disposed ship's company who are kept orderly and, I flatter myself, well regulated, without exercising severity or rigour. The officers continue as I wish them. Captain Maxwell, [of the marines] who joined some time ago, is an active, diligent officer in his corps; and Mr. Packwood, as well as Mr. Holliday, our new chaplain, are very good men in their respective stations.'[11]

On 29 July St Vincent ordered Saumarez to take command of the inshore squadron stationed off the Black Rocks, arguably the position of greatest responsibility within the whole fleet. Often shrouded in thick fog, with hidden dangers in the form of submerged rocks and shoals, the Black Rocks, situated eleven miles south-west from Ushant, were the least desirable station imaginable for any ship of the line. Frequently operating against both wind and tide and exposed to enemy fire from Brest Water, the sailors in the Channel Fleet called the region 'New Siberia' and St Vincent would soon come to call it 'the Elysian Lake'. Drawing from an admittedly small pool of suitable candidates, Saumarez was the most obvious choice for this important command. The ship's now under his command were drawn under rotation from the main fleet and upon Saumarez's arrival off the Black Rocks consisted of four 74s, *Magnificent*, Edward Bowater, *Defiance*, Thomas Shivers, *Marlborough*, Thomas Sotheby, and *Edgar*, Edward Buller. With the recent arrival of Napoleon at Brest there seemed a real possibility that the French might attempt to put to sea. If they did Saumarez had been ordered to harass the enemy's rear until the arrival of the main fleet.

On 17 August *Caesar* left her station to return to Cawsand Bay to re-provision. On his return to the Black Rocks on 3 September Saumarez received intelligence that the Brest Fleet intended to put to sea '*On dit*, but I do not believe it, that the French fleet is to be ordered out by the First Consul, at all risks' he wrote to Martha. 'We may therefore expect to make minced meat out of them with our seventeen three-deckers. We remain in sight of the enemy unmolested by them. To-day I had the colours hoisted, to show them Sunday was not expunged from *our* calendar; and divine service was performed on board.'[12] News was expected any day from Paris where Napoleon had entered into negotiations with the Austrians and Saumarez had now formed: 'very sanguine hopes that peace will shortly extend its blessed influence over these countries'.[13] Peace, he hoped, would also allow him 'the satisfaction to enjoy without interruption the sweets of domestic comfort'.[14] Writing to his wife on 12 September Saumarez told Martha he hoped that his girls would continue with their French grammar, even though they much preferred dancing, as it would prove a good grounding for other languages and he requested that James, who was then leaning the Greek alphabet, sent him a copy at the earliest opportunity.

For several months a rumour had been floating about that the service was about to make a large number of promotions to flag rank in order to reach those deserving captains stuck further down the list. Having missed out on the last round of promotions in February 1799 Saumarez now sought assistance from his commander-in-chief and St Vincent promised to use his influence at the Admiralty to help obtain a long-overdue advancement to Saumarez's career. With winter fast approaching Saumarez sent St Vincent an updated list of rendezvous points for his squadron. On 15 September his commander-in-chief sent this reply. 'Nothing can be more appropriate than the different rendezvous you have sent me a copy of; your change of position must fluctuate according to the sudden changes of weather, which are to be looked for soon. I repose such unbounded confidence in your zeal and judgement that I sleep as soundly as if I had the keys of Brest in my possession.'[15]

On 23 September the annual September gales arrived and the Channel Fleet followed its usual procedure of abandoning its blockade of Brest and heading for the safety of Torbay. However, instead of following the fleet back to Britain, Saumarez took his squadron and sailed south along the French coast. Later that evening *Caesar*, *Pompee*, *Captain*, *Marlborough*, the frigate *Sirius* and the fireship *Megaera*, dropped anchor in Douarnenez Bay, ten miles south of Brest. Anchoring just out of range of the shore batteries Saumarez's ships struck their topmasts and lower yards and rode out the storm using the enemy's own anchorage, a large sheltered bay protected from the sea by the Crozon peninsular. The following morning stores and provisions were removed from *Marlborough* and Captain Sotheby's ship sailed to Torbay with Saumarez's dispatches and a letter to Martha describing recent events. 'We anchored at eleven last night, and this morning found ourselves in one of the finest bays I have ever seen. It is far more spacious than Torbay, and much more enclosed; consequently more secure against all winds. It is the same distance from Brest by sea as Dartmouth is from Torbay; and by land the same as from Brixham. It abounds with the finest fish, of which we shall profit.'[16] Later that day *Montagu* and the frigate *Naiad* dropped anchor in the bay. The weather continued to worsen and by 25 September had developed into a severe gale. The following day the wind shifted to the north and Saumarez attempted to put to sea but by the evening the wind had changed direction yet again forcing Saumarez back into the bay. By midday on 27 September the wind was once again blowing from the north and Saumarez's ship's bent their sails and headed out of the bay, *Pompee* losing her bower anchor as she weighed. Setting off under a full press of sail by next morning Saumarez's squadron were off St Matthews Point where they were able to observe the twenty-two ships of the Brest Fleet at anchor.

On 29 September Saumarez received several letters from Martha mentioning her intentions of returning to Guernsey from Bath.

Saumarez had originally suggested the idea on a false assumption that the war would soon be over and it would be safe to return home but with hostilities continuing he had now become 'a very coward on the idea'[17] and wished he had never suggested it. On 4 October Saumarez wrote. 'I find the rumours of peace are vanished, and that war is determined upon ... There is no doubt the French are much distressed for provisions in the neighbourhood of Brest, and that discontent prevails upon their troops, who are ill-paid, ill-fed, and badly clothed. It is horrid to see the leading men of all nations so infatuated for war, at a time peace is so much to be desired for the sake of humanity.'[18]

When Spencer learned that St Vincent had returned to Torbay with the bulk of his fleet due to the September gales he enquired whether or not the advanced squadron might be replaced with frigates to avoid the loss of several valuable ships of the line. St Vincent replied: 'My dear Lord- frigates are not worth a pin off Brest; the enemy out numbers them and drives them off at will. Sir James Saumarez is at anchor in Douarnenez Bay and in greater safety than we are here.'[19] Hearing this, on 30 September Spencer sent the following letter to Saumarez: 'I was much pleased to find that you had got hold of that anchorage, as I felt very uneasy at your absence during the late gales. I should rather doubt whether that bay could be capacious enough for a large fleet to anchor in without danger from the batteries; but I have always hoped that some of our small squadron might avail themselves of that resource on such an occasion as that which has presented itself to you.'[20] St Vincent also sent his approval, but 'Old Jarvie' blew hot and cold towards the officers in his fleet and his letter came just days after he had written to Spencer berating the commander of his inshore squadron. 'Sir James Saumarez does not stand the work at the advanced post with the firmness I had expected; whence it is evident that the man who faces the Frenchman or Spaniard with intrepidity, does not always encounter rocks or shoals with the same feeling; would to God that the promotion had taken place and I might get at Captain Thornbrough.'[21] The captain of *Formidable*, Edward Thornbrough was a favourite of St Vincent who was eventually promoted to flag rank in January 1801. (True to form, St Vincent would later complain of his leadership qualities.)

The winds having finally abated, Saumarez's squadron resumed its station off the Black Rocks on 14 October and the Channel Fleet once again took up its blockade of Brest. Saumarez's boats were frequently employed chasing enemy vessels attempting to enter Brest and the squadron was also approached by several vessels from Guernsey. Saumarez had to stop these traders from selling spirits to his men and hoped they would not give a bad account of their countryman on their return to Guernsey. The squadron had also captured two small islands, which provided an additional supply of beef and fresh vegetables for the squadron. In addition Saumarez had also purchased a small cow from Captain Buller, which, at a cost of only three guineas, was now providing him with fresh milk.

On 17 October Saumarez received a note from St Vincent informing him that he expected Saumarez's flag to be raised aboard *Caesar* in a few days. Saumarez also learned that the commander-in-chief intended to make Jahleel Brenton his flag-captain. Recently promoted but without a ship to command, Brenton had arrived in the fleet on 23 September and had gone aboard *Ville de Paris* as a volunteer. Spotting an opportunity to advance the career of an officer he greatly admired, St Vincent suggested that Brenton spend some time with the advanced squadron aboard *Caesar*. Entering the navy in 1781 aged eleven Brenton had served as a lieutenant under Jervis at the Battle of Cape St Vincent. As commander of the brig *Speedy* his spirited actions against Spanish gunboats in the Straits of Gibraltar in November 1799 led, with the enthusiastic backing of St Vincent, to his promotion to post captain later that year. Upon his arrival aboard *Caesar* Saumarez found Brenton to be a 'sensible, good officer, and of great experience'[22] and wrote that he could think of no one he would prefer to have as a flag-captain. Grateful for Brenton's company, Saumarez was sorry to see him leave *Caesar* and return to the flagship on 21 October.

After nearly a fortnight at the Black Rocks a strong westerly wind on 26 October forced Saumarez to once again seek shelter in Douarnenez Bay. That evening *Megaera* anchored in the bay and Saumarez learned that St Vincent intended to pass the command of the fleet at sea to Hyde Parker and spend the winter ashore at Torbay due to poor health. Saumarez was still waiting for news regarding his promotion and feared he would grow 'sulky and impatient'[23] if he were kept at sea for much longer, performing the duties of an admiral without a flag. Saumarez had now spent nearly two months at sea, cruising off the Black Rocks where any lapse in concentration could end in disaster. From a fellow officer St Vincent now heard that Saumarez appeared, to quote Shakespeare's *Henry IV*, as 'thin as a shotten herring'.[24]

In the middle of another severe gale on 9 November *Ville de Paris* made the signal for *Megaera*. When Captain Hill went aboard the flagship St Vincent told him to go into Douarnenez Bay with dispatches for Saumarez. From the quarterdeck of St Vincent's flagship Hill could clearly see the inshore squadron which had been blown from its safe anchorage and were now nine miles off the weather bow of *Ville de Paris*.

'No, no,' insisted St Vincent 'they are in Douarnenez Bay.'[25] St Vincent's flag-captain, Troubridge, turned to Hill and whispered 'He wishes them there, but sees them just as plainly as you do.'[26] Hill duly returned to *Megaera* and delivered St Vincent's dispatches as ordered. The storm had caused little damage to *Caesar* apart from the loss of some storm sails and by 11.00pm she had resumed her former station. Towards the end of the month the French began lowering the masts and removing the stores from their blockaded ships for the winter. It was a victory hard earned by Saumarez and his fellow captains.

On 2 December Saumarez finally heard from St Vincent: 'The *Impetueux* took in her guns this day, and Sir Edward Pellew will receive his orders tomorrow morning; and, if the wind favours his getting out of Hamoaze, he will be with you in the course of the week. You will receive by him orders to proceed to Spithead.'[27] This was the news Saumarez had been waiting for, but it was not all to his liking: he was finally being relieved, but by St Vincent's new favourite, Pellew, an officer Saumarez had not spoken to since their falling out over prize money almost six years earlier.

Impetueux arrived off the Black Rocks on 12 December and Saumarez handed over command of the inshore squadron to Pellew, bringing to an end his five-month cruise. *Caesar* departed the Black Rocks and arrived at Torbay on 14 December. As requested, Saumarez went ashore and met with St Vincent at his residence at Tor Abbey to discuss his recent cruise. Saumarez informed his commander-in-chief that it was his considered opinion that the French fleet at Brest would put to sea as soon as the weather improved.

Upon her arrival at Spithead on 21 December *Caesar*, a new and untested design of ship, was found to have suffered so much from the rigours of her recent cruise that she was urgently in need of repair. Most worryingly of all were the signs that the hull had started to hog, that is, her bow and stern drooping down, causing her keel to arch upwards. From 1797 the Admiralty had begun strengthening structurally-weak ships either by diagonal bracing or by sheathing the hull in plank. *Caesar* was in such a poor condition that both measures were required. The right-angled wooden brackets that supported the deck beams were reinforced with bracing pieces and the hull was sheathed in plank from the top of the side to six strakes below the wale. Repairs completed, *Caesar* came out of dock on 6 January 1801 and received her guns and six months' worth of provisions.

Chapter 14

The Battle of Algeciras: January 1801 – November 1801

Whilst St Vincent's Channel Fleet had successfully maintained its blockade of Brest, preventing the French fleet from sailing, elsewhere there was little for Britain to celebrate. The Anglo-Russian expedition of August 1799 against the French-backed Batavian Republic (Holland) had ended in disaster and in June 1800 the Austrian army was decisively beaten by Napoleon, now First Consul of France, at Marengo. Following the battle the Austrians and French entered into negotiations which eventually led to the cessation of all Austrian operations in the peninsula and their evacuation from northern Italy.

Having defeated the Austrians at Marengo – effectively ending the Second Coalition against France – Napoleon once again turned his attention to Britain. Whilst he might not be able to destroy her powerful navy in battle, he could deny her the equipment and raw materials needed to maintain her ships. Most of this came in via the Baltic States, Russia, Sweden, Prussia and Denmark. When Napoleon waived the right to search Danish and Swedish ships, Denmark's Crown Prince responded, as anticipated, by ordering that Danish frigate captains should no longer allow the British to stop and search the vessels under their protection. In a move designed to destabilise the Anglo Russian alliance Napoleon also promised to hand Malta over to Tsar Paul, Grand Master of the island's ruling order, the Knights Hospitaller, if the French garrison held out against the British. However, in September 1800 French resistance on Malta finally collapsed and the British assumed control over the island. Left out of discussions regarding Malta's future, the Tsar responded by placing an embargo on the 200 or so British ships then in Russian ports and seizing the British crews in St Petersburg, marching them inland in chains through the cold Russian winter. On 16 December Russia, Denmark, Sweden and Prussia signed the Northern Convention, an alliance that closed the Baltic to British trade.

Between them these four Baltic states now controlled a nominal force of up to ninety-six ships of the line. On 13 January 1801 news of the agreement reached Britain. In response the government placed an embargo on all Danish and Swedish ships in British ports and ordered that any encountered at sea were to be captured. Britain also sent a special envoy to begin negotiations with the Crown Prince of Denmark. If British diplomacy was the carrot then the stick came in the form of the Baltic Fleet. Headed by Admiral Hyde Parker with Nelson acting as his second-in-command, it had orders to attack Copenhagen if negotiations failed.

In December 1800 a joint naval and military force commanded by Lord Keith and General Abercromby sailed from Gibraltar for Egypt. To counter this threat Napoleon immediately ordered reinforcements into the Mediterranean. On 23 January Rear Admiral Ganteaume left Brest with a squadron of seven ships, taking advantage of bad weather that had forced the Channel Fleet back to Torbay. Passing through the Straits Ganteaume discovered from a captured Royal Navy frigate that he was now being pursued by the six ships under Admiral Warren from Cadiz. Ganteaume immediately altered course for Toulon, anchoring in the port on 19 February, just days before the arrival of Warren's ships. Though now blockaded, Ganteaume was immediately ordered back to sea by Napoleon. He was to head to Egypt and if possible land troops at Alexandria.

On 1 January 1801 the long-awaited promotion of flag officers took place and Saumarez was made rear admiral of the blue and ordered to hoist his flag aboard *Caesar*. As was widely anticipated, Brenton was appointed his flag-captain. Following his promotion to the rank of commander First Lieutenant Henryson left the ship and his place was taken by John Lamburn. Lieutenant Tancock rejoined the ship as second lieutenant following a request to the Admiralty from Saumarez and Phillip Dumaresq was made flag-lieutenant. Saumarez hoisted his flag aboard *Caesar* on 24 February, and the following day the ship sailed from Spithead to join the Channel Fleet, still sheltering at Torbay. On 7 March the fleet returned to Brest and Saumarez resumed command of the advanced squadron, relieving Admiral Thornbrough of that duty

On 19 February 1801 William Pitt had been forced to resign as Prime Minister due to a disagreement with the King over the question of Catholic emancipation and was replaced by the Speaker of the House, Henry Addington. Among his first appointments Addington made St Vincent First Lord of the Admiralty. To the relief of many of Saumarez's fellow officers, St Vincent was now replaced as commander-in-chief of the Channel Fleet by Admiral William Cornwallis.

The British under Abercromby arrived at Aboukir Bay on 2 March. Troops were eventually landed ashore and the British advanced on Alexandria. During heavy fighting on 22 March Abercromby, far too old to be leading an assault, was mortally wounded. The British advance eventually ground to a halt and Abercromby's replacement, General Hutchinson, turned the army round and headed off towards Cairo.

On 20 March a severe gale forced Saumarez's squadron to once again seek the safety of Douarnenez Bay. As they entered the bay they came under converging fire from the batteries at the Bec de la Chevre and the Bec du Raz. Anchoring in the east of the bay, out of range of the enemy guns, Saumarez remained at Douarnenez until 25 March when, after two attempts to work out of the bay, the squadron returned to the Black Rocks.

Negotiations between Britain and Denmark having failed, on 2 April Nelson took a detachment of Parker's fleet, ten ships of the line together with a collection of frigates, sloops and fireships, and attacked the Danish blockships defending the capital, Copenhagen. Two British ships grounded on the approach and the remainder anchored so far away from the Danish defences that they were almost at the limits of effective gunnery. The Danes fought with great bravery and determination and, with his ammunition running low and casualties mounting, Nelson proposed a ceasefire, which the Danish Crown Prince, watching the battle from the shore, accepted. During the battle Parker's flagship famously raised the signal of recall but this was ignored by Nelson. After the ceasefire Nelson entered into negotiations with the Danish Crown Prince during which news came through that the Tsar was dead and that Russian foreign policy was being reversed.

In mid-April a cutter arrived in the Channel Fleet bearing reports of Nelson's victory at Copenhagen and the British landings in Egypt. Returning to the Black Rocks from a visit to the flagship with copies of these reports Saumarez ordered that *Caesar*'s company be turned up. However, by the time they had assembled Saumarez was far too overcome with emotion to read the accounts aloud to his men. Brenton took over and upon hearing the news of the British victories *Caesar*'s people gave three rousing cheers.

After several abortive attempts to evade Warren's blockade of Toulon, Ganteaume finally managed to put to sea on 27 April. However, there was a sudden outbreak of typhus amongst his squadron and Ganteaume was forced to transfer the men worst affected by the illness to *Indomptable*, *Formidable* and *Dessaix*. These three ships were ordered back to Toulon under Ganteaume's second-in-command, Rear Admiral

Linois, while he continued on with his remaining ships of the line towards Alexandria.

Following a cruise of fourteen weeks Saumarez was relieved by Thornbrough on 1 June and the following day *Caesar* arrived in Cawsand Bay. On 4 June Saumarez received word from St Vincent that he was to be placed in command of a detached squadron 'destined for a very important service at no great distance from home'.[1] The Admiralty had received word that five Spanish ships of the line had sailed from Ferrol to Cadiz and Saumarez was now ordered to blockade the Spanish port, to follow the enemy fleet if it had already sailed and to keep a lookout for any French squadron that might attempt to link up with the Spanish, using his best endeavours to take or destroy it. St Vincent's orders promised some real action and came as a great relief to Saumarez, his officers and crew who were all heartily sick of blockade duty.

On 16 June Saumarez's squadron bent their sails and headed out of the English Channel and into the Bay of Biscay. Saumarez's ships included four 74-gun Third Rates; *Pompee*, Charles Stirling; *Spencer*, Henry Darby; *Hannibal*, Solomon Ferris; and *Audacious*, Shuldham Peard (recently released by the French), along with the 32-gun frigate *Thames*, Aiskew Hollis. On 26 June the squadron reached the Tagus where they were joined by the 38-gun *Phaeton*, James Morris and two more 74s, Richard Keats's *Superb* and Samuel Hood's *Venerable*. The ships now proceeded towards their final destination, Cadiz, arriving at the port on 28 June. For the next week the squadron cruised offshore, with *Superb* stationed off Lagos as a lookout to the west and *Thames* in the straits to the east.

Having managed to find 1,500 experienced sailors at Toulon to man his ships, Linois received fresh instructions from Paris. He was to join up with the twelve Spanish ships at Cadiz, sail to Italy, embark troops then continue on to Egypt and attack the British rear. However, when Linois reached Gibraltar he captured the brig *Speedy* and learned of the arrival of Saumarez's squadron off Cadiz. Not wishing to fight a much-superior force, Linois changed course and on 4 July brought his ships to anchor close to the shore of Algeciras Bay, in full view of the British at Gibraltar.

On the morning of 5 July Saumarez received a despatch from Captain George Dundas, patrolling the Straits in the sloop *Calpé*, informing him that three French ships of the line and a frigate had been spotted in the Straits headed for Algeciras. Saumarez immediately recalled *Superb* and he gave the order for *Pompée*, *Hannibal*, *Spencer*, *Audacious* and *Venerable* to make sail and proceed to the Straits. At 11.00am divine service was held aboard *Caesar*. It was a beautiful morning with the lightest of breezes coming in from west. Saumarez stood with his officers on the quarterdeck whilst the ship's band and the marines stood above them on the poop deck. The crew, arranged into their various divisions on the quarterdeck, were all dressed in white, as was customary aboard Saumarez's ship whilst it was in the Mediterranean. *Caesar*'s people knew they were hours away from a possible battle in which many would lose their lives and Brenton noted that the occasion was 'solemn and deeply impressive'.[2] When the service was over Saumarez and Brenton sat down to discuss the forthcoming battle. According to Brenton Saumarez remained 'calm, cheerful and collected'. He was 'quite aware of the difficulties we had to encounter and fully determined to overcome them if possible'.[3] Saumarez now issued his final instructions. Owing to Hood's knowledge of the local waters *Venerable* would lead the attack, passing the enemy ships without anchoring. The other ships of the line would then anchor abreast of the enemy ships and the batteries guarding the bay. *Superb* and *Thames* were to remain under sail and 'annoy the enemy's batteries and gunboats'.[4]

Algeciras Bay is situated roughly six miles west of Gibraltar. Open to the east, it is a bay with shallow water and hidden rocks and at that time was heavily defended. These defences included a battery of seven 24-pounder guns on the island of Isla Verda, situated close to the town with the forts of Santa Garcia and San Jago, with its five 18-pounders, further south. Prior to the battle there were also around fourteen gunboats present in the bay. Linois had arranged his ships in a line extremely close to the shore, both beneath the guns of the shore batteries and between the gun batteries that extended out into the bay. The ships were anchored 500 yards apart with *Formidable* at the head of the line followed by *Dessaix* and *Indomptable*. It was an extremely strong defensive position.

At 2.00pm *Caesar* made the signal for the other ships to prepare for battle and for anchoring at the stern. They closed to within seven or eight miles of the Rock but then the wind died away and did not pick up again until early the next morning when a light breeze sprang up from the north-west. As the British ships approached the bay, *Superb* and the brig *Pasely* still some distance to the rear, Saumarez and Brenton prepared for the coming battle by looking through Brenton's signal-book, the two men familiarising themselves with the signals they were most likely to need during the attack. At 4.00am *Venerable* signalled that she had sighted the French ships, they were in the process of warping closer to the shore, seeking out the protection of the batteries that defended the bay. *Caesar* beat to quarters and she made the signal to engage the enemy ships on passing them.

At 7.45am the lead British ships rounded Cabrita Point and were engaged by the shore batteries, the gunboats in the bay and by the battery on Isla Verda. In the light and variable winds *Venerable* quickly became becalmed and was passed by *Pompée and Audacious*. *Pompée* took up a position within pistol shot off the starboard bow of *Formidable* but the lack of wind meant that *Audacious* and *Venerable* were forced to drop anchor before they reached their intended positions, *Audacious* ended up some distance across from the French ship *Indomptable* whilst *Venerable* anchored between *Dessaix* and *Formidable*. The remaining three British ships, *Caesar*, *Spencer* and *Hannibal*, were now roughly three miles astern of the other ships. The French gunners waited until they were sure the British were in range. *Indomptable* was the first French ship to open fire, followed soon after by *Formidable*. At 9.00am *Caesar* fired her first shots of the battle and fifteen minutes later came to anchor on *Dessaix*'s starboard bow between *Pompée* and *Venerable*.

At 9.35am *Spencer* dropped anchor between Saumarez's flagship and *Hannibal*. After half an hour of sustained fire from the British Linois's ships began warping closer to the shore and Saumarez ordered his own ships to follow. *Pompée* cut her cables but the ship immediately swung round with the current and was powerless to stop *Formidable* raking her now-exposed bows. Unable to bring her guns to bear on the enemy ships, *Pompée* now redirected her fire to the battery of San Iago but soon drifted into a position where she could no longer fire at any useful targets and was also preventing *Venerable* from firing at the enemy. Saumarez sent Brenton aboard *Spencer* to request that Captain Darby 'weigh and work up to the enemy',[5] he then sent a signal for *Hannibal* to assist *Pompée*. Intending to pass between *Formidable* and the shore to draw the French ship's fire away from *Pompée*, Captain Ferris first sailed northwards before attempting to wear round. Saumarez sent boats from *Caesar* and *Venerable* to assist in the manoeuvre but they were still making their way across to *Hannibal* when the ship ran aground close to the battery at San Iago. Immediately coming under fire from the French ships and the shore batteries, *Hannibal* returned fire with as many of her guns as she could bring to bear.

The British ships now attempted to take advantage of a fresh breeze which had blown up from the north-east. His main mast badly wounded and with sails and rigging shot away Hood eventually managed to get *Venerable* close enough to *Indomptable* to open fire on the French ship. In response Linois threw a signal out to his ships

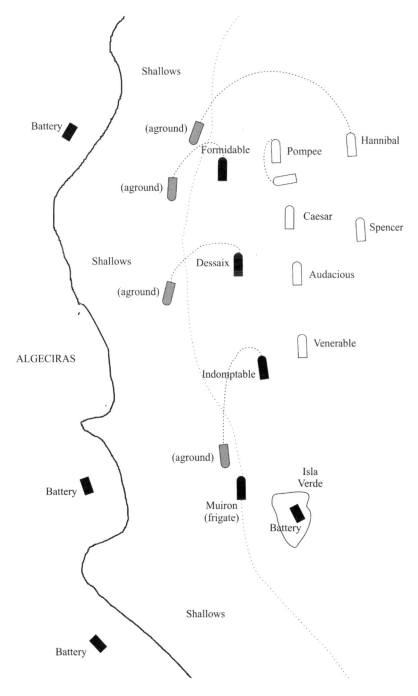

Shallows

Battery

(aground)

Formidable

Pompee

Hannibal

(aground)

Caesar

Spencer

Shallows

Dessaix

(aground)

Audacious

Venerable

Indomptable

(aground)

Battery

Isla
Verde

ALGECIRAS

Muiron
(frigate)

Battery

Shallows

Battery

The Battle of Algeciras, 6 July 1801.

instructing them to cut their cables and run themselves aground in order to lure the British closer to the shore batteries. *Formidable* beached with her larboard guns facing the enemy, *Dessaix* grounded on a shoal directly in front of the town of Algeciras and *Indomptable* ended up on a shoal to the north-east of Isla Verda.

Shortly after 11.00 another breeze blew up and Saumarez ordered his ships to cut their cables. *Caesar* wore round *Venerable* and *Audacious* before firing several broadsides into the bows of *Indomptable*, eventually bringing down her fore topmast. But then *Audacious* drifted in front of Saumarez's flagship, bringing her attack to a halt. *Venerable* and *Spencer* cut their cables to assist *Caesar* but a combination of wounded masts, damaged rigging and ripped sails prevented the ships from taking advantage of the wind before it dropped once again. With *Caesar* now drifting dangerously close to the island battery, Brenton ordered the last boat to be lowered to send a warp across to *Audacious*, however, the boat was discovered to be shot to pieces. Before anyone could stop him a young sailor from the mizzen-top, Michael Collins, grabbed the cable and dived into the sea from *Caesar*'s taffrail, swimming the fifty yards to *Audacious* where the cable was retrieved.

At 11.30am Sterling cut *Pompee*'s anchor cables, his ship was pulled out of action and towed across the bay to Gibraltar. All attempts to get *Hannibal* afloat had failed. By now her fore and main masts had been shot away, most of her guns had been knocked out and there had been a fearsome loss of life aboard ship. Captain Ferris ordered his officers and men below and struck his flag. He later reported to Saumarez that he had found it 'impossible to do anything either for the preservation of the ship or the good of the service'.[6] A boat from *Formidable* came alongside and *Hannibal* was boarded. Having no flag of their own the French officers simply re-hoisted the English colours upside down. The boarders had only one thing on their mind and in their haste to get at the British officers' trunks they trod over the dead and injured lying in the cockpit and the cable-tiers. Captain Ferris had not been able to return to his cabin to retrieve the papers in his desk as it would have meant stepping over the wounded but this proved no obstacle for the French who trampled many injured men to death in their urge to plunder. It was now that the boats sent from *Caesar* and *Venerable* finally reached *Hannibal*. The men from the boats insisted on going aboard the captured British ship and were immediately taken prisoner.

Audacious had drifted beneath the guns of the battery on Isla Verde and the Spanish gunners were using heated shot to try and set Peard's ship on fire. Ordering her one remaining anchor cable to be cut, *Audacious* was tacked back to Gibraltar. Having watched *Hannibal*'s flag being lowered, at 1.30pm, with the wind still unpredictable and his ships now drifting away from the French and towards the enemy battery, Saumarez reluctantly called off the attack and ordered a withdrawal to Gibraltar, leaving Ferris's ship in the hands of the enemy. The battle had lasted for nearly four hours and casualties amongst the British ships had been severe; *Caesar* had lost her master, William Grave, six seamen and two marines. Twenty-five of Saumarez's men were wounded and eight men had been taken prisoner aboard *Hannibal*. *Pompée* had also lost her master along with one midshipman, ten seamen and three marines. Three lieutenants and sixty-six other men were wounded aboard Stirling's ship. *Spencer* had lost six men with a further twenty-seven wounded, whilst *Venerable* had lost eight men, one a midshipman, with a further twenty-five wounded. Worst of all were the losses aboard *Hannibal*. Seventy-five men aboard the captured British ship were dead and sixty-two wounded.

On his arrival at Gibraltar Saumarez sent Brenton ashore to meet with General O'Hara, who had watched the battle from his official residence. He then retired to his cabin, where he remained until the following morning. He had caused a great deal of damage to the French squadron but he had still lost the battle. Worse still, a British ship of the line was now in enemy hands. To Martha he wrote 'I should be miserable had I to reproach myself for having undertaken the enterprise on light grounds, or with having failed in the planning and execution; but, on the contrary it is admitted by everyone to have been most judicious. It is therefore only in the result that I have been unfortunate.'[7] In another letter to his brother Richard, Saumarez wrote: 'Everything was done that depended on myself, both in the planning and executing the business; but I cannot be accountable for the accidents that prevented its success.'[8] Saumarez was certain that *Pompée* would have silenced the French flagship 'had not an unfortunate flaw of wind broke her sheer; from that moment she was unable to bring one of her guns to bear on the enemy's ship'.[9]

Having satisfied himself that he had done all he could to ensure a British victory, Saumarez's attention quickly turned to the crew of *Hannibal*, now languishing in a disused stable without water or anyone to care for the wounded. Saumarez sent Brenton with a flag of truce to request that Linois release Captain Ferris and the ship's officers but Linois replied that he could not act without first receiving permission from the Minister of Marine in Paris, although he did parole Ferris. Upon his release *Hannibal*'s captain reported to Saumarez that the French squadron were unlikely to be repaired in under three weeks. Ferris was immediately ordered to England aboard the lugger *Plymouth* with copies of Saumarez's dispatches and a message for his superiors in London. 'Tell the Admiralty, Sir, that I feel convinced I shall soon have an opportunity of attacking the enemy again and that they may depend on my availing myself of it.'[10] Saumarez made several more requests to Linois for the wounded prisoners to be released but they were all refused.

Having issued his crews with an extra allowance of wine, repairs to the ships began. In this Saumarez was greatly assisted by his friend and colleague, Alexander Ball, who had left Malta and was now Commissioner of the Navy at Gibraltar. *Pompée* was in such a crippled state that there was possibility of her being ready in time for any further action, so Saumarez authorised the distribution of her crew to the other ships. His own flagship, *Caesar*, was in just as bad a state. By 9 July she had been warped into the mole where her shattered mainmast, shot through in five places, was removed and a replacement installed. That same day *Superb*, which had been watching the Spanish fleet at Cadiz, appeared in the offing flying the signal 'Enemy at sea' from her halyards. Soon after her arrival, a squadron of six Spanish ships of the line, including two massive First Rates, put to in Algeciras Bay. These ships had been requested by Linois, from the Spanish commander at Cadiz, Don Jose Massaredo. Saumarez now wrote to Keith in Egypt requesting immediate assistance. Fearing that *Caesar* would not be ready in time for the imminent battle he moved his flag across to *Audacious* and informed Brenton that he intended to transfer *Caesar*'s men to the other ships in the squadron. *Caesar*'s people responded to this threat by promising Brenton that they would work day and night until the ship was repaired and ready for action. The men proved as good as their word and worked sixteen-hour shifts in order to get *Caesar* repaired. Brenton, who reputedly did not sleep at all, was forced to order the exhausted men to rest and save themselves for the upcoming battle. He proudly recorded that there were no cases of drunkenness or desertion amongst the men who had been sent ashore for powder and other stores. During this period several wounded men escaped from hospital, returned to the squadron and hid aboard their ships.

By 11 July Saumarez was still concerned that repairs to his flagship would not be completed in time. Worried that his crew would soon be unfit for action when turned over to the other ships he ordered all work on *Caesar* to cease, telling Brenton 'you have now done all in your power; you must make up your mind to the disappointment'.[11] Saumarez and Brenton were due to dine with the governor that evening but Brenton asked to be excused and told Saumarez that if the ship was still not repaired when he returned that evening then he would have the people ready for distribution around the squadron. Saumarez agreed and went on shore. Directed by Brenton, *Caesar*'s crew now set about making the ship look ready for sea; the topgallant yards were sent up, sails bent and *Caesar*'s running rigging got in order. When Saumarez returned from his dinner he was delighted with what he saw and quickly abandoned all thoughts of removing his flag to *Audacious*.

At dawn on 12 July the French and Spanish ships were spotted with their yards across and sails bent. They put to sea around midday whilst *Caesar* and the other British ships were still receiving powder, shot and other stores. At 2.30pm, with the sea wall crowded with spectators and the band playing 'Britons Strike Home', *Caesar* warped from the mole and half an hour later joined the other British ships already out in the bay, firing a salute to the town and re-hoisting Saumarez's flag.

The French and Spanish ships were headed for the safety of Cadiz, sailing in two squadrons; Linois's ships were leading five Spanish ships, *Real Carlos, Hermenegildo, San Fernando, Argonauta* and *San Augustin* and the French ship, *St Antoine*, all under the command of Vice Admiral Juan Joaquin Moreno. The 112-gun *Real Carlos* and *Hermenegildo* were two of the largest ships then afloat and this combined force was now twice the size of Saumarez's fleet. Saumarez was still hourly expecting for reinforcements from Keith, according to Brenton it was his intention to 'throw his whole force upon whatever part of the enemy's line he might be able to reach; depending upon the talents of his captains and the discipline of his ships to make up for the disparity of force, especially in a night action'.[12]

At 7.00pm Saumarez's squadron assembled at Europa Point on Gibraltar's southern tip, as the sun set around an hour later the British squadron was still trailing some way behind the combined fleet. Repairs to the ships had still not been completed, they were all handling badly and as a result they were unable to gain on the French. Saumarez now ordered his one undamaged ship, *Superb*, to go on ahead and attack the rear of the enemy line. *Superb* hoisted more sail and soon passed *Caesar* and the other British ships and disappeared into the night. Sailing with no lights or signals, by 11.20pm *Superb* had closed in to within several hundred yards of *Real Carlos* without being seen and was able to fire off several broadsides. Vice Admiral Moreno was no longer aboard his flagship as he had transferred to the frigate *Sabina* and the Spanish First Rate's captain and officers were all relaxing and eating supper. Panicking, *Real Carlos*'s gun crews opened fire in all directions. Several shots hit *Hermenegildo*, sailing ahead of her compatriot, which immediately returned fire. The two Spanish 112-gun First Rates now began trading broadsides with one another. After *Superb* fired her third broadside at *Real Carlos* the Spanish ship lost her fore topmast and as the sail fell across the forecastle guns their discharges set it ablaze. Observing that the Spanish ship was now on fire Keats broke off the attack to go after *Saint Antoine* which had been spotted off *Superb*'s starboard bow. With her crew distracted by the fire spreading across her deck *Real Carlos* ran into *Hermenegildo* which she also set ablaze.

Watching this chaos unfold from *Caesar* Saumarez gripped Brenton's shoulder and pointed across to the burning ships, exclaiming 'My God, Sir, look there! The day is ours.'[13] The flames shot up both ships rigging, igniting their sails and illuminating the ships Spanish colours. As the flames, which could be seen as far away as Gibraltar, consumed the masts and the rigging the two burning ships finally separated and slowly drifted apart.

The action between *Superb* and *Saint Antoine* was short and brutal. By 12.20pm the French ship had ceased firing and had begun hailing that she had surrendered. She was unable to strike her colours however, as her flag had become tangled up with the rigging. *Caesar* and *Venerable* now arrived in quick succession and continued firing at *Saint Antoine* until Keats signalled that she had in fact surrendered. *Caesar*'s damaged masts had been put under so much strain that it was necessary to close-reef the main topsail and take in the fore topsail, and now, as the wind again dropped, *Caesar* began rolling on the swells, adding to the strain on the masts.

Just after midnight the flames of *Real Carlos* finally reached her magazine and she blew up. *San Hermenegildo* was destroyed in a similar fashion some fifteen minutes later; the force of these huge explosions could be felt as far away as Cadiz. Almost 2,000 Spanish sailors died in the explosions and Saumarez, who had witnessed the destruction of *L'Orient* at the Nile later wrote 'So awful a scene I have never yet witnessed.'[14] *Caesar* was soon enveloped in a cloud of thick, acrid smoke that lay on the surface of the water and quickly spread throughout the ship, causing some of her people to mistakenly believe that their own ship was on fire.

Whilst *Superb* remained by *Saint Antoine* the rest of Saumarez's squadron now gave chase to the remaining French and Spanish ships which had become dispersed. By dawn Hood's ship *Venerable* was closing in on *Formidable* with the aid of the lightest of airs coming in off the shore. *Formidable* had spent the night imitating the British signal lights. Although she had avoided being attacked by the British ships, this did result in her coming under fire from both Spanish First Rates. At around 5.00am the French ship finally hoisted her colours and opened fire on *Venerable* with her stern chasers. *Caesar*, now completely becalmed, was still a mile and a half away with her boats deployed in an attempt to tow her nearer to the action. At around 6.45am *Venerable* lost her main mast, allowing *Formidable* to slowly pull away, still firing her stern chasers as she attempted to follow the other French ships headed for Cadiz. The action continued for another hour and a half until *Venerable*'s weakened foremast also came crashing down. Unable to manoeuvre she ran aground twelve miles south of Cadiz. Ten minutes later Hood's ship also lost her mizzen mast. Saumarez, worried that *Venerable* might follow *Hannibal* into enemy hands, sent Brenton with orders for Hood to burn his ship and transfer his people to *Thames*. Brenton was rowed across to the 'perfect wreck'[15] of *Venerable* and, with shot from *Formidable*'s stern chasers flying over his head, stepped onto her quarterdeck where he discovered her captain calmly sitting on one of the guns. Hood told Brenton 'Tell Sir James I hope it is not yet so bad with old *Venerable*; I hope to get her off soon.' adding 'Let the *Thames* stay by me, in readiness to receive our people. These rascals shall not have her.'[16] With the appearance of *Audacious* and *Superb* the combined fleet retreated back to Cadiz. A fresh breeze soon sprang up enabling *Thames* to heave *Venerable* off the shoal. *Spencer* arrived and Darby soon had Hood's ship under tow, heading back towards Gibraltar along with the rest of Saumarez's squadron.

At around 8.00am, with the French and Spanish ships still visible as they headed back to Cadiz, Saumarez retired to his cabin and began writing his despatches to the Admiralty. He also wrote to his brother Richard to inform him of the 'wonderful and most awful event of last night' – a victory which he ascribed to the intervention of an 'all-merciful PROVIDENCE'.[17]

By the following morning *Venerable*'s people had completed the task of repairing their ship, cutting away the damaged rigging and shattered masts and installing jury masts. At 6.00pm Hood's ship, no longer under tow, anchored along with the rest of the squadron and their prize at Gibraltar. The rocks overhanging the bay were crowded with onlookers enthusiastically rejoicing at news of the victory. The royal standard had been raised and a 21-gun salute was fired at the nearby King's Bastion as *Caesar* came to anchor, the whole fortress illuminated in celebration of the victory. Although heavily outnumbered and outgunned Saumarez's squadron had succeeded in destroying two massive Spanish First Rates and capturing one French ship of 74 guns. The following day Saumarez sat down in his cabin to write a general memorandum to his ships: 'Rear-admiral Sir James Saumarez has the happiness to offer his most heartfelt congratulations to the captains, officers, and men of the ships he had the honour to command', adding 'to the discipline and valour of British seamen is to be ascribed their great superiority over the enemy, who, although more than triple the force of the English squadron in number of guns and weight of metal, have been so signally defeated'.[18] Now that the battle had ended *Caesar's* people were suddenly overcome with exhaustion. Those men that did not collapse on the spot were dead on their feet, incapable of further action.

News of the 5 July battle and the loss of *Hannibal* reached Britain through the French papers a full week before the Admiralty received Saumarez's dispatches reporting his subsequent victory. In response it was immediately decided to send four ships of the line cruising off Ireland, *Warrior, Defence, Bellona* and *Russell*, to reinforce the Cadiz squadron. On 9 August these ships fell in with *Pompée* and *Superb* which had resumed the blockade of Cadiz.

Sailing aboard the brig *Louisa* Saumarez's flag-lieutenant Philip Dumaresq arrived with Saumarez's dispatches at Mount's Bay, Cornwall on 30 July. At the Admiralty he was received by St Vincent who shook his hand warmly and declared: 'I knew it, I knew it. I knew the man. I knew what he could do. It is the most daring thing that has been done this war. It is the first thing. I knew it would be so.'[19] St Vincent immediately wrote out Dumaresq's commission for commander along with a letter of congratulation to Lady Saumarez which he entrusted to Dumaresq before sending him on to meet the Prime Minister. To Saumarez he wrote: 'The astonishing effort made to refit the crippled ships at Gibraltar Mole surpasses everything of the kind within my experience, and the final success in making so great an impression on the very superior force of the enemy crowns the whole.'[20] Saumarez also received a letter from his son James, then aged twelve, explaining that the governor of Guernsey had organised a bonfire in celebration of the victory and that 'Uncle John had all the colours you had taken hung upon the outside of Grandpa's house which made a great shew.'[21] Saumarez's sister-in-law, Martha, wrote exultantly, 'You are now the theme of every conversation, the toast of every table, the hero of every woman and the boast of every Englishman ... we had the rascally French despatches a full ten days before we received yours; and, when we did receive the first account, your brother Richard was not satisfied. He feared the business was not done, and his mind dwelt upon it with anxiety. At last, on the 1st August, and not before, all our fears were removed.'[22]

Saumarez was kept busy after the battle, first with the exchange of prisoners and then with the numerous appointments that always followed a large fleet battle. Having written to the governor of

Algeciras, the Spanish sailors saved from *Real Carlos* were sent ashore. Then, after writing to Massaredo and Dumanoir at Cadiz, it was agreed that *Hannibal*'s men could be exchanged for the crew of *Saint Antoine*. Commander George Dundas of *Calpe* was made captain of *Saint Antoine* (renamed *San Antonio* by the British) and *Caesar*'s first lieutenant, John Lamburn, was promoted to captain of *Calpe*. Saumarez also promoted Mr. Beard, *Caesar*'s master's mate, *Thames*'s purser and several of her warrant officers to positions aboard *San Antonio* and he also made his secretary the purser aboard *Thames*.

As a reward for his victory Saumarez was given the Freedom of the City of London along with a 100-guinea sword. From the Lords there were tributes from Nelson, the Duke of Clarence and even from St Vincent. In Nelson's speech, his first to the House, came the belated acknowledgment that Saumarez had been his second-in-command at the Nile. Whilst St Vincent had been fulsome in his praises Saumarez had still not heard anything regarding the customary promotion of officers following the battle or what honour the government might bestow upon him. 'I shall certainly think myself entitled to a high mark of distinction,' he wrote to Martha, 'but past experience has taught me what an individual, unsupported by interest, has to expect.'[23] In mid-October Saumarez finally learned that he was to be made a Knight of the Bath; he had been expecting to receive a peerage as had been the case with Duncan following the Battle of Camperdown and Nelson after the Nile and considered the 'red riband but a poor reward'[24] for his victory and yet further proof that his services were being disregarded just as they had been after the Nile. Despite being aware that he might be accused of ingratitude, he nevertheless wrote letters questioning the award to St Vincent and Troubridge.

On top of his disappointment over the lack of a peerage Saumarez now learned that the Admiralty had rejected all his battlefield promotions (apart from that of Dundas to *San Antonio*) as they had not been cleared by his commander-in-chief, Keith. Saumarez was particularly infuriated to learn that Lamburn was to be sent back to *Caesar* whilst *Venerable* and *Superb*'s first lieutenants were to be promoted. (Saumarez had allowed Hood and Keats to send their own reports of the battle to the Admiralty along with his dispatches.) To Troubridge Saumarez wrote: 'I leave it to you to decide … what I must feel at this moment to find Mr Lamburn sent back, and the lieutenants of the *Superb* and *Venerable* alone promoted. I cannot but view it as a great injustice done me, and am very sorry to say it mortifies me more than I can express.'[25] To his brother Richard he wrote in much stronger terms. 'The conduct of Lord St Vincent has been scandalous, and what

Mr Tucker [his secretary] points out only proves to me he is the tool of his lordship. Lord St Vincent has proved he has no claims from me. I shall soon resume my calm and forbearance, but I have been deeply affected by the conduct of the Admiralty towards me.'[26]

Repairs to *Caesar* completed, Saumarez made two attempts to rejoin his squadron off Cadiz where Linois was still bottled up but it was not until 15 August that he finally reached his station. Saumarez now received word that he was to be reinforced with a squadron of four ships commanded by Sir John Borlase Warren. *Bellona* and *Audacious* were sent to Gibraltar to refit and *Phaeton* left with despatches for Keith, escorting a convoy of merchantmen into the Mediterranean.

Owing to its importance, the Admiralty had been decided to strengthen and separate the Cadiz station from the rest of Keith's fleet. On 14 August Nepean wrote to Saumarez to inform him that the squadron was to be placed under the command of Vice Admiral Charles Pole. This news was accompanied by a letter from St Vincent explaining, in sympathetic terms, that Saumarez could not continue in command owing to his lack of seniority. However, Saumarez immediately took this as a slur on his abilities and wrote a formal letter of complaint. St Vincent wrote back expressing his surprise at the contents of his letter and pointed out that Saumarez would now be second-in-command whereas under Keith he had been two positions lower. To Addington he wrote: 'What shall I say upon Sir James Saumarez his expectations, which are worked up to a pitch beyond all comparisons.'[27] Saumarez also received a tremendous rebuke from Nepean. 'Their Lordships cannot consider you a competent judge of the extent of the force which may be proper for them to appropriate. They cannot but disprove of your having made this complaint and hope that on cooler reflection you will see the impropriety of prescribing to their Lordships the line of conduct they should pursue.'[28] On 31 August Vice Admiral Pole arrived on station aboard his flagship *St George*, his reinforcements, *Dreadnought*, *Russell* and *Powerful*, bringing the squadron up to twelve ships of the line. Saumarez immediately asked permission to return home but his request was denied. However, it did not take long for his humour to improve. On 2 October he wrote to Martha: 'I should tell thee Admiral Pole and I are on the very first footing. I felt a little hurt at the circumstance of his taking my command, but the sulky fit soon wore off and we have been on the best of terms.'[29] Saumarez remained on station until 14 November when the squadron sailed to Gibraltar following the news of a peace treaty between England and France, the preliminaries of which had been signed on 1 October 1801.

Chapter 15

The Peace of Amiens: November 1801 – May 1803

By the summer of 1801 Napoleon had been thwarted in his plan to shut British trade out of the Baltic, his army in Egypt was still stranded and his alliance with Russia had also failed. At the same time eight years of costly war had almost bankrupted Britain. The increase in taxes to pay for the war along with a series of poor harvests had led to a rise in the price of food, resulting in widespread unrest and rioting. All a starving, war-weary British population wanted was peace. Peace also suited Napoleon as it would give him a chance to re-stock his war chest and reassess the strategic situation. Saumarez's victory at Algeciras meant that Napoleon had lost control of the Mediterranean and there was now no longer any possibility of relieving his army in Egypt. Furthermore, the loss of two Spanish First Rates at Algeciras had also led to a breakdown in Franco-Spanish relations, with the Spanish government demanding the return of its ships then stationed at Brest. On 20 July a peace treaty between Spain and Portugal was signed and the Spanish government now informed Napoleon that it wished to terminate as soon as possible 'an alliance which had become irksome to the court of Madrid'.[1]

After month of negotiations led by Addington's Foreign Secretary, Lord Hawkesbury, and his French counterpart, Talleyrand, on 1 October a preliminary peace deal was signed between Britain and France. Britain agreed to hand over almost all the territories taken during the war including Malta, Minorca and the Cape of Good Hope. In return France agreed to withdraw her troops from Naples and the Papal States, restore Egypt to the Ottoman Empire and recognise the neutrality of Holland and Switzerland. There were joyful scenes when news of the peace reached Saumarez's squadron, the men cheering wildly from the rigging of their ships and throwing their hats in the air. Expecting that they would soon be sailing for home a large number of men, most

131

notably from *St George,* also kicked their shoes overboard. Word that hostilities between Britain and Spain had also ceased soon reached the squadron and on 11 November Vice Admiral Pole relinquished his command and sailed for England. There being no reason to remain at Cadiz any longer Saumarez proceeded to Gibraltar with his squadron, *Caesar, Dreadnought, Spencer, Vanguard, Defence, Bellona, Zealous, Warrior, Trial* and *Powerful.* At Gibraltar Saumarez found Sir John Borlase Warren and his squadron of four ships of the line at anchor.

At midday on 16 November the Gibraltar garrison formed under arms with their colours and marched in two lines from the Great Parade to the Grand Parade to watch General O'Hara confer the Order of the Bath on Saumarez. The garrison was followed by a procession involving over 200 sailors, marines and civilians. Also marching with the procession were Captains Darby and Brenton. At the Grand Parade a podium had been set up in front of the Royal Pavilion where General O'Hara and Saumarez sat down next to one another. Having received the Order of the Bath from O'Hara Saumarez was given three 21-gun salutes from the Saluting Battery, the South Battery and Jumper's Battery. Several ships in the bay also joined in the salutes.

Saumarez remained at Gibraltar for the rest of 1801, with little to do except kick his heels and worry about a steadily worsening toothache. On 5 January 1802 he received a letter from Lord Eldon informing him that the thanks of both Houses of Parliament had been voted to the officers and crews of the Cadiz squadron for their victory over the fleets of France and Spain. In his reply to the Lord Chancellor Saumarez wrote: 'Having on four occasions been honoured with the thanks of their lordships when commander of a line-of-battle ship in different general actions, this very high mark of distinction cannot but be more particularly gratifying to my feelings when entrusted with the command of his Majesty's squadron.'[2]

The celebratory mood amongst Saumarez's squadron soon changed when the men learned that four ships, *Warrior, Defence, Bellona* and *Zealous,* were being dispatched to the West Indies. Several of these ships refused to weigh anchor and Saumarez and Brenton were forced to go aboard these vessels and speak to the men. The sailors were eventually persuaded to return to duty but they did so with no great enthusiasm, hauling in anchor cables at a snail's pace. On 25 January the squadron was surprised by the appearance of four French ships of the line and a frigate which had been spotted headed eastwards through the Straits. Having sighted the enemy the crews aboard the disaffected ships immediately forgot their grievances and returned to work, hauling up anchor cables and setting sails in lightning-quick time. Saumarez correctly guessed that the enemy ships belonged to Admiral Ganteaume – part of a much larger fleet of thirty-five ships of the line and twenty-one frigates commanded by Admirals Ganteaume, Villaret and Linois, together with five Spanish ships under Don Gravina, carrying an army of 21,000 men for an assault on the former French slave colony of San Domingo. Saumarez detached *Warrior*, *Defence*, *Bellona* and *Zealous* with orders to follow the French and link up with Duckworth at Jamaica. He also sent *Phaeton*, Captain Hope, to England to warn the Admiralty.

After eight months away at sea Saumarez was once again suffering the usual anguish caused by prolonged separation from his wife and family and he now learned that Martha was enduring a particularly harsh winter with their five children at Bath: 'My fingers can hardly hold my pen, they are almost frozen'[3] she wrote, 'but the ice can do no more, it does not reach my heart for it beats as warmly as ever and in all seasons is ever wholly thine.'[4] On 17 February Saumarez wrote. 'A few days more and I trust to have my orders to proceed homewards, as we understand from different quarters the Peace is finally concluded.'[5] Saumarez's optimism was misplaced as it would be another six months before he saw his wife and family again.

Eight days after the writing of this letter, Gibraltar was shocked by the sudden death of General O'Hara, governor of the Rock since 1795, who died following a short illness on the morning of 25 February. Saumarez despatched *Penelope*, Captain Blackwood, to Britain with the news of O'Hara's death and the flags on all the ships in the harbour were lowered to half-mast. On 3 March the squadron's boats rowed in procession to the Ragged Staff, while minute guns were fired by the flagship and the garrison. Saumarez and Major General Charles Barnett, the garrison commander, performed the duties of chief mourners.

In early February Brenton had received news of the death of his father, Rear Admiral Jahleel Brenton, and requested permission to return home. Saumarez was sorry to lose his trusted flag-captain but realised that his duties now lay elsewhere. However, Brenton did not want to leave until the definitive peace treaty was signed between Britain and France. With peace imminent the Admiralty had decided to reduce Saumarez's squadron and as the frigate *Santa Dorothea* was now preparing to return home Saumarez authorised Brenton to exchange commands with her captain, Hugh Downman, an experienced officer who had fought aboard *Victory* at the Battle of Cape St Vincent. When news reached Gibraltar that a peace treaty between Britain and France had been signed on 25 March Brenton sailed for home, his ship arriving at Portsmouth on 7 April.

One of the various provisions of the Treaty of Amiens was that the British hand the island of Minorca, captured in 1798, back to Spain. On 24 April Keith, who had arrived a month earlier from Malta, sent the following orders to Saumarez: 'Whereas orders may be immediately expected for the evacuation of the island of Minorca, and as I think it is indispensable that the service should be conducted by an officer of rank, ability and experience you are hereby required and directed to proceed thither in his Majesty's ship the *Caesar*, to be in readiness to take you upon the charge and execution of that duty.'[6] With her new flag-captain, Downman, now aboard, *Caesar* sailed from Gibraltar on 1 May in company with *Généreux*, Captain Cornwall and *Dreadnought*, Captain Vashon. Arriving at Port Mahon five days later, Saumarez met with Major-General William Clephane, commander of British troops on Minorca, to discuss the evacuation of the island and the embarkation of the 5,247 troops once the Treaty of Amiens was ratified. During these discussions it was decided that Saumarez would sail with the last division of troops to England whilst *Généreux* would sail with the first ten troopships bearing the 79th Regiment to Gibraltar and *Dreadnought* would escort the 40th Regiment directly to England. *Dreadnought* sailed on 2 June and the troop-ships that had sailed to Gibraltar with *Généreux* returned to Minorca to allow the evacuation of troops to continue.

On 16 June Clephane handed over the keys of Fort George to the Spanish Captain-General Don Juan Nines y Felia, and the British flag was lowered over Minorca for the last time. Clephane boarded the frigate *Pomone* for his passage to England and the following day *Caesar* left Port Mahon, escorting the last division of troops to Gibraltar. Arriving at the Rock on 24 June, Saumarez discovered that Keith had already sailed for England, leaving instructions for him to follow with the remaining three ships of the line and the troopships from Minorca. *Caesar* sailed from Gibraltar on 30 June and arrived at Spithead on 23 July. Two weeks later, on 7 August, she dropped anchor at Portsmouth where, according to the *Naval Chronicle*, she was 'received as an old friend returned to port after a long absence'.[7] Saumarez immediately struck his flag and set off for London with Martha who had arrived from Guernsey aboard the cutter *Pigmy*.

In September Saumarez was presented with a large silver vase valued at £200 that had been sent from Guernsey in acknowledgement of his services to Britain and the Channel Islands. The vase was inscribed: 'The inhabitants of Guernsey to their gallant countryman, Rear Admiral Sir James Saumarez, Bart and K. B. Whose suavity of manner and private virtues have long engaged their esteem and affection, and whose brilliant achievements have not only immortalised his name but will for ever reflect lustre on his native isle, and add to the glory of the British empire.'[8]

By the end of 1802 the brief peace between Britain and France was beginning to look untenable. Napoleon was making aggressive moves towards Switzerland and Holland and continued to exclude British trade from Continental ports. In October the Admiralty ordered all its ships in port to take on four months' worth of stores and to prepare for sea. Whilst Napoleon had used the peace to rebuild his fleet, Britain, her economy stretched to breaking-point after nine years of war, had done the opposite. Ships had been decommissioned and around 40,000 seamen had been released from their duties. Addington's administration, First Lord included, had been convinced that the peace would last and St Vincent had been more interested in rooting out corruption, both real and imagined, in the navy's dockyards than maintaining the navy as an effective fighting force. In November the government asked for 30,000 more seamen for the navy, an increase of 20,000 over the normal peacetime establishment. Amongst the various rumours flying about in the press was a suggestion that Saumarez would soon hoist his flag aboard *Blenheim* and proceed in her to Malta.

The rumours in the papers proved to be false and for the time being Saumarez remained in Britain. In January 1803 Saumarez was at Sheerness, presiding over the court martial of Captain John Ferrier who was accused of false muster and of using un-officer like language to his boatswain whilst in command of the frigate *Fortunée*. A minimum of five captains were required to sit in judgement at a court martial and it could often take several months for the required number to assemble. Ferrier had had to wait four months for his court martial by which time he had moved to the 74-gun *Albion*. The court found that Ferrier's choice of language had been improper but that the charge of false muster was malicious and ill-founded. He was honourably acquitted of all charges.

As a reward for his victory over the French and Spanish fleets at Algeciras, on 3 March Saumarez received the freedom of the City of London at a ceremony attended by the Lord Mayor, the Chamberlain and several of Saumarez's friends and colleagues. In his speech the Chamberlain stated that Saumarez's victory had equalled those of Essex, Blake Rooke and Walter, all freemen of the City. Presented with a dress sword valued at 100 guineas that bore both his and the City's coats of arms, Saumarez, in full dress uniform, thanked the chamberlain and said he would be proud to draw the weapon in defence of King and country. Following a recommendation by St Vincent to Addington, later that month Saumarez was granted an annuity of £1200 for life by the King.

On 8 March 1803 George III delivered a speech to Parliament in which he stated that due to military activity in the ports of France and Holland he had found it necessary to 'adopt additional measures of precaution for the security of his dominions'.[9] Britain and France entered into negotiations in an effort to save the fragile peace. The talks came to nothing, though they did give Britain the time it needed to begin rebuilding her navy. On 11 March 1803 Saumarez was appointed commander-in-chief the Nore, hoisting his flag aboard the 64-gun *Zealand* at Sheerness. His flag-captain was William Mitchell, an officer who had joined the navy as an able seaman and was rumoured to have been flogged through the fleet for desertion. Saumarez did not remain at the Nore for long however. War with France was imminent and his talents were needed elsewhere.

Chapter 16

Commander-in-Chief, Channel Islands: May 1803 – February 1808

On 18 May 1803 Britain declared war on France. Before the month was out French troops had entered Naples and the Papal States and Napoleon had once again turned his attention to an invasion of Britain, touring the Channel ports where an army of 160,000 men had begun to assemble. Britain responded to the renewed threat of invasion threat with a variety of measures, including the building a line of Martello towers along the south coast and calling for volunteers to help defend the country. At sea, Cornwallis resumed the blockade of Brest and Nelson, placed in charge of the Mediterranean Fleet, was tasked with keeping an eye on the French fleet at Toulon and protecting both Malta and Sicily.

With Britain once again under threat of invasion the Channel Islands resumed their front-line role, vulnerable to attack but also a perfect location to observe the troop and ship movements taking place along the French coast. The new Lieutenant-Governor of Guernsey, Sir John Doyle, quickly set about making improvements to Forts Grey, Hommet and Le Marchant which were all hastily enlarged and reinforced and the island also gained its first Martello towers. The garrison on the island also grew in size so that by 1805 it numbered over 4,000, around one-fifth of the islands population. In order to move troops around Guernsey's quickly, Doyle also built the island's first proper roads.

Owing to his expert knowledge of Guernsey and Jersey, on 18 May 1803 Saumarez was made Commander-in-Chief, Channel Islands, and was ordered to hoist his flag aboard the 50-gun *Grampus*, Thomas Caulfield.

This was of course an ideal posting for Saumarez as he would now be in almost daily contact with his wife and family. Sailing from the Nore aboard the brig *Kite*, his vessel fell in with *Grampus* en route to the Channel Islands and both ships arrived at St Pierre's Road on 19 May, joining the squadron of six frigates and six brigs and cutters busy protecting the waters around the Channel Islands and cruising off the enemy coast observing troop movements.

With ships sailing perilously close to the enemy shore in all weathers the operations carried out by Saumarez's squadron would be a constant source of danger. However, the rapid mobilisation of the navy had meant manning ships with men who were poorly trained and ill-disciplined. On one occasion whilst cruising off Guernsey during a heavy gale a recently-captured Dutch prize ship was spotted drifting towards *Grampus*. *Grampus*'s crew, pressed men and quota men from the jails, were slow to react to the danger and Caulfield, a man with a normally relaxed attitude towards discipline, was forced to personally start men with a length of rope to force them into action and save the ship. Passing so close to *Grampus* that she carried away her bowsprit yard, the prize drifted onto the rocks astern of Saumarez's flagship where she was lost.

With his move to the Channel Islands Saumarez had been reunited with his former flag-captain, Jahleel Brenton, now captain of the 38-gun *Minerve*. Brenton had only recently joined his ship, having spent several months ashore recuperating from a head injury caused by a falling block. On the night of 2 July Brenton's ship was cruising off of Cherbourg in thick fog when she ran aground on one of the submerged breakwaters that was being built at the port. The fog now chose this moment to lift and the batteries on the Ile Pélée, little more than half a mile distant, opened fire on the stricken British ship. Two enemy brigs also headed out from the port towards *Minerve*, stationing themselves across *Minerve*'s bows from where they could rake Brenton's ship whilst he could not bring any of his guns to bear. *Minerve*'s kedge anchor was carried out in one of the ship's boats. The anchor cable was soon shot away but the line was eventually re-established and the ship was slowly hauled off the breakwater and into deep water. At this critical moment the wind suddenly dropped and the tide pushed *Minerve* further back into the harbour where she grounded on a second set of submerged stones. It was now 6.00am and the tide had begun to fall. Eleven of *Minerve*'s crew were dead and a further sixteen were wounded. Realising that the situation was now hopeless, Brenton lowered his flag and surrendered his ship. Most of *Minerve*'s crew would remain prisoners until the end of the war but in October 1806 Brenton was exchanged for Captain Louis-Antoine Infernet, captured at Trafalgar in 1805.

As the build-up of French forces continued along the coast Saumarez tested the possibility of an enemy landing on Guernsey, sailing with Sir John Doyle to a spot on the south side of the island that the governor had claimed was inaccessible from the sea. A party of men were landed ashore and, having seen the ease with which they climbed to the top of the hill overlooking the bay, Doyle admitted that this spot, together with several other locations along the coast, would need additional fortifications.

In September a plan was devised to attack the invasion vessels assembling at Granville, south of Cherbourg. Saumarez temporarily transferred his flag to the frigate *Cerberus*, William Selby, for the duration of the operation, sailing from Guernsey on 13 September with a force consisting of two ship-sloops *Charwell* and *Kite* and the bomb vessels *Sulphur* and *Terror*. Saumarez arrived off Granville on the evening of 13 September and, having reconnoitred the assembled invasion craft together with the different batteries that were protecting them, dropped anchor as close to Granville as the tide would allow, with only sixteen feet of water beneath *Cerberus*'s keel at low tide. *Terror* grounded on the approach and it was not until 2.00am that her captain, George Hardinge, was able to place his ship in the position assigned to him and open fire with his two mortars. Saumarez's squadron immediately received return fire from the batteries overlooking the town and from several gun-vessels stationed at the entrance to the harbour. The bombardment was kept up for almost four hours until shortly before 6.00am when Saumarez called a halt to the action and anchored with *Terror* and *Charwell*, Philip Dumaresq, a short distance from Granville. *Sulphur*, Nicholas McCleod, whose poor sailing had prevented her joining in the bombardment arrived soon after and anchored alongside the rest of the squadron. That evening a few more shells were thrown towards Granville from both bomb vessels, but at too great a distance to have had any effect. Losses during the operation were minimal, just two men injured by splinters aboard *Terror*.

The following morning, whilst it was still dark, the squadron returned to Granville to resume the bombardment. On the approach *Cerberus* ran aground on a sandbank but *Terror* and *Sulphur* took their positions and opened fire on the enemy positions around 5.00am. Around twenty enemy gunboats now emerged from the harbour, drew themselves up into a line and returned fire. Nine gunboats attempted to approach the stricken *Cerberus* but were beaten back by *Charwell*, *Kite*, Philip Pipon, and *Cerberus*'s own launch, commanded by Lieutenant

Mansell, which was armed with carronades. By now the tide had dropped around six feet, exposing *Cerberus's* hull to enemy shot. The ship had also started to list so her topmasts were struck to prevent her from rolling completely over onto her side. Saumarez had been stood on the quarterdeck alongside his secretary, Samuel Champion, but Champion had beaten a hasty retreat when his leg was suddenly grazed by shot. Saumarez, however, refused to leave the quarterdeck and would not even consider moving his flag to another ship. After almost three hours aground *Cerberus* was finally re-floated. The bombardment continued until 10.30am when Saumarez ordered a withdrawal due to the falling tide. The squadron returned to Guernsey and, *Grampus* having sailed for Portsmouth, on 17 September Saumarez's flag was re-hoisted aboard *Diomede*. Saumarez had been impressed by Lieutenant Mansell's command of *Cerberus* whilst she lay aground and he was moved to *Diomede* as Saumarez's flag-lieutenant. Following the operation Saumarez had written to his brother Richard describing the action: 'You will be glad to find that, thanks to Providence the business of Granville has gone off as well as possible, although we have not succeeded in entirely destroying the enemy's gun-vessels. I have to regret that, in the execution of my orders, many of the harmless inhabitants of the town, and their dwellings, must have suffered very considerably … I am quite exhausted by fatigue, having had no rest since I left the island. Lady S. was unapprised of what was going forward, as well as yourself: but you must approve of the motives which urged me to conceal it from you.'[1]

The blockade of the French coast from Le Havre to Ushant continued throughout the remainder of 1803. In November *Diomede* was sent to Portsmouth for a refit and Saumarez shifted his flag back to *Cerberus*, though he spent most of his time ashore with his family, carrying out the duties of a port-admiral. On 10 December the newly launched 36-gun *Shannon* was wrecked in a gale off Cape la Hogue and on 31 December the gun-brig *Grappler* was lost off the Iles de Chausey having been ordered there by Saumarez to supply a group of French prisoners with two weeks' worth of provisions. The crews from both these vessels were rescued by the French and made prisoners.

On 6 January 1804 *Diomede* returned to Guernsey. It was now *Cerberus's* turn to sail to Portsmouth for a refit. Hoisting his flag aboard *Diomede*, Saumarez requested the services of Captain Hugh Downman, the officer who had briefly served as his flag-captain aboard *Caesar* after Brenton had left the ship following the Second Battle of Algeciras. Operations against the French invasion fleet continued into the New Year. On 31 January 1804 the frigate *Hydra* discovered a convoy of gunboats struggling along the coast and succeeded in separating and taking four vessels from it. On 17 March *Loire* captured the privateer *Braave* after a chase of seven hours. The following day *Tartar* captured the brig *Jeune Henri* and in April the brig-sloop *Sylph* destroyed several gun-vessels in the Race of Alderney and *Hydra* captured a privateer off Cherbourg.

In May 1804 Addington's weak government collapsed and Pitt returned as Prime Minister. St Vincent was quickly replaced as First Lord by Henry Dundas, Lord Melville, a close friend and political ally of Pitt. St Vincent had not been a popular First Lord, his reforms, criticised by Pitt whilst in opposition, had crippled the dockyards and many officers felt they had been poorly treated. Addington, now serving as a member of Pitt's government, offered St Vincent the command of the Channel Fleet but the stubborn old admiral refused to serve afloat whilst Pitt was still Prime Minister. By now the threat of invasion had begun to recede. Napoleon was having trouble getting enough transports built and those he did have were both unseaworthy and hard to manoeuvre. Boulogne had gained a new basin capable of holding 1,000 landing craft but the harbour still dried out at low tide and the maximum amount of landing craft that ever managed to sail together was 100. During a trial embarkation thirty landing craft were wrecked and several hundred men were lost due to high winds.

On 8 October Saumarez sent the ship-sloop *Albacore* to chase after a large group of gunboats that had been observed making their way along the French coast from the south. By that evening Captain Henniker had forced five enemy vessels to anchor beneath the battery at Flamanville. The following morning *Albacore* anchored with springs close to the enemy vessels and opened fire, driving the gunboats on shore. As the surf crashed over the stricken vessels their crews abandoned ship, dragging their injured colleagues with them. During the attack *Albacore* had received fire from the battery at Flamanville and from the enemy gunboats. Henniker had not lost any men but *Albacore*'s hull had been struck in several places and her rigging had received considerable damage.

On 2 December 1804 Napoleon was crowned Emperor of France during a lavish ceremony at Notre Dame Cathedral. That same month his faltering invasion plans received a boost when Spain declared war against Britain, at a stroke doubling the number of ships available to France. Whilst Cornwallis continued blockading the twenty-one ships of Admiral Ganteaume at Brest and Nelson kept an eye on Villeneuve's fleet at Toulon, Calder began blockading the Spanish at Ferrol and Orde was dispatched to Cadiz.

Napoleon now put all his efforts into getting the fleets at Brest, Toulon, Cadiz and Ferrol out of port to form one large combined fleet to assist in the invasion of England. Villeneuve, Ganteaume and Missiessy at Rochefort were to break out of port as soon as the opportunity arose, gather up whatever Spanish ships were available at Cadiz and Ferrol then head off into the Caribbean. Napoleon anticipated that the British would sail to the West Indies to come to the assistance of these distant, British-held islands. In the West Indies the French and Spanish fleets would join up to form a combined force of around forty French and twenty Spanish ships, they would then return to the Channel to cover Napoleon's invasion of England.

On 17 December *Niobe* entered Guernsey Road during a gale and collided with *Thisbe*, taking off her bowsprit and figurehead. Guernsey Road was a notoriously dangerous anchorage in bad weather, with ships frequently dragging their anchors and being lost. At the height of the storm, around midnight, *Thisbe*'s anchor cable parted and she was driven towards the rocks. However, just before the ship was wrecked a line was bent to the spare anchor and the danger was averted. *Sylph* and *Niobe* had begun pitching so violently they were both forced to cut away their masts and *Thisbe*'s foremast was also cut down. At around 4.00am the gale finally began to blow itself out. Before the gale struck *Thisbe* had been preparing to sail to Jersey with a spare anchor and cable for *Severn*, the flagship of Commodore d'Auvergne, which was lying in Grouville Bay with a broken rudder. Already disabled and without an anchor to secure her, *Severn* was driven ashore during the storm and wrecked. Thankfully her crew had all been taken off and there was no loss of life.

On 11 January 1805 Rear Admiral Missiessy slipped out of Rochefort during a snowstorm. Six days later Villeneuve left Toulon and set sail for the West Indies. However, two days out of Toulon he ran into bad weather and had to return to port. Missiessy continued on to the Caribbean with his four ships of the line and sloops transporting 3,500 troops but by the time he arrived at Martinique towards the end of February Napoleon had issued a new invasion plan. Ganteaume was to sail from Brest, collect the ships at Ferrol and sail to Martinique where Villeneuve and Missiessy would be waiting. This combined fleet would then return under the command of Ganteaume to cover the invasion of Britain. On 30 March 1805 Villeneuve left Toulon and sailed through the straits of Gibraltar. Collecting Vice Admiral Don Federico Gravina's squadron at Cadiz the combined fleet sailed for Martinique. Having received intelligence of Villeneuve's movements, Nelson set off in pursuit. Meanwhile, Ganteaume remained stuck in port, having been refused permission by Napoleon to fight his way past Cornwallis. On 28 March Missiessy finally gave up waiting for Ganteaume and the Combined Fleet and sailed for home.

Villeneuve and Gravina arrived at Martinique on 16 May. On 4 June Villeneuve attacked a British convoy, took possession of several ships, and discovered that Nelson was in the West Indies. His men, poorly trained and sick, were in no condition to fight the battle-hardened British so Villeneuve ignored his orders and immediately sailed for home. The brig *Curieux*, returning to Britain with Nelson's dispatches, spotted Villeneuve headed for Ferrol and was able to warn the Admiralty. Cornwallis was immediately ordered to lift the blockade of Rochefort in order for his squadron to join Calder off Ferrol. Calder's fleet of fifteen ships of the line met Villeneuve and Gravina's combined fleet of twenty ships of the line on 22 July. The Spanish, who did the bulk of the fighting, lost two ships, the British none. Villeneuve despaired at the fighting abilities of his own ships. The action, fought in fog was largely inconclusive and Calder chose not to re-engage when the opportunity arose, seemingly intent on protecting his prizes.

On 10 August the cutter *Pigmy*, Lieutenant Smith, ran aground on a falling tide when leaving Saint Aubin, Jersey. The vessel was secured and her kedge anchor rowed out whilst boats from other vessels began removing her guns, ammunition and stores. Finally Smith's crew began to cut down *Pigmy*'s masts so that she could be floated off the reef with the returning tide. However, *Pigmy*'s hull had been badly damaged and when the tide eventually returned she rapidly began filling with water and had to be abandoned. Smith was court-martialled at Portsmouth on 20 August. The court censured the pilot but honourably acquitted Smith, his officers and crew.

Following his bruising encounter with Calder, Villeneuve returned to Cadiz, arriving in port on 21 August. His ships now combined with those of the Cadiz station, Nelson began a loose blockade of the Spanish port to tempt Villeneuve back to sea. On 18 October Villeneuve learned that six of Nelson's ships of the line had been dispatched to Gibraltar for provisions, reducing the strength of the British fleet. Villeneuve took the bait and by the afternoon of 20 October the Combined Fleet was back at sea, headed south.

On 18 October Nelson had received a packet of newspapers and some wine from Saumarez at Guernsey. Nelson's letter of thanks to Saumarez was one of the last he would ever pen: 'In whatever manner, my dear Sir James, I may be able to meet your wishes, I desire you will let me know. Our friends at Cadiz are ready to come forth and I hope they will not escape me ... I have to thank you for your great attention about my wine and for recommending me some excellent champagne. I beg my most respectful compliments to Lady Saumarez.'[2] The following day Nelson wrote a letter to Collingwood which he ended: 'I had a letter from Sir James Saumarez yesterday, of October 1st. He sent me some papers. I take it very kind of him.'[3]

On 21 October the British and Combined Fleets finally met one another off the south-west coast of Spain at Cape Trafalgar. The battle was a brutal, vicious encounter, unlike any Nelson had been in before. At its height he was hit in the shoulder by a musket ball which punctured his lung and shattered his spine, he was taken below, face covered so as not to upset *Victory*'s people. Nelson died knowing that the battle had been won and that seventeen enemy ships were now in British hands. The destruction of the Combined Fleet had ended all of Napoleon's grand invasion plans, and left Britain master of both the Channel and the Mediterranean. Napoleon would begin a programme of rapid shipbuilding to restore his navy, but the haste in which these ships were built meant that they were leaky, unseaworthy and generally unfit for purpose.

On 9 November Saumarez was promoted Rear Admiral of the Red. With the threat of invasion now over several of the vessels under Saumarez's command were needed elsewhere and on 26 November *Diomede* sailed as part of an expedition under Commodore Sir Home Popham to take the Cape of Good Hope from the Dutch. As a consequence Saumarez hoisted his flag aboard the 36-gun *Inconstant*, Edward Dickson.

On 23 January 1806 William Pitt died of bowel cancer, forcing a change in government. Three weeks later Lord Grenville became Prime Minister and he formed the 'Ministry of All the Talents', selecting his cabinet from members of all the various political factions, not just his own. Amongst his other appointments Barham was replaced as first lord at the Admiralty by Lord Howick. The death of Pitt and the change of government tempted the 71-year-old St Vincent back to sea and in February, to the consternation of many in the service, he resumed command of the Channel Fleet, hoisting his flag aboard the 110-gun *Hibernia* in Cawsand Bay.

At 8.00am on 26 April the gun-brig *Rebuff*, Commander Charles Shackleton, was cruising seven leagues north-west of Guernsey in company with the revenue cutters *Drake* and *Beagle* when she fell in with the 16-gun French privateer *Sorciere*, four days out of Saint-Malo. *Sorciere* was a fast sailing vessel that had done a great deal of damage to British trade, particularly off the coast of Ireland. Shackleton gave chase but his vessel was a poor sailer and had trouble remaining in contact with *Sorciere*. Thankfully, at around 2.00pm he was joined by the privateer *Mayflower*, Commander James Laine. *Mayflower* quickly overhauled *Sorciere* and at around 4.30pm the French privateer surrendered to Laine's faster, better-armed vessel.

On 27 May Saumarez was at the Admiralty for a meeting with the new First Lord. Having been confirmed as commander-in-chief of the Channel Islands Station under the new administration by Howick, Saumarez requested that he be provided with an additional two fireships. From London Saumarez travelled to Portsmouth and following an overnight stay at the Fountain Inn returned to Guernsey aboard the sloop *Charwell*, Commander Dumaresq, on 3 June.

On 9 September *Constance*, Alexander Burrowes, and the gun-brigs *Strenuous*, John Nugent, and *Sharpshooter*, John Goldie, attacked a French frigate and drove her on shore to the west of Cape Frehel. With the weather rapidly deteriorating the British left the French frigate to her fate and returned to their anchorage at the Iles Chausey twenty miles south-west of Jersey. On 12 October *Constance*, *Strenuous* and *Sheldrake*, John Thicknesse, returned to sea. The same enemy frigate that had been spotted the previous month had been sighted off Saint-Malo and the British squadron now gave chase. The frigate turned and headed for the Bouche d'Arkie, anchoring with springs on her cables beneath a battery supported by troops and field guns. Dropping anchor within pistol shot of the battery the British squadron opened fire. During the two-hour action the French frigate, *Salamandre*, and *Constance* both ran aground and Captain Burrowes was killed by grape shot. Totally disabled, *Salamandre* finally hauled down her colours and *Sheldrake*'s first lieutenant, Richard Kevern, took possession of her. Despite repeated attempts, neither *Salamandre* or *Constance* could be got off. *Salamandre* was burnt and *Constance* was abandoned. The following morning *Sheldrake* and *Strenuous* returned to discover *Constance* lying on her back, a total wreck. Writing to the Admiralty on 15 October Saumarez lamented the loss of Burrowes but applauded the efforts of Thicknesse and his crew to prevent *Sheldrake* from falling into enemy hands.

Following the British victory at Trafalgar Saumarez's command had been reduced in size and from late October 1806 to January 1807 he hoisted his flag aboard whatever frigate was at anchor at Guernsey Road. On 23 October he shifted his flag from *Inconstant* to *Uranie*, and on 3 November from *Uranie* to *Crocodile*. From 11 December Saumarez's flag flew aboard *Brilliant*, shifting once again on 28 January 1807 to the 38-gun *Spartan*. Two days later *Spartan* left Guernsey for Ushant, taking Saumarez to a new, more active command, along the French coast.

In October 1806 St Vincent had gone ashore for the winter, leaving his second-in-command, Sir Charles Cotton, in effective control of the blockade of Brest. Cotton had served as the Channel Fleet's second-in-command since April 1802, carrying out the role twice under St Vincent and once under Cornwallis. However, in December 1806 Cotton was offered, and accepted, his own command at Newfoundland. St Vincent readily understood the difficulties now faced by the new First Lord, Thomas Grenville, in finding a suitable replacement for Cotton, an officer with years of experience in a challenging role: 'I do not know one flag-officer upon half pay, senior to Sir C. Cotton, whom, if I filled the station you do, I could confide in to guard the port of Brest. There is such a deficiency of nerve under responsibility, that I see officers of the greatest promise and acquired character sink beneath its weight.'[4] After several false starts, the Admiralty's attention eventually fell on Saumarez. Though still a junior flag officer he had experienced the rigours of close blockade under St Vincent's strict regime and the two men had worked well together. When Saumarez's name was first mooted Grenville had commented: 'Saumarez would certainly do extremely well; could not be displeasing to Lord St Vincent; would be acceptable to the fleet; and would enjoy the confidence of the country.'[5] The First Lord did, however, doubt that Saumarez could be tempted away from his command of the Channel Islands where the rewards were high and the stresses low. St Vincent sent his approval, writing 'No Officer on the Flag List of the Navy is better qualified to command the squadrons before Brest, or so well, as Sir James Saumarez.'[6] The major stumbling-block, Saumarez's lack of seniority, was addressed on 13 December 1806 with a promotion to Vice Admiral of the Blue. Saumarez proved Grenville wrong by immediately accepting the position of St Vincent's second-in-command. Arriving in the Channel Fleet aboard *Spartan* on 29 January, he hoisted his newly-assigned blue flag aboard the 112-gun *San Josef*, Captain John Conn. In mid-March Saumarez's flagship was caught in squally weather off Ushant and she limped back to Cawsand Bay with ten inches of water in her hold. Saumarez now shifted his flag to *Prince of Wales*, William Bedford, to allow *San Josef* to go into port for long overdue repairs.

In the spring of 1807 Grenville's government collapsed due to disagreements over the question of Catholic emancipation and the Duke of Portland became Prime Minister. With a Pittite once again in power on 26 March St Vincent wrote to the Admiralty, claiming his health was now so bad he could no longer continue as the Channel Fleet's commander-in-chief. Alan Gardner was appointed as his replacement, hoisting his flag aboard *Ville de Paris* on 14 May.

On 6 June *Hibernia* arrived off Ushant and Saumarez shifted his flag to Captain Conn's ship to allow *Prince of Wales* to return to Cawsand Bay to refit. *Hibernia* cruised off Ushant for the next fortnight, visiting the in-shore squadron at the Black Rocks on 9 July. Upon accepting command of the fleet Gardner had requested that Sir John Duckworth, who was then in the Dardanelles, serve as his-second-in-command. Duckworth returned to Britain on 26 May and immediately went on leave. On 20 July he hoisted his flag aboard *Royal George* at Plymouth and sailed for the Channel Fleet. Saumarez had no desire to be demoted from second to third-in-command under Gardner and Duckworth and so he struck his flag and went ashore that same day. On 1 August he had an interview with the new First Lord, Mulgrave, at the Admiralty. It was a lengthy meeting and Mulgrave, a former general, must have been impressed by the Channel Fleet's outgoing second-in-command for in the months that followed he would take every opportunity to advance Saumarez's career. His first move was to offer him his old position as Commander-in-Chief of the Channel Islands which Saumarez accepted without any hesitation. Having attended the King's levée at Buckingham House on 5 August Saumarez returned to Guernsey to take up his new command, hoisting his flag aboard *Inconstant* on 24 August.

On 1 September the 22-gun frigate *Boreas*, Robert Scott, arrived at Guernsey from Portsmouth. Launched in April 1806, *Boreas* had been commissioned for service in July of that year under the command of the newly promoted Scott, an officer whom Saumarez greatly admired. On 2 October *Boreas* captured the French privateer *Victoire*, out of Morlaix after a four-hour chase. *Victoire* had with her an American prize vessel which was retaken by Scott. Six days later *Boreas*, in company with the 28-gun *Brilliant*, Thomas Smyth, captured the Danish vessel *St Hans*. After just a few short months on station Scott had proved to Saumarez that he was a valuable and enterprising officer who had shown 'the greatest zeal and attachment for his Majesty's service'.[7]

On the afternoon of 21 November *Boreas* was ordered to search for a pilot-boat that had been blown off the coast of Guernsey in a gale. The vessel was soon picked up and taken under tow but about 5.00pm it was discovered that the strong winds had driven *Boreas* towards the dangerous Hannois Rocks, two miles south-west of Guernsey. Orders were given to put the helm down but *Boreas* struck the submerged rocks and ran aground. Her hull was ripped open by the impact and she began filling with water. The crew of the pilot-cutter now cut the tow and shamefully abandoned *Boreas* to her fate. As the ship began to heel over onto her larboard side Scott gave orders for the masts to be cut

147

down. Realising that his ship was beyond saving, Scott ordered the crew to be given a tot of rum each and the ship's boats to be lowered. The gig was dispatched to obtain assistance and the launch and the cutter were ordered to take the sick and land them at Hannois Point, then return to *Boreas*. With *Boreas* firing distress guns in the distance the launch reached Hannois Point but most of the crew, pressed men and privateers, immediately deserted on reaching safety. Undermanned and struggling against the wind and tide, the launch spent several fruitless hours attempting to make it back to *Boreas*. News of the emergency reached St Peter Port around 2.00am and Saumarez immediately dispatched *Jamaica* and *Brilliant* to Hanois Point. However, by the time they arrived *Boreas* was a total wreck and his remaining crew, over 100 men, were all dead. Only the men in the boats, six men aboard the gig and thirty seamen aboard the launch and cutter were saved. Saumarez reported the loss to the Admiralty the following day: 'With feelings of utmost regret, I have to inform you that the gallant officer, Capt. Scott, from whose valour and talents the country had reasons to expect so much, is now no more. The *Boreas*, which under his command has rendered such essential services upon this station, run upon the Hannois Rocks about six o'clock yesterday evening, when standing in for this island, the wind blowing with great violence at North-East . .. Captain Scott, with the greater part of her crew are lost.'[8] Saumarez would later provide *Boreas*'s survivors with clothing and pay for coffins and other burial expenses.

On 23 January 1808 Mulgrave wrote to Saumarez to offer him the command of the East Indies station, replacing Edward Pellew who had resigned his commission. This would be a lucrative command with plenty of prize money to be had. However, it was also a distant station, far from the dramatic events being played out in Europe and there was little chance of any major fleet action. The extreme distance also meant that communication with home would take up to a year. Saumarez could barely stand a week without contact from his wife and family and hoped to be employed on a more active station much closer to home where his services might be yet be rewarded with the peerage many though long overdue. On 30 January Saumarez wrote to Mulgrave from Guernsey to decline the offer, citing ill health as a reason, an explanation frequently used by officers when turning down a promotion: 'I cannot sufficiently express my grateful acknowledgements for the obliging manner in which your lordship has been pleased to propose to me the command in the East Indies, which I should be most happy to profit by, did the state of my health hold out any prospect of my fulfilling so important a trust with satisfaction to myself or the benefit of the country.

I am therefore, though reluctantly, compelled to decline this mark of your lordship's kindness.'[9]

Undeterred, on 20 February Mulgrave wrote to Saumarez offering him another command, this time much closer to home: 'It is my intention to send a squadron into the Baltic, consisting of not less than twelve or thirteen sail of the line. If your health should be such as to admit of your taking the command of this fleet, I know of no arrangement, which I can make that would be so satisfactory to myself, as to entrust the important service of attempting to destroy the Russian fleet, and of affording protection to his majesty's firm and faithful ally, Sweden, to your direction.'[10] On 27 February Saumarez wrote to Mulgrave gratefully accepting the command. He would spend the next five years in charge of the Baltic Fleet, by the end of his tenure one of the largest and most important fleets in the Royal Navy.

Chapter 17

The Baltic:
February 1808 – March 1808

Deeply religious and, by all accounts, slightly mad, King Gustav IV of Sweden had a deep-seated hatred of Napoleon, referring to him as the 'Beast of the Apocalypse'. In 1805 he had joined Britain, Austria and Russia in the war against France and in return the British government agreed to pay for additional Swedish troops to assist both in her defence and her territorial ambitions. At that time the geopolitical situation in the Baltic was a complicated one. Finland had belonged to Sweden for almost 700 years but was coveted by her domineering neighbour Russia whilst Sweden herself had ambitions towards Norway, which at that time belonged to Denmark.

In response to the naval blockade of the French coast begun by Britain in May 1806 Napoleon issued the Berlin Decree. From November 1806 any ally of France was forbidden from trading with Britain. Napoleon's economic blockade of Britain proved hard to enforce, indeed France herself continued to purchase British goods covertly (the French army was one of the largest purchasers of indigo dye from India). Spain and Russia presented large holes in his Continental System though which goods continued to flow unchecked and in 1807 Napoleon declared war Russia. (He would invade Spain the following year.) The first meeting between French and Russian armies at Preussisch-Eylau in eastern Prussia proved inconclusive but at the battle of Friedland in June 1807 Napoleon inflicted a heavy defeat on the Russians. The following month Alexander met with Napoleon at Tilsit and signed a peace treaty that included an agreement by Russia to adopt the Continental System. In Britain the news of the treaty came with a false rumour that it also contained secret articles that would revive the armed neutrality of the Baltic States. With France and Russia now exerting pressure on neutral Denmark to side with them in the war against Britain, on 14 July Mulgrave suggested sending a fleet to the Baltic to prevent the Danish navy falling into Napoleon's hands. A sizable fleet was assembled under Lord Gambier and sailed to the Baltic where it met up with British troops under General Cathcart at Stralsund. On 16 August British troops were landed on Zealand. Danish forces were quickly brushed aside and Copenhagen surrounded. From 2 September the Danish capital was subjected to a daily bombardment from the British army and the Royal Navy out at sea. On 7 September, with large parts of Copenhagen in flames, the Danes finally surrendered and their entire fleet (eighteen ships of the line and fifty-two smaller vessels) was removed to Britain together with 20,000 tons of naval stores. This humiliating defeat had the opposite effect to that intended by the British government on the Danes, who, up to that point, had made every effort to remain neutral, for they threw their lot in with the French and would remain their staunchest ally till the end of the war.

As a consequence of Tilsit and the Russian adoption of the Continental System, the Tsar had demanded that Sweden, Denmark and Prussia close their ports to British trade and that Sweden also declare war on Britain, threatening to invade Finland if she did not. Gustav IV understood the importance of trade with Britain (as Alexander would later) and refused these demands, consequently, on 21 February 1808 Russia declared war on Sweden, Russian troops crossing the Finnish border nine days later. Napoleon also sent an army, led by Marshal Bernadotte and made up largely from Spanish troops, to Holstein, south of Denmark, ready to attack Sweden from the south if the opportunity presented itself. It was now that the Admiralty decided to send a sizable fleet to the Baltic and began to look for a commander-in-chief with the requisite skills to handle the complicated political and military situation that had developed in the region. Whoever they chose would have to ensure that trade continued to flow in and out of the Baltic past the Danish and Norwegian gunboats and privateers now operating in the Sound and the Great Belt, the only two routes in and out of the region. Most importantly, with Russia acting belligerently towards Sweden the eventual commander-in-chief of the Baltic fleet would have to decide if and when to carry out military operations against Britain's former ally. On top of this, the Swedish Crown Prince had his own territorial ambitions and would also need careful handling, his last military campaign having ended in an ignominious retreat.

Of the senior flag officers available, both Keith and Cornwallis had struck their flags and were now ashore, the unfortunate Calder had fallen out of favour after Finisterre and Warren, despite his proven diplomatic skills, was considered 'good for nothing but fine weather and easy sailing'.[1] This left just three officers with the qualities needed to command the Baltic Fleet; Pellew, Collingwood and Saumarez. Pellew was a capable commander and had recently resigned his command of the East Indies fleet but was still on station waiting for his replacement. He had also had a falling out with the highly-regarded joint commander of the East Indies Station, Thomas Troubridge, a protégée of St Vincent's, that would have done him no favours at the Admiralty. Nelson's second-in-command at Trafalgar, Cuthbert Collingwood, was skilled in fleet action but since Nelson's death he had been tied down in the Mediterranean under increasingly failing health. Furthermore, the government was reluctant to move him as he would be succeeded by the Duke of Clarence (the future William IV) whose senior position on the Admiral's list had nothing at all to do with his limited abilities as a commander. The last flag officer on the Admiralty's shortlist was Saumarez. An experienced commander, he had a proven track record in both fleet battle and blockade, and, as his prolonged correspondence with the governor of Cadiz also attested, diplomacy. He was respected by both senior officers and those serving under him and was capable of making important decisions without recourse to his superiors.

Accepting the position of Baltic Fleet commander, in his letter to Mulgrave of 27 February Saumarez wrote. 'I feel most deeply impressed with the very obliging manner in which your lordship has been pleased to offer me the command of the squadron proposed to be sent to the Baltic. It is with great diffidence that I undertake a trust of so high and great importance, having ever made it the principle of my life to go upon any service where my exertions for my king and country would be deemed most useful.'[2] For his rear admirals Mulgrave had proposed Richard Keats and Samuel Hood. Both men had served under Saumarez at Algeciras (Hood and Saumarez had also fought together at the Nile) and both men had recent experience of the Baltic, having served as part of Gambier's fleet. Saumarez was pleased with Mulgrave's choice. 'The two officers selected to co-operate with me, are possessed of the highest merit; and, of all the others, those I should have been happy to apply for, had they not been previously appointed.'[3] Saumarez requested that Philip Dumaresq serve as his flag-captain and George Hope was appointed as Captain of the Fleet. Hope was an experienced officer who had captained *Defence* at Trafalgar, His ship had been heavily engaged with the Spanish ship *San Ildefonso*, eventually forcing her surrender. Hope was one of the few captains to anchor his prize during the storm that followed the battle and as a result *San Ildefonso* was one of only four ships that made it back to Britain out of the twenty-two ships taken during the battle.

It was eventually agreed that Saumarez could have *Victory* as his flagship. Now over forty years old, she was still regarded as one of the finest three-deckers in the navy and was highly sought-after. Following Trafalgar the ship had undergone a lengthy refit to repair battle damage. It was also decided to take the opportunity to lighten the ship to save her ageing timbers. Her heavy oak masts and spars were removed and elm and ash replacements installed. The 24-pounders on the middle deck were replaced with lighter 18-pounders, two lower-deck 32-pounders were removed completely and the four 68-pounder carronades on the upper deck that had done so much damage at Trafalgar were replaced by smaller 32-pounders. With her draft now reduced from twenty-one to nineteen feet *Victory* was well suited for operations in the Baltic.

Saumarez hauled down his flag aboard *Inconstant* on 12 March and was replaced as commander-in-chief of the Channel Islands by Sir Edmund Nagle. On 14 March 1808 Denmark declared war on Sweden. In a move that surprised his generals Gustav decided not to concentrate his efforts on defending Finland from the Russians but instead invaded Norway. The British government now decided to send 10,000 troops under General Sir John Moore to Sweden. However, from his conversation with the Secretary for War, Lord Castlereagh, it was apparent to Moore that the government had no clear idea what to do with his army once they were in Sweden. Whilst Saumarez waited in London for his final instructions word of his appointment reached the press. *The Times* of 13 April surmised that the Baltic Fleet would either invade Norway, attack Cronstadt, or capture the Danish islands off the coast of Sweden but Saumarez understood that its role would be purely defensive. On 24 April he wrote to Martha: 'The most we can expect is that of contributing our aid to the defence of Sweden, in which we shall succeed – but as to anything further, the Country will I fear be much disappointed.'[4]

On 16 April Saumarez received his final instructions from the Admiralty. He had specific orders to prevent the passage of French troops and their supplies from the Continent into Zealand; to protect Skåne (Danish territory lost to Sweden in 1660), to watch the Jutland and to prevent the passage of any French troops into Norway. He was also 'to cause the coast of Norway to be menaced by the ships which may be stationed in the Cattegat [*sic*] as far as is consistent with a due attention to other important objects to be provided for'.[5] To assist in the safe passage of Saumarez's ships through the Kattegat he was advised to secure the lighthouse on the Danish island of Anholt. He was also to evaluate the capture of Bornholm and Eartholms to see if these two islands could be used as bases for future operations. Furthermore, Saumarez was told 'to consider as one of the principle objects of the service on which you are employed the affording every protection in your power to the trade of His Majesty's subjects by granting convoy from time to time ... to the said trade to and from the different ports of the Baltic.'[6]

By 1800 northern Europe (Prussia, Poland, Sweden, Denmark and Russia) accounted for 49 per cent of all shipping leaving London. Exports to St Petersburg alone were worth £1 million. In 1805 it was estimated that the export of British produce and manufactured goods to the region was more than double all of Europe put together. In 1805 11,537 vessels passed though the Sound, over half of which were bound for Britain. The Royal Navy also depended on the Baltic states for its naval stores: oak from Hamburg and Danzig, fir from Norway, hemp from Riga and St Petersburg, iron, pitch and tar from Sweden and tallow from Russia. In 1801 the Royal Dockyards required 36,000 loads of timber, 1,400 tons of iron, 5,500 barrels of pitch, 18,800 barrels of tar and 371,000 deals. In 1801 the total quantity of imported hemp, used in the construction of sails and cordage, was 36,000 tons, half of which went to the Royal Navy. Russian hemp was considered to be the best in the world: the navy had repeatedly tried but failed to find any suitable alternatives.

Britain had responded to Napoleon's Continental System with her own Orders of Council. Allies of Great Britain and neutral countries were forbidden from trading with France and the Royal Navy was ordered to blockade French and allied ports and any port that refused to trade with Britain. Three-quarters of Russia's commerce was carried by British merchants and it was hoped that growing economic difficulties caused by the Orders of Council would eventually force the tsar to abandon his ill-advised alliance with Napoleon.

Chapter 18

Commander-in-Chief, Baltic Fleet: March 1808 – December 1808

Having received his final instructions from Mulgrave, Saumarez left London for Sheerness, hoisting his flag aboard *Victory* on 18 March. On the 31st Saumarez's baggage was taken aboard his flagship from the gun-brig *Escort* and the following day she proceeded to the Nore, anchoring alongside *Namur* and *Dictator*. On 30 April *Victory* weighed anchor and sailed for the Baltic in company with the gun-brigs *Rose* and *Wrangler*. Held up by bad weather the ships arrived in Gothenburg on 7 May. Hood had been in the Sound with *Centaur*, *Goliath*, *Vanguard*, *Orion*, *Implacable* and *Dictator* since early April and the arrival of *Victory* brought the Baltic Fleet up to seven ships of the line. On the day of Saumarez's arrival news came through of the loss of the fortress of Sveaborg, close to Helsingfors (Helsinki). Home to the 100-odd galleys of the Shallows Fleet, the loss of Sveaborg ripped a hole in Sweden's eastern defences that the British could not fill for they had no vessels suitable for operations along the Finnish coast.

On 17 May Moore's 140 troop-ships arrived off Copenhagen, escorted by *Mars*, the flagship of Rear Admiral Keats, *Audacious*, Thomas Gosselin, the brig-sloop *Magnet*, a cutter and six gun-brigs. Over the next few days several more troop-ships, stragglers from the main convoy, arrived in Flemish Road. The Swedish ambassador in London, Carl Adlerberg, had insisted that British troops would be warmly welcomed in Sweden. However, Gustav refused to allow their disembarkation until he had discussed their future use with Moore. Gustav objected to the fact that the British troops were to act independently from the Swedish army and remain under the direct control of Moore who could withdraw them from operations if they were needed elsewhere. Gustav proposed that Moore's troops either invade Zealand, defended by 28,000 Danish troops, or assist in a joint attack on Norway which was defended by 44,000 French, Dutch and Spanish troops. Both schemes were wildly ambitious and had little to do with the reality on the ground. The Swedish army was already fully employed and troops could not be spared for either enterprise without compromising current operations. However, whilst Moore did not agree with either strategy he could offer no alternative and so he dispatched his quartermaster general, Colonel Murray, to London for further instructions. On 9 June Saumarez wrote: 'Our impatience to receive the further directions for the movements of the troops can be easier conceived than described ... I am anxious to be left to my own means for the execution of the important service entrusted to me without being shackled as we have so long been from uncertainty of the manner in which the troops are to be employ'd.'[1] On 10 June *Superb* arrived off Gothenburg in company with *Africa* and Keats transferred his flag to her from *Mars*.

When Murray eventually returned from London it was with 'inexplicit and contradictory'[2] orders from Castlereagh that in public agreed with Gustav's demands but in private allowed Moore to withdraw his troops and return home if he disagreed with the Swedish monarch's orders. Moore now decided to travel to Stockholm and meet with the King in person. This proved disastrous as negotiations rapidly broke down. With Moore insisting he could do no more than comply with his orders Gustav became infuriated with the British general's intransigence and refused permission for him to leave Stockholm. Moore eventually escaped the capital dressed in civilian clothes and, after a journey of four days, arrived aboard *Victory*, at anchor in Flemish Road, on the evening of 29 June in the middle of a ball Saumarez was holding for the ladies of Gothenburg. Moore told Saumarez he intended to return home and the next morning *Victory* weighed anchor and withdrew to Wingo Sound (Vinga Sand), some fourteen miles from Gothenburg. In a letter to the British Minister Plenipotentiary in Stockholm, Edward Thornton, Moore later revealed: 'Had I not escaped it was the intention of Sir James to have threatened to withdraw his Fleet from the defences of the Sound & Belt if I was not released.'[3]

On 3 July Moore transferred to *Audacious* and the order was given for his ship to weigh anchor and return to Yarmouth with the transports. Saumarez was somewhat relieved to see the back of Moore for ever since his arrival in the Baltic *Victory* had been in use as a headquarters for both army and navy, disrupting Saumarez's daily routine. In his

The Baltic in 1808.

letter to Martha of 3 July Saumarez wrote: 'The last has been to me a Week of considerable anxiety and bustle … You cannot conceive how pleasant I feel to be disembarrassed from so great a clog as I have been encumbered with.'[4]

Still awaiting fresh instructions from the Admiralty. Saumarez now decided to sail for the Baltic. Prior to Moore's return home Saumarez had to hold his main force at Wingo in support of Moore and had only been able to send small detachments under Hood and Keats into the Great Belt and Baltic to assist in convoy protection. But now he was free to take his fleet into the Baltic to support Swedish operations in Finland and to engage the Russian fleet if the opportunity arose. *Victory* and *Superb* weighed anchor on 5 July. As the two ships made their way through the Belt Saumarez wrote to Martha 'This station affords much greater anxiety than the Channel Islands and I may add than any other Station I have hitherto been upon and its being so perfectly novel in all respects makes it the more interesting ... I have the satisfaction to say that I never enjoyed greater comfort aboard any Ship than I do in this, the officers all being very estimable characters and most of them my own selection, particularly Dumaresq who is everything that can be wished.'[5]

Intending, if possible, to engage the Russian fleet, Saumarez had already sent a despatch to Hood ordering him to collect all the ships under his command and rendezvous at the southern end of the Danish islands. He would, however, still need to maintain a force to combat the Danish gunboats operating against British and Swedish shipping in the region. Saumarez had already given this some thought and just three weeks after his arrival in the Baltic had written to Mulgrave requesting the services of a third flag-officer, Rear Admiral Thomas Bertie, who had briefly served under Saumarez during the blockade of Cadiz in 1801, to take command of the four ships of the line currently protecting shipping in the Sound. Accepting his appointment, on 24 June Bertie had written to Saumarez: 'I had rather serve under your Command than any other person I know in the Service.'[6]

On 4 June the gun-brig *Tickler* was cruising off Langeland when she was attacked by four Danish gunboats. With little wind to assist her *Tickler* could not outmanoeuvre these oared vessels and could only engage the enemy with her bow chasers. *Tickler's* commander, John Skinner, was killed early on in the action and his vessel was eventually forced to surrender with almost half her crew dead and the rest injured. Five days later a flotilla of Danish gunboats and mortar vessels out of Copenhagen attacked a convoy of seventy merchant vessels becalmed in the southern part of the Sound. Situated towards the rear of the convoy *Turbulent*, Commander Wood, was surrounded by gunboats and after a sustained attack was captured along with eleven merchant ships. The British gun-brigs were proving to be ineffective against the Danish gunboats and Saumarez was now forced to augment the convoy escorts with a ship of the line. But even his larger ships were not immune to attack from these Danish 'mosquitos'. On 26 June the 64-gun *Dictator*, stationed outside Køge Bay, was attacked by six gunboats which were able to rake the larger British ship's stern with virtual impunity. *Dictator* was saved by the timely appearance of several gun-brigs escorting a convoy through the Sound. Several British seamen had been injured in the engagement and *Dictator*'s sails and rigging had been severely damaged.

Victory and *Superb*'s progress through the Belt was held up by light and contrary winds together with the difficulty of navigating two large ships in shallow waters. On 25 July Saumarez fell in with Hood's ships off Møn. He now received his first dispatches from the Admiralty in several weeks and they contained a complaint from the Secretary to the Admiralty, William Pole, over the loss of *Turbulent* and the merchant ships the previous month. Asked whether the force under his command had been 'distributed in the most judicious manner as well for the protection of the Baltic trade as for affording assistance to the king's ally', Saumarez replied tersely: 'When it is considered that above three hundred sail of vessels have gone under convoy to the Baltic in the face of the immense flotilla which the enemy have collected in Zealand, it cannot be matter of surprise that 16 of that number should have fallen in their hands.'[7] Passing through the Great Belt, the ships under Saumarez's protection were never more than three miles away from enemy shore positions and under the constant threat of attack from Danish gunboats, but losses such as those suffered in June were rare. Following the capture of *Turbulent* Saumarez had entered into discussions with the Danish Admiralty concerning the exchange of the captured British seamen. He hoped that if these discussions went well they might eventually develop into peace negotiations.

With his squadrons combined, Saumarez now had eight ships of the line, *Victory*, *Superb*, *Centaur*, *Implacable*, *Mars*, *Dictator*, *Africa* and *Goliath*. This was a large enough force to cope with the Russian fleet but if their eleven ships combined with the Swedish fleet, also eleven ships, he would have to retreat back through the Great Belt. A week before Saumarez had sailed for the Baltic Gustav had embarked aboard one of his yachts for a cruise, appointing a regency to act during his absence but telling no-one his intentions. A significant number of Gustav's ministers had been pressing for a peace deal with Russia and whilst it was perfectly possible that Gustav might have been sailing to Finland to support his troops, Saumarez found his actions suspicious and, following Moore's detention in Stockholm, feared that Gustav was on a personal mission to make peace with Russia.

On 16 July Rear Admiral Bertie arrived off Viken. The following day he hoisted his flag aboard Archibald Dickson's *Orion*. Receiving orders from Saumarez to take command of the ships in the Sound, he would remain on that station until 31 December. In late July Saumarez assisted in the transportation of several members of the exiled French royal family, including King Louis XVIII's consort, the Countess de Lille, to England. Saumarez also managed to find passage aboard *Euryalus* for his old acquaintance the Duke d'Havre and his family.

Having received a report from a Swedish cutter watching the eastern Baltic coast that the French had embarked troops and artillery for the invasion of Sweden, Saumarez sent Keats to Straslund for further intelligence. Returning on 29 July Keats informed Saumarez that whilst the French had been embarked the vessels had not yet made any effort to put to sea. Saumarez waited two more days for dispatches from London then decided to return to Stockholm as *Victory* had on board the subsidy that had been promised to Sweden by the British government and Thornton had also suggested a meeting with Gustav. At the same time Keats was dispatched to the Danish island of Funen.

Not long after Moore's departure from the fleet Saumarez had received despatches intended for the general asking if he could assist in the evacuation of Spanish troops from Funen. The troops, 10,000 men commanded by the Marques de la Romana, were part of Marshal Bernadotte's Hanseatic Army that had assembled in Holstein for the invasion of Sweden. Relations between the French and Spanish had always been poor but they deteriorated even further with Napoleon's invasion of Spain in March 1808. Bernadotte had tried to prevent news of the invasion reaching Romana, but eventually the Spanish commander learned of the capture of Barcelona and Figueras and the brutal crushing of an uprising in Madrid. On 24 June news reached Funen that the Spanish royal family had been forced into exile by Napoleon and his brother Joseph proclaimed king. With the Spanish troops on Funen refusing to sign an oath of allegiance to their new king, Romana was now contacted by the Scottish Catholic priest and British spy James Robertson, and learned that most of the Spanish provinces were in open revolt against the French. Robertson and Romana now discussed the possibility of British ships assisting in the evacuation of the Spanish troops from Langeland, a small Danish island situated to the south-east of Funen.

Sailing south with *Superb, Mars, Brunswick* and *Edgar*, on 5 August Keats was met at Langeland by the schooner *Mosquito* which was carrying dispatches for Saumarez. When Keats forwarded these to his commander-in-chief Saumarez was pleased to note that the measures he was pursuing in Funen 'were exactly what was pointed out in my instructions from Government'.[8] Keats' first contact with the Spanish troops came with the arrival aboard *Mosquito* of a lieutenant in Romana's Catalonian regiment, Don Antonio Fabragues, who gave details of the number and disposition of Romana's men. Keats now proceeded under a flag of truce to Funen's main port, Nyborg. Spurred into action by news of a surprise visit by Bernadotte to Funen, on 7 August Romana made his move and seized Nyborg. Two Danish vessels were moored across the harbour but were soon captured by boats led by *Edgar*'s captain, James McNamara, with support from the Spanish troops.

Threatened by this show of force, Nyborg's governor made enough transports available to move the 9,000 Spanish from Funen to Langeland where they joined the 3,000 troops already on the island. Saumarez had already ordered two victuallers from Gothenburg and Keats thought Langeland a productive island 'where they could support themselves until the transports were ready'.

On 4 August Saumarez reached Karlskrona, where he visited the dockyard, met with the Swedish heads of department and dined with the captains. He also met with the outgoing commander-in-chief of the Swedish fleet, Admiral Cederström, who had been dismissed by Gustav simply for allowing some Russian frigates into Finnish waters. At Karlskrona Captain Hope leaned that his wife was seriously ill. Requesting permission to return home, Hope left *Victory* on 5 August.

On 11 August Saumarez received a letter from Gustav requesting that he send all the ships of the line he could spare to participate in joint operations with the Swedish navy in the Gulf of Finland. However, Saumarez delayed sailing to Hangö Udd to await the arrival of victuallers from England that had been held up by contrary winds. Receiving a report that contact had been made with Romana's troops and that 12,000 men were waiting to return to Spain, Saumarez now decided to sail for the Belt. On 15 August, whilst en route to Funen, Saumarez received word that Keats had begun the evacuation of Romana's men, taking two Danish vessels in the process. Saumarez applauded Keats' skill and judgement and praised the efforts of the men under his command.

On 18 August *Victory* joined *Superb*, *Mars*, *Brunswick* and *Edgar* at anchor off Funen and Romana went aboard the British flagship to meet with Saumarez. With the help of *Victory*'s boats, by 21 August the Spanish had completed their embarkation aboard Keats's ships and a hastily assembled flotilla of sixty-odd Danish sloops. Before the Spanish troops sailed there was one last meeting between Romana and

Saumarez aboard *Victory*. Arriving at Gothenburg, the Governor-General of Scania refused to allow Romana's men to land as they were foreign troops (the invalids were allowed ashore) and they had to wait for the arrival of transports from Britain to complete their journey to Spain. Rather than sending his own report of the operation to the Admiralty Saumarez was happy to send Keats's dispatches instead and they were enthusiastically received by Mulgrave, who commended them to the king. To Martha Saumarez wrote: 'Admiral Keats has been indefatigable in the management of this intricate business, which will add greatly to his well earned fame, and I hope will draw upon him some mark of Royal favour, which he so justly merits.'[10]

On 7 August Cederström's replacement, Admiral Nauckhoff, wrote to Saumarez to inform him that the Russian fleet, nine ships of the line and eight frigates, had emerged from Cronstadt and attacked the three Swedish ships of the line and two frigates that had been patrolling off Hangö Udd, at the entrance to the Gulf of Finland. As requested by Nauckhoff Saumarez now detached two ships, Hood's *Centaur* and *Implacable*, Byam Martin, to reinforce the Swedish fleet.

Nauckhoff's fleet had been cruising off the Gulf of Finland for several months, his eleven poorly maintained ships of the line were worn out and their inexperienced crews, made up mostly of conscripts, were in poor health and morale was low. Scurvy was rife and one ship had already been loaded with the fleet's sick and sent back to Karlskrona. *Centaur* and *Implacable* joined the Swedish fleet at Utö, fifty miles west of Hangö Udd, on 20 August. On 25 August Nauckhoff's ships weighed anchor and began a pursuit of the Russian fleet. By dawn the following morning the faster sailing British ships were ten miles to the windward of the Swedish fleet and in range of the 80-gun *Sevolod*, which had become separated from the rest of her fleet in the night. *Sevolod* opened fire but within half an hour *Implacable*'s superior gunnery had forced Captain Rudno to haul down his colours. With the rest of the Russian fleet now bearing down on *Centaur* and *Implacable*, there was no chance to put a prize crew aboard *Sevolod* and so Hood hoisted the signal of recall. As the two British ships withdrew, Rudno's ship was taken under tow. However, once the slight damage to *Implacable* had been repaired she and *Centaur* began to chase after the retreating Russian ships, forcing them to abandon the slower-sailing *Sevolod*. The Russian fleet now turned and headed for the port of Rogervik (Paldiski in modern-day Estonia). *Sevolod* attempted to follow them but grounded on a shoal at the entrance to the harbour. As *Centaur* approached *Sevolod* she was afloat and riding at her anchors, but an attempt to board the Russian ship ended in the two vessels colliding and running aground. Once

Implacable had pulled Hood's flagship free *Sevolod*'s remaining crew were taken prisoner and the ship burnt.

Saumarez had now sailed north with *Mars*, *Goliath* and *Africa* in the hope of joining Nauckhoff's fleet off Hangö Udd. On 30 August Saumarez fell in with the Swedish frigate *Camilla* and learned that that the Russians had been pursued into Rogervick. The ships were cleared for action and around 2.00pm the Swedish fleet with *Centaur* and *Implacable* in company was seen at anchor outside the Russian port. Saumarez's ships dropped anchor and Hood and Nauckhoff came aboard *Victory* to give Saumarez an update of the situation. Whilst the Swedish fleet had remained at anchor off Rogervik the Russians had been busy fortifying their position, securing their ships with cables and establishing shore batteries at the entrance to the harbour. Saumarez's first instinct had been to attack the Russians at anchor but he was dissuaded from this by Hood, Martin and Nauckhoff. Martin later wrote to his brother: 'It is impossible for me to find any language capable of conveying to you the admiration I have of Sir James Saumarez's zeal and anxiety to get at the enemy, and he has once or twice nearly determined to hazard, or rather (as it would inevitably be) to sacrifice, his fleet in order to have the glory of destroying the Russians.'[11] To attack the strongly-defended Russians with an experienced British fleet would have been hazardous enough; to attack with the poorly-maintained Swedish ships would only end in disappointment – if not disaster. Saumarez would later explain his decision not to attack the Russians in a letter to Martha: 'I had so many discouraging circumstances to encounter, particularly in the decided opinions of those in whom I had most to confide, meaning Sir Saml. Hood and Captain Martin (as well as I believe all the other officers) that I felt myself obliged most reluctantly to resign my intentions.'[12] However, Saumarez was still very much a fighting admiral and he admitted in confidence to Martha that he would 'always retain the unpleasant reflexion that if I had follow'd my own opinion, things would have been better'.[13]

On 31 August Saumarez went aboard Nauckhoff's flagship *Gustav IV Adolph* for a meeting with the Swedish admiral and the following day he embarked aboard *Rose* with Rear Admiral Hood to reconnoitre the enemy position. Twenty-seven enemy guns were counted guarding the eastern side of the harbour at Rogervik and a further fifteen were counted on the opposite shore. Saumarez returned to *Victory* and later that day his flagship returned to Rogervik in company with *Mars*, *Goliath* and the bomb vessel *Thunder*. Sailing close to the westernmost enemy shore *Victory* fired a starboard broadside which was returned by the battery of guns guarding that side of the harbour. Next *Thunder* was sent in to test the enemy defences.

Having determined that his bomb vessels could not get close enough to the enemy to be of any use and having been persuaded against a fleet attack, Saumarez now decided to burn the Russian fleet at anchor: 'a mode of warfare which should never be resorted to except in cases of extremity.'[14] Four fireships were ordered from Karlskrona by Nauckhoff and Saumarez also ordered the conversion of the ship-sloop *Erebus* and the cutter *Baltic*. Whilst waiting for his fireships to be made ready a Russian officer now came aboard Saumarez's flagship under a flag of truce apparently to discuss the exchange of Russian prisoners taken from *Sevolod*. Meeting with Captain Dumaresq the Russian officer insisted he could not speak English. However, Lieutenant John Ross happened to come on *Victory*'s quarterdeck and recognised the Russian as an officer who had served for several years in the Royal Navy and who understood English perfectly well. Before he left the ship to report to Admiral Khanikov, the slightly-embarrassed officer, Skripeetzen, was taken below to see *Victory*'s gun decks cleared for action. Extra shot had been piled up alongside the long guns, some of it 'franked' in chalk by the crew with messages such as 'Post-paid' and 'Free, George Canning'.

With the fireships now ready for action Ross was sent aboard *Gustav IV Adolph* with instructions for Nauckhoff. He would remain aboard the Swedish flagship to assist with signals and help the Swedish fleet to come into action during the upcoming attack. Still lacking a captain of the fleet, Saumarez appointed Martin to that position. Martin was succeeded as captain of *Implacable* by *Rose*'s commander, Philip Pipon. Before the attack commenced Rogervik was reconnoitred one last time by *Salsette* in company with the Swedish frigate *Camilla* at which point it was discovered that the Russians had run out a boom in front of their ships to prevent enemy fireships from getting in amongst them.

Denied an attack by the stout Russian defences, now the weather turned against the British. By the following morning the wind had veered to the south and over the next eight days it blew a strong gale. Hoping to prevent unnecessary bloodshed 'betwixt nations that ought to be in perpetual amity',[15] on 3 September Saumarez sent a flag of truce to Khanikov and proposed terms that involved the surrender of half his fleet whilst allowing the remainder, including the flagship, safe passage to Cronstadt. Khanikov replied that he would rather burn his whole fleet than surrender. The 24-hour truce came to an end at sunset on 4 September and Saumarez began fitting out more fireships. On 7 September Saumarez sent Khanikov a parcel of recently arrived newspapers containing news of the uprisings against Napoleon in

Spain. Having received fruit and vegetables in return Saumarez now sent another gift, this time of English porter and coffee. When she heard about this exchange of gifts Martha wrote. 'I am delighted with the reciprocal courtesy that has passed between Thee and the Russian Admiral, it affords a pleasing contrast to the horrors of war.'[16] Saumarez had not yet admitted to his wife that he had been ill for some time, suffering from stomach pains almost since his arrival in Gothenburg. By the time of his arrival off Rogervik he was suffering from severe chest pain and, according to *Victory*'s surgeon, Valentine Duke, passed several sleepless nights in considerable distress. There were numerous consultations with other surgeons in the fleet and Hood kept Saumarez supplied with arrowroot. To his wife Saumarez would only admit to suffering from a heavy cold but to his brother Richard he wrote: 'I can assure that all the illnesses I can recollect from my first coming to sea except on one important occasion, has not been equal to what I have suffered in this late attack even for forty eight hours only. I was for a considerable time in great doubt if I should ever recover.'[17] Saumarez was thankful for the assistance of his new captain of the fleet, Byam Martin, on 10 September he wrote to Martha: 'Captain Martin is everything that I can wish – he is a most excellent worthy man and I am now very glad to have consented to the arrangement, altho' I was at first rather averse to it.'[18]

Eventually the weather abated and on the evening of 13 September *Erebus* and the Swedish fireships made another sortie into Rogervik. However, one of the Swedish vessels, a Russian prize brig, could not cope with the heavy swell and had to be abandoned. Following this setback, and with the light now failing, the vessels were forced to withdraw. Finally admitting defeat Saumarez ordered the Swedish fireships to be returned to Karlskrona and *Erebus* and *Baltic* restored to their former state.

Having learned that the Russian Minister of Marine, Admiral Paul Tchichagoff, was expected to arrive in Rogervik from St Petersburg, Thornton had decided to travel to Rogervik to see Saumarez. Arriving aboard *Victory* on the evening of 13 September, Thornton learned of Saumarez's surrender proposal and was asked what instructions he had received from the government 'relative to any overtures to a Peace with Russia', as Saumarez believed that, given 'the present situation of the Russian fleet, they would be glad to avail themselves of any opportunity to enter upon a negotiation with Great Britain and her ally'.[19] For several days prior to Thornton's arrival Saumarez had been pondering sending a peace proposal directly to the Tsar. He could now discuss the idea with the British ambassador. As originally written

Saumarez's letter described the Spanish revolt against France and Wellington's victory at Vimeiro. It also contained references to Austria and Denmark, which following discussions with Thornton, were omitted from the final copy dated 17 September:

> Your imperial Majesty is probably uniformed of the events that have recently taken place in the southern parts of Europe. Spain had succeeded in rescuing herself from the usurpation and tyranny of the ruler of France. Portugal has also extricated herself from the baneful hands of the enemy of all independent states; the whole of the French forces in that country having been compelled to surrender to the British army under Sir Arthur Wellesley. It is hoped that those events will induce the powers of the continent to unite with Great Britain to restore that peace so highly to be desired for the welfare of mankind.
>
> Knowing it to be the object most at heart of my gracious sovereign, and that of his Majesty's ally, the King of Sweden, should your imperial Majesty be impressed with the same sentiments, nothing will afford me greater happiness than to have the honour of imparting them to my government, and to desist from further hostile operations, upon condition that your majesty will give orders to your forces to desist from hostilities against England and her ally, and to withdraw your forces from Swedish Finland.

Saumarez's letter was addressed to the Tsar through Tchichagoff and Thornton agreed to send his own letter to the Russian minister. Unfortunately, by the time Saumarez's letter reached Alexander he had left for a meeting with Napoleon at Erfurt. Napoleon and Alexander read Saumarez's letter as a formal overture for peace from the British government and the two emperors offered to send plenipotentiaries to whichever city George III chose to send his own diplomats. Napoleon suggested discussions based on the principle that the parties to any treaty could retain possession of territory acquired by force during the war. Napoleon knew his conditions would be unacceptable to the British government as it would mean the Spanish crown remaining in the hands of the French. With Canning insisting that there be representatives of both the old Spanish regime and the Swedish government at any meeting the peace discussions quickly broke down.

By late September disease was so rampant amongst the Swedish fleet that it was becoming clear to Saumarez that he would not be able to maintain his blockade of Rogervik for very much longer. Following a tour of the Swedish ships, *Victory*'s surgeon, Valentine Duke, had reported that 'scurvy of the most obstinate and dangerous nature, threatens the safety of the whole fleet … already twelve hundred men have been sent to hospital – every hour is adding to the number of sick'.[20] Following his own tour of the Swedish squadron Saumarez reported his findings back to the Admiralty: 'I found 1500 Sick all much affected by scurvy, accompanied with dysentery, low fever, and a few Cattarhal complaints.' Furthermore, 'in their hospitals I found 3864 suffering under similar disease'.[21] Saumarez's own mysterious illness was still troubling him and on 26 September he wrote to the Lord Commissioner Sir Richard Bickerton: 'I have wished as long as it lay in my power to conceal from my friends the very ill state of my health, but it has of late become so much impaired as to render it indispensable for me to return to England as soon as the Service will permit.'[22] Saumarez told Bickerton that he intended to remain off Rogervik for as long as the weather allowed, then sail for home. On 28 September Hope returned from leave having buried his wife and exchanged commands with Martin who sailed for England with Saumarez's dispatches. Saumarez maintained the blockade of Rogervik until 30 September when, rather than risk being iced in for the winter, he took the bulk of the combined fleet south to Karlskrona, leaving *Mars*, *Orion* and *Goliath* together with the frigates *Ariel* and *Alaart* to cruise between Dagerort and the coast of Sweden to protect trade and to stop the Russian fleet entering the Baltic. At Karlskrona a further 3,000 Swedish sick were landed and the hospitals supplied with medicines from the British fleet. The British had plenty of medicine to spare, for amongst the 11,000 seamen of their fleet there had only been four reported cases of scurvy and thirty-two cases of venereal disease.

Whilst *Victory* was at anchor at Karlskrona a visit was made to Saumarez's flagship by Admirals Palmquist, von Rosenstein, Nauckhoff and Captain Tornquist. Meeting Saumarez in his Great Cabin the conversation inevitably turned to early careers at which point Saumarez discovered that all four Swedish officers had served in the French navy during the American War of Independence and had taken part in the Battle of the Saintes. When Tornquist discovered that Saumarez had captained *Russell* during the same battle he rose from his chair and shook Saumarez warmly by the hand. The battle was fought again and, according to Lieutenant Ross who was also present, the Swedish officers were all firmly convinced that it was *Russell*, not *Canada*, that had engaged several enemy ships before pushing up to the Comte de Grasse's flagship, *Ville de Paris*. Furthermore, both von Rosenstein and Palmquist agreed that de Grasse would have escaped to leeward were it not for *Russell*.

On 4 October *Mars* reconnoitred Rogervik and observed that the Russian fleet had left the port and was proceeding up the Gulf of Finland to Cronstadt, leaving behind one of their frigates which had been driven ashore by a severe gale and was now a complete wreck. With the Russian fleet sailing for home and the weather worsening further naval operations in the region were unlikely and so Saumarez decided to take the ships under his command and return to Gothenburg.

Unaware that he had received the support of the Admiralty in his decision to blockade rather than to attack the Russians at Rogervik, Saumarez was now preparing for the inevitable criticism he felt he would receive for failing to engage the Russian fleet. On 24 October he wrote to Martha: 'Altho' it has not terminated equal to my expectations I am well convinced ev'ry thing has been done that could depend on me – and that the country will be satisfied of it, altho' I know John Bull is disappointed when success does not correspond with expectation.'[23] When Martha heard that Saumarez had entered into peace negotiations with the Russians she was not the least bit surprised and wrote to her husband to tell him that this was 'the highest Triumph to thy humane and beneficent heart'.[24]

Victory dropped anchor in Hawke Road on 28 October. On his arrival in Gothenburg Saumarez received orders from the Admiralty dated 15 October directing him to return with his ships to the Downs, leaving Keats at Wingo with a reduced squadron (*Superb, Brunswick, Orion, Edgar, Dictator*, the frigates *Salsette* and *Tribune* and eighteen assorted smaller vessels). *Goliath* and *Vanguard*, having already been ordered home for repair, Saumarez left directions for Captain Lukin to follow in *Mars*, and ordered the ships returning to England to leave all available provisions with Keats. On 3 November *Victory* sailed for England in company with *Centaur* and *Implacable*, escorting a convoy of several hundred merchant ships on the voyage back to the Downs.

Chapter 19

Saumarez:
British Diplomat Afloat:
November 1808 – December 1809

Victory arrived at the Downs on 8 November 1808. Saumarez went ashore and the following day was at the Admiralty for a meeting with Mulgrave. Saumarez had already been rebuked by the Admiralty for entering into discussions with the Russian admiral, Khanikov, and on 16 November, whilst still in London, he received a memorandum from the Lords Commissioners demanding answers to several questions. Having received complaints from various merchants, the Admiralty wanted to know why Saumarez had repeatedly allowed delays to the convoys to occur. They also wanted to know why had he quit Rogervik before the bad weather had actually set in, allowing the Russians escape back to Cronstadt, why had he felt authorised to write his letter to the Tsar but did not report the matter to the Admiralty and why he had not informed them about a letter sent to him from Gustav on 15 October instructing him to remain off Rogervik.

Somewhat surprised by this letter, Saumarez informed the Lords Commissioners that 'there is no part of my conduct from my first appointment to the command in the Baltic to the present time that I am not perfectly ready to have submitted to the strictest investigation'.[1] Using convoy reports and letters to and from the Swedish monarch Saumarez was able to provide satisfactory answer all of the Admiralty's questions other than the query regarding his letter to the Tsar. In writing to the Tsar directly Saumarez had exceeded his instructions from the Admiralty but, more damagingly, his superiors had only learned of the letter's existence through the Foreign Office after Thornton had informed Canning of his discussions with Saumarez. In defending his actions Saumarez pointed out that the letter was written with the agreement of Thornton and Admiral Nauckhoff and that Thornton thought 'that much good might come from it and that he was not aware of it doing any possible harm'.[2] Secondly, he had understood it to be the case that when an opportunity for peace between Great Britain and Russia offered itself it was to be 'eagerly embraced':[3] such a moment had occurred with the news of events in Spain and Portugal. With little advice coming from home Saumarez had been forced to use his own initiative, having first discussed his plan with those who were in the best position to assist him. It was not poor advice but poor timing upon which Saumarez's plan had foundered: had the Tsar received Saumarez's letter on his return from Erfurt the outcome might have been very different. On 16 December Saumarez received a mild rebuke from the Admiralty, Pole informing him that 'their Lordships are of opinion that officers employed on Military Service cannot be justified in stepping beyond the line of their professional duty, by entering into Political Negociations with the Enemy, unless especially directed to do so by their instructions'.[4] Rebuked at home for entering into negotiations with a belligerent nation, in the Baltic Saumarez's conciliatory letter to the Tsar was seen favourably by the Russians and would not be forgotten.

By early 1809 the Russian army had gained control of Finland and, having crossed the frozen Gulf of Bothnia, had marched into northern Sweden. Meanwhile, in the south a Danish army of 30,000 men was gathering in Zealand ready to cross the frozen Sound into Scania. With Gustav refusing to abandon his alliance with Great Britain and instead raising new taxes in order to continue the war, a group of army officers led by General Adlercreutz now began plotting to overthrow the king. As the commander of the Western Army, Colonel Aldersparre, marched his army from Värmland towards Stockholm Gustav raided the treasury and attempted to flee the capital. On the morning of 9 March Adlercreutz and his co-conspirators arrived at the palace for the king's levée and told Gustav he must not leave Stockholm. When Gustav refused demands to annul his recently-imposed taxes and call a Diet he was arrested. The King was taken to his family home at Drottningholm and a proclamation was issued declaring that he was unable to govern and had been replaced by his elderly uncle, the Duke of Sodermania.

In London there was an immediate fear that the new Swedish government would seek an alliance with France but the new Foreign Secretary, Baron Lagerbjelke, insisted that relations with Britain would remain the same. With Britain now refusing to officially recognise the new Swedish government, Saumarez was instructed to consider the protection of trade his principal object for the season ahead. He was also ordered to watch, and if possible, attack the Russian fleet; to give protection to any Swedish ship that requested it and to source water and supplies so as not to be dependent on Swedish ports. Saumarez would once again hoist his flag aboard *Victory* with Dumaresq as his flag-captain and Hope as captain of the fleet.

Victory sailed from the Nore on 27 April in company with *Minotaur*. Both ships arrived off Gothenburg on 4 May and dropped anchor alongside *Centaur, Implacable, Dictator* and the frigates *Alexandria* and *Erebus*. On 9 May Rear Admiral Manley Dixon arrived in Wingo Sound aboard *Temeraire*. Dixon was now ordered to sail for the Belt to relieve Keats whose services were required for an expedition bound for Walcheren that was currently assembling in England. That same day Hood sailed home due to illness having been in the Baltic just over a month. On 11 May Saumarez received a letter intended for Hood from Augustus Foster, the British legation secretary, announcing his appointment as the new chargé d'affaires.

On 12 May the Swedish Diet declared that Gustav and his son had lost all rights to the throne. At a meeting with Foster on 15 May Lagerbjelke put the Swedish case to Foster. Sweden wished to 'remain in amity and maintain her commercial intercourse with Great Britain'[5] and was now concerned about the build-up of forces in Finland preparing for 'the immediate invasion of this country'.[6] Appeals had been made to Napoleon to lead the peace negotiations but the Emperor had 'evaded the frequent solicitations of Sweden to take into his own hands the management of the negotiations'.[7] Sweden would need naval assistance to protect herself against Russia and Denmark and Lagerbjelke made an appeal to Saumarez through Foster to 'send such a force into the Baltic Sea as to render it dangerous for the Russians to make any attempt with ships-of-the-line against the harbours or to carry an invading force against the coast of Sweden'.[8] Saumarez was also asked to detach enough smaller vessels to Norrköping, Stockholm and Gälve to prevent Russians troops launching an attack from Åbo. Along with his public correspondence Foster also sent Saumarez a private letter revealing his own personal appraisal of the situation. Foster had found the Swedes to be 'in a most deplorable state, they cannot, I believe, collect 10,000 men: without your assistance they must perish or yield'.[9]

Both Keats and Hood had been suspicious of the new Swedish government, but Saumarez, who relayed his junior officers' fears back to Foster, remained 'perfectly convinced of the good disposition of the present government of Sweden towards our country'.[10] On his arrival off Gothenburg Saumarez received several letters from Swedish officers with whom he had served the previous year welcoming him back to the Baltic. From Nauckhoff Saumarez learned that the Duke of Sodermania had written to the British government asking for Lieutenant Ross to be promoted to captain and that *Victory's* surgeon, Valentine Duke, was to be awarded two medical honours and a gold medal in recognition of his services to the Swedish fleet. Nauckhoff was himself grateful to Saumarez for 'the many kindnesses and favours shown by your excellency to my nephew Mr Nordenskjold who, I hope had done all that is possible to be worthy of your goodness'.[11]

In Saumarez's orders for 1809 emphasis had been made on securing supplies of water for the fleet. With the recent change of government there was no guarantee that Swedish ports would remain open to British ships and, as Hood had pointed out, obtaining reliable sources of water would be one of the biggest challenges faced by the British fleet. As if to reinforce this point, on 19 May eighty-three men from *Ardent*, Robert Honeyman, were captured whilst watering on the Danish island of Romso. Saumarez's concern over water supplies led to him assigning each ship a weekly expense of water that was not to be exceeded. In addition, along with the report of the sick, every captain was required to send Saumarez a weekly return of the water remaining aboard their ships.

One item from left over from the previous year's instructions which Saumarez was once again asked to investigate was the occupation of Anholt, a low-lying island surrounded by dangerous reefs and shoals situated at the entrance to the Baltic Sea. To aid navigation a lighthouse had been built on the island in the 1780s but it was decommissioned by the Danes shortly after their declaration of war against Sweden in March 1808. Later that year a British lightship, *Proselyte*, was briefly stationed off the island to aid passing convoys but she had struck Anholt Reef during the winter and was wrecked.

Convinced that Anholt would providing a safe anchorage for merchant ships and also prove to be 'of considerable importance in furnishing Supplies of Water to his Majesty's fleet',[12] Saumarez decided to seize the island. The governor of Anholt was sent for and offered surrender terms which he refused. Saumarez now ordered an attack on the island, sailing there in company with the 64-gun *Standard*, Aiskew Hollis, the 36-gun *Owen Glendower* and the sloops *Avenger*, *Rose* and *Ranger*. On 18 May a detachment of marines under Captain Nicholls was put ashore and stormed the island's batteries. Following a brief battle the Danish garrison of 130 men surrendered. The lighthouse was reinstated and Saumarez appointed Captain Nicholls as the island's governor. The Admiralty would later confirm Nicholl's appointment as governor and also arrange for an additional 150 marines to be sent to the island. Saumarez's suspicions concerning Anholt proved correct. A midshipman serving aboard *Majestic*, John Boteler later recollected: 'The peculiarity of this sandy island was that fresh water was to be had at any part, even within twenty yards of the sea, we had only to sink an empty flour cask in the sand and it would instantly be filled.'[13] Fresh water was also found on Gotska Sandön, near Gotland, and, having persisted in digging wells in different parts of the island of Nargen, Saumarez discovered fresh water there too. On 5 June Saumarez wrote to Martha: 'The weather is still very cold for the season, but the men very comfortable and healthy – it is impossible for a fleet to be more healthy than that at present with me.'[14]

Following the capture of the eighty-three men from *Ardent* Dixon had ordered *Melpomene*, Frederick Warren, to sail to Nyborg under a flag of truce to arrange their release. Returning to the British squadron on the afternoon of 20 May she was followed by a flotilla of thirty Danish gunboats but was soon forced to anchor when the wind dropped. The gunboats waited until night before they attacked. With no wind *Melpomene* could not manoeuvre to bring any of her guns to bear on the enemy vessels swarming round her and for the next two hours the gunboats, armed with 24-pounders, attacked with virtual impunity. Finally the wind picked up, *Melpomene* was able to perform a fighting retreat and she was soon joined by *Temeraire* who had at last spotted Warren's blue distress lights. *Melpomene*'s sails and rigging had been badly cut up, her bowsprit was badly damaged, several guns had been knocked out and she had over a hundred grapeshot embedded in her hull. Five of *Melpomene*'s crew now lay dead and there were a further twenty-nine wounded. Surveying the devastation all around him after the battle Warren struggled to contain his emotions. Carpenters from *Temeraire* were sent to assist in the repairs, spending five days aboard *Melpomene*, but her damage was so great that two months later she was forced to return to Britain for proper repairs.

Still lacking instructions from London but with the knowledge of the meeting between Foster and Lagerbjelke, Saumarez now decided to take his fleet through Danish waters into the Baltic. Leaving Gothenburg on 24 May Saumarez reached Karlskrona on 4 June where he notified the local commander, Admiral Puke, that he was on his way up the Baltic with part of the fleet under his command assigned to defend Sweden against a Russian attack. On 16 June Hood's replacement, Rear Admiral Francis Pickmore, arrived off Karlskrona aboard his flagship *St George*, in company with *Saturn* and two more ships. Keats having departed for England, Manley Dixon was now directed to shift his flag to *Ruby*, she having a shallower draft than *Temeraire*, and take command of the ships in the Belt. *Bellerophon* and *Minotaur* were sent on ahead into the Gulf of Finland and *Rose* was sent south to the Prussian seaport of Pillau. *Cruiser* and *Tilsit* were both sent to Kolberg and *Tartar* was dispatched to Rügen, off Stralsund. Stripped of territory by Napoleon following a series of crushing defeats and forced to accept his Continental System, Prussia was an unwilling ally of France and was a good source for intelligence regarding French troop movements and activities. Prussia would also prove to be a good source of wood and water, the port of Danzig eventually supplying Saumarez's fleet with around fifty barrels of water a day.

On 22 June *Victory* sailed from Karlskrona in company with *St George*, *Temeraire*, *Implacable*, *Saturn*, *Rose* and *Wrangler*. Six days later *Minotaur* and *Bellerophon* rejoined Saumarez's fleet. Whilst cruising off Dagerort on 19 June their boats had been in action against three Danish privateers, setting them on fire and also spiking the guns of a nearby battery. *Temeraire* now spoke to a Prussian merchantman and learned that the Russian fleet had been spotted cruising in the Gulf of Finland. A message was sent to *Victory* and Saumarez immediately ordered *Temeraire* and *St George* to sail to Reval. The two ships anchored off Nargen, eight miles from Reval, where they waited for the arrival of the rest of the British fleet.

On 29 June the Duke of Sodermania was crowned Carl XIII at a ceremony to which Saumarez had been invited but could not attend as he was en route to the Gulf of Finland. Old and infirm, Charles XIII was without an heir and the search immediately began for a new Crown Prince. King Frederik VI of Denmark put his own name forward as a means of uniting all of Scandinavia but the Swedes eventually settled on Prince Christian August, Frederik's cousin and his viceroy in Norway. Prior to Charles's coronation Saumarez had learned that he was to be awarded the Swedish Order of the Sword in recognition of his services to the country. This caused a slight problem as the British government had not yet officially recognised Charles XIII as King of Sweden and could therefore not give Saumarez permission to wear the decoration.

By 12 July *Victory* was stationed off the island of Nargen. Here Saumarez found not only water but also trees that could be cut down for spars. The island's governor had already surrendered to the British and on 26 July Saumarez went ashore to declare that the British had taken possession of the island. The British soon began cutting down trees across the island and in August Saumarez organised the transportation of 5,188 pine sticks back to Britain. From Nargean Saumarez resumed contact with the Russians. When a captured English seaman was returned under a flag of truce along with a quantity of melons and vegetables, Saumarez responded by sending the Russian commander a gift of some English porter. A subsequent supply of melons and vegetables was exchanged for cheese, sugar and coffee. Saumarez did not ignore the strategic situation, however. At Foster's suggestion Baron Von Platen, the king's aide de camp, was invited aboard *Victory* to discuss ways in which Saumarez's ships might assist Swedish troops who were attempting to encircle the Russians in East Bothnia. Platen was confident that the appearance of a British squadron 'would give more weight to the negociation than any other blockade in the Gulf of Finlandia'.[15] Saumarez agreed to send *Tribune, Rose* and a gun-brig to cruise off the Aland Islands. For his visit on 23 July Platen brought with him the decorations of the Order of the Sword, that had earlier been conferred Saumarez by Charles XIII

On 8 July 270 men in boats from *Implacable, Bellerophon, Melpomene* and *Prometheus* took part in a night attack on a convoy of Russian gunboats and merchantmen out of Porkala, capturing six of the eight gunboats and the twelve merchantmen. Seventeen British seamen were killed including the leader of the attack, *Implacable*'s first lieutenant, Joseph Hawkey, cut down by grapeshot in the process of boarding one of the gunboats. Whilst praising Martin's attack in public, in private Saumarez expressed his concerns over the loss of life it had caused. To Martha he wrote: 'The Admiralty may probably approve of it, but in my Opinion it was too hazardous a service to order the Boats upon.'[16] On 31 July Saumarez issued a memorandum to all captains and commanders banning further boat attacks unless there were 'very strong grounds for the expectation that the service will be accomplished without too severe a loss'.[17] Martin's raid may have been risky but it had resulted in an end to Russian activity in the Gulf of Finland; Saumarez reported: 'since the attack upon the gunboats, not a vessel has been seen upon the coast; and I hope effectually to prevent any supplies getting to the Russian troops in Finland excepting overland, which must tend to retard all their operations exceedingly.'[18]

Whilst the Russian threat had been neutralised, Danish vessels still remained a danger to shipping in the Great Belt, which, as Boteler later recalled, was 'swarming with privateers and row-boats'.[19] On 10 August the former Danish brig *Allart* was recaptured following an attack by fifteen gunboats. Two days later *Monkey* and *Lynx* captured three privateers operating off the Danish coast but on 2 September the gun-brig *Minx*, stationed off the Skaw to provide a warning light to passing convoys, was taken by a flotilla of Danish gunboats.

Though reinforced by Saumarez the Swedish attack at Vasa did not go as planned. General Wachtmeister landed with 7,000 men but the bulk of the Russian troops were allowed to escape. A subsequent Swedish defeat at the Battle of Umeå led to the Russians having the upper hand at the peace talks that followed. Under pressure from Napoleon Russia now demanded that Sweden make peace with France, Denmark and Norway, adopt the Continental System, end its alliance with England and cede Finland. The Treaty of Fredrikshamn, signed on 17 September after a month's negotiations, was a disaster for Sweden as she lost almost a third of her territory. Russia took possession of Finland together with the strategically-important Åland Islands and Sweden was forced to accept the Continental System, although the import of goods such as cotton, coffee, sugar, indigo and various other manufactured goods was still allowed.

Further to his successful blockade of the Russian fleet at Reval, Saumarez had also stationed *Bellerophon* and *Defence* in Makiluoto Bay to interrupt the supplies passing along the coast of Finland intended for Russian troops fighting in East Bothnia. The British had captured around ninety Russian vessels operating in the Gulf of Finland, twenty of which were directly involved in supplying the Russian army. A further 340 Danish privateers and gunboats were also taken in the Great Belt. At the conclusion of the peace Platen wrote a grateful letter to Saumarez: 'We cannot yet deny that in a high degree we are indebted to you for our existing as a state. I therefore anew congratulate myself on our personal acquaintance as it enables me to express to you my thankfulness, confident as I am that these are the feelings of the whole nation'.[20] With Sweden having been forced to accept the Continental System, Platen now sought to reassure Saumarez: 'I am authorised to say that no alteration will take place ... Our ports are open to so brave an ally, to so successful a protector for so many sails as your excellency judges fit to send into them.'[21]

With Sweden and Russia having formally declared a peace it was no longer necessary for Saumarez to blockade the Russians at Reval and so *Victory* returned to Karlskrona with *Temeraire* and *St George*, arriving there on 5 October. There Saumarez received an invitation from Rear Admiral Palmquist to attend a dinner celebrating Charles XIII's birthday, Saumarez could not attend as the new Swedish king had still not been formally recognised by the British government but Saumarez allowed Pickmore, Hope and the other captains to dine with Palmquist.

On 25 October the fiftieth anniversary of King George's coronation was celebrated by the British fleet. Saumarez's ships were dressed in all their colours and at midday *Victory* fired a fifty gun salute, the other ships twenty-one guns each. The ship's bands played 'God Save the King' and 'Rule Britannia' and in the evening there was a display of fireworks and rockets. Saumarez held a dinner for his fleet's senior officers aboard *Victory* and the men were given a double allowance of grog.

On 27 October Charles XIII issued a formal proclamation closing all Swedish ports to British merchant ships and ships of war after 15 November, the date previously arranged by Saumarez for the last convoy of the season to sail from the Baltic. *Victory* remained at Karlskrona until 1 November when she sailed for Hawke Road, Anholt, escorting a convoy through the Belt and visiting the different stations. On 23 November *Victory* finally sailed for home. She arrived at Yarmouth on 27 November and from there sailed to the Downs where Saumarez and Hope went ashore. On 29 November Saumarez attended the King's levée at Buckingham House along with the Dukes of York, Kent and Sussex. Also in attendance was Richard Wellesley, the newly-appointed Foreign Secretary (elder brother of Viscount Wellington). Saumarez remained in London until the New Year when he sailed for Guernsey aboard the sloop *Rose*.

Chapter 20

The Prince of Ponte Corvo: January–December 1810

Following lengthy negotiations, a peace treaty was eventually signed between France and Sweden in Copenhagen on 6 January 1810. In return for Pomerania, Swedish territory in Prussia seized by Napoleon in August 1807, Sweden agreed to adopt the Continental System, with various concessions such as the import of salt aboard neutral ships. On 13 January the new governor of Gothenburg, Count von Rosen issued ordered that: 'Ships flying the English flag are not allowed, unless suffering from substantial damage at sea and needing assistance, to enter a major port or to pass or lie under the guns of the fortress that commands its entrance.'[1]

The small island of Fotö, three miles north of Wingo Sound, was not a major port but by 1810 it had grown into an important centre for smuggling and the Swedish were perfectly aware of, indeed happily tolerated, its existence. Manned by Britons and protected by Saumarez's fleet, it contained shops, offices and warehouses. Following the issue of von Rosen's orders the British eventually received assurances that, in the event of boisterous weather, British convoys could use the small mainland harbour of Matvik, just five miles east of Carlshamn.

Even though she had been spared the worst of the Baltic weather by her early return to port, *Victory* had still suffered substantial damage during her last cruise and on her arrival back in Britain was reported to be leaking eight to ten inches of water an hour. Saumarez's flagship spent 24 January to 12 February at dry dock at Portsmouth. At a cost of £11,043 her hull was re-coppered and she was also fitted with beam end chocks and iron plate knees to replace defective wooden hanging knees.

On 8 April the new French chargé d'affaires, Monsieur Desaugiers, arrived in Stockholm to ensure Sweden complied with Napoleon's Continental System. At the same time the Swedish ambassador, Carl

Brinkman, was recalled from London. For the time being Foster continued as the chargé d'affaires in Stockholm and the two consuls, Charles Fenwick in Halsingbourg and John Smith in Gothenburg, also remained at their posts. Meanwhile, in London the former Swedish ambassador, Baron Rehausen, maintained an unofficial link between the two governments.

On 22 March Saumarez arrived at Portsmouth aboard the frigate *Hussar* from Guernsey. His instructions from the Admiralty for the new season were similar to those issued the previous year. He was to protect British trade; maintain a presence off the southern coast of the Baltic and keep an eye on the Russian fleet and attack it if the opportunity availed itself. New for this year, however, were the instructions to also keep an eye on the Swedish fleet. Finally he was to ensure his fleet had regular supplies of water. Throughout 1809 Saumarez had to arrange regular provisions for 12,000 men, and on his return to Britain he had suggested changes to the Victualling system, requesting fewer but larger shipments planned well in advance. It was eventually decided that the Victualling Board would communicate directly with Saumarez and not via the Admiralty concerning provisions for the personnel of his fleet, now numbering 15,000 men.

On 17 April Saumarez wrote to Dixon at Yarmouth and ordered him to proceed to the Great Belt with his flagship *Vanguard*, *Ganges*, *Plantagenet*, *Hero* and *Dictator*. *Victory* dropped down from Spithead to Yarmouth and on 10 May she hoisted Saumarez's flag and sailed from Yarmouth in company with *St George* (the flagship of Rear Admiral Robert Reynolds who had now replaced Pickmore), *Formidable*, *Mars Resolution*, *Stately* and *Africa*. Now with nineteen ships of the line, four frigates and eighteen smaller vessels under his command, on his return to Hawke Road on 22 May Saumarez was happy to find 'everything much the same as when I left last year – the Swedes as disposed to be friendly to us as ever, but apprehensive that we will not let them preserve their neutrality much longer'.[2] On 2 June *Victory* sailed from Hawke Road to Hanö. With Dixon cruising the Great Belt with five ships of the line Saumarez ordered Reynolds to the eastern entrance of the Belt with a detachment of four ships of the line, *St George*, *Formidable*, *Resolution* and *Standard*.

Saumarez had only received his instructions Wellesley on 11 May, when he was already en route to the Baltic. The new foreign secretary had instructed Saumarez to treat Swedish ports as hostile. No coastal trading was to be allowed between them except for ships with London-issued licences. He was also permitted to pursue enemy vessels into neutral ports or those excluding British vessels. Finally Saumarez was given permission, if all other options had failed, to commence hostilities against Sweden.

Along with his instructions from Wellesley Saumarez also received his first letters from home. From Martha he learned of the collapse of a local bank that was causing much distress. Saumarez advised his wife: 'It is our part to afford any relief to the industrious and who have families that may need it and two or three hundred pounds cannot be better applied ... The [fall] in the stocks makes our loss the greater – *mais n'importe*. Providence will always make up to us the deficiency.'[3] Writing to Martha on the same subject a month later Saumarez told his wife that there was no better use of the money entrusted to them by Providence 'than in bestowing it on those who are in need'.[4]

Wellesley's orders regarding coastal trading had created such alarm in Sweden that, according to Foster, 'even private individuals are afraid to take their passage in the packet boats, between Sweden and Straslund, without they have letters from me'.[5] Saumarez had already recognised that these orders would be seen as an inflammatory measure in Sweden as they would have affected both the Swedish economy and the supply of food to the country. He told Martha: 'They are under the greatest alarm at the measures I have been ordered to adopt against their trade – and which alone would have been a subject of the greatest distress to Sweden, but when added to their other disastrous events must involve them in deeper ruin.'[6] Reluctant to enforce Wellesley's instructions, Saumarez decided to wait until he had 'an opportunity of communicating with the Consul at Gothenburg and some of the principal merchants, who appeared perfectly satisfied with the indulgence I allowed to the trade of Sweden under the existing circumstances'.[7]

Two days after his arrival in Sweden Saumarez had received further instructions from Wellesley, this time regarding the Danish port of Elsinore, where ships were forced to stop and pay for entrance to the Sound. Wellesley now instructed Saumarez to blockade the port. By giving ships an excuse not to stop there the government hoped to inflict further damage on the Danish economy. However, enforcing the blockade would not be an easy task as Saumarez's ships would have to stop vessels bound for Elsinore together with those that were simply sailing down the Sound.

On 6 June Wellesley had a change of mind regarding his earlier instructions and ordered Saumarez not to interfere with Swedish coastal trading and to release any vessels already captured by the British. Thanks to Saumarez's lengthy 'discussions' with Smith and the local merchants, there were none. On 28 June the new First Lord, Charles Yorke, sent a note of apology to Saumarez: 'It seems evident that your first instructions warranted what you are said to have done and that they required explanation. That which [you] have now received will. I trust, postpone, if not prevent, an actual rupture with Sweden which is very desirable to avoid if possible. At the same time I feel for all your difficulties.'[8]

Following French pressure on the Swedish government, on 6 June Foster learned he was being given forty hours' notice to quit the country. Fenwick and Smith would both remain, but now as private citizens. This left Saumarez as the de facto official British representative in the Baltic. Easing the burden on Saumarez were the unofficial links between the British and Swedish governments; the English businessman George Foy in Stockholm and the former Swedish Ambassador Baron Rehausen in London. Foy, a friend of Thornton, would deal directly with the Swedish Foreign Minister, von Engeström and Rehausen, who was married to an Englishwoman, would have regular meetings with the British Foreign Minister, Wellesley.

In late May the delicately-balanced diplomatic relationship between Britain and Sweden was thrown into turmoil following the death of the Swedish Crown Prince whilst attending a military parade. There were persistent rumours that Christian August had been poisoned and at his funeral, held on 20 June, an angry mob attacked Count Fersen, who was reputed to be a supporter of Gustav's son, stripped him naked and beat him to death. Saumarez recoiled at the barbarity of the mob but nonetheless suspected the guiding hand of Providence: 'If he was accessory to the death of the Prince Royal are we not to wonder at Providence having permitted his suffering a violent death.'[9] The Swedish Parliament, the Riksdag, now began the process of electing a new Crown Prince. There were four main candidates: Frederik VI, King of Denmark; the dead Crown Prince's younger brother, the Duke of Augustenborg; the Prince of Oldenbourg and Marshal Bernadotte. Assessing the situation, Baron Mörner, Riksdag member and early advocate of Bernadotte, declared: 'Sweden does not need a Dane, or a Russian, or a boy whose long minority would do us an injury.'[10] Oldenbourg was soon ruled out as he was too closely connected to the Russian royal family. Frederik VI initially thought he had French support but Napoleon eventually chose to back Bernadotte 'as an honourable monument to my reign and an extension of my glory'.[11] Having assured Frederik of his support, Napoleon sent a secret message to Count Wrede, president of the Riksdag committee, to back Bernadotte. At the first round of elections, held on 8 August, eleven members of the Riksdag voted for Augustenborg and only one for Bernadotte, but by the time of the second round of elections a week later Bernadotte received ten votes to Augustenborg's two. Charles XIII now personally recommended Bernadotte to the Riksdag and on 21 August he was universally endorsed by the Diet's four estates.

Although his claim to the Swedish succession had been supported by the French emperor, Bernadotte and Napoleon had an uneasy relationship, with enmity apparent on both sides. Bernadotte had originally been chosen as the commander of the Army of Italy but Napoleon had outmanoeuvred his rival and persuaded the Directory to award him the position instead and to make Bernadotte the French ambassador to Austria. In August 1798 Bernadotte married Désirée Clary, a former fiancée of Napoleon and the sister-in-law of his brother Joseph. Bernadotte was amongst the original group of officers appointed as Marshals of France when Napoleon became Emperor but he was never given the command of French troops. Instead they were variously Bavarians, Poles, Dutch, Spanish and Saxons. In 1806 Bernadotte had been rebuked by Napoleon for not coming to the aid of Marshal Louis-Nicholas Davout at the Battle of Auerstadt. At the Battle of Wagram three years later Bernadotte ignored Napoleon's order not to retreat. This, together with his subsequent Order of the Day claiming that the French victory was largely due to the efforts of his Saxon troops, resulted in his dismissal from the Grande Armée. Bernadotte's already poor standing with Napoleon was not helped by the fact that it was his Spanish troops who had deserted from Denmark in 1808, destroying the emperor's invasion plans. However, Bernadotte was a popular choice with the Swedish military and von Rosen declared that: 'If Prince Ponte Corvo [Bernadotte] will be a successor to the throne we will get a good man.'[12] Amongst the people he was fondly remembered for his friendly treatment of Swedish prisoners following the capture of Lübeck.

On 21 August Krusenstjerna came aboard *Victory* to inform Saumarez that the Riksdag would appoint Bernadotte as the new Crown Prince. This news came as a shock to Saumarez who had assumed that the late prince would be succeeded by Augustenborg. 'The election of a general officer in the service of the most inveterate enemy that England had to oppose would be highly obnoxious to His Majesty's Government',[13] he complained. Krusenstjerna tried to reassure Saumarez, explaining, as Baron Mörner had earlier pointed out, that this was the only choice possible and that Bernadotte's nomination had not involved Napoleon. Furthermore, Bernadotte 'had professed his firm intentions, as far as depended on him, to maintain the relative situations between England

and Sweden'.[14] The new Crown Prince was also keen to assure Saumarez that he was the only candidate 'who would have the firmness to oppose the intentions of Bonaparte or the agents and ministers in the intercourse with other countries'.[15] Saumarez remained doubtful and thought that the election of Bernadotte had been made 'with a view of detaching the country from all intercourse with England'.[16]

In September the new French minister, Baron Alquier, arrived in Stockholm from Denmark. That same month several events occurred that might easily have resulted in a dramatic escalation of tensions had a less capable officer been in charge of British affairs in the Baltic. Since the signing of the peace between France and Sweden French privateers had been using Stralsund and Danish vessels had also started to appear in Swedish ports. On 14 September Captain James Newman of the 74-gun *Hero* sent a boat with twenty men to attempt to cut out a Danish privateer threatening a convoy under his protection that had sought shelter in the harbour of Marstrand, twenty miles north of Gothenburg. The privateer was boarded but could not be cut out and was run ashore. The men returned to their boat, *Dasher*, but she ran aground and came under attack from a detachment of Swedish troops from Carlsten Castle. A midshipman was killed and another officer wounded. *Dasher* was eventually forced to surrender and was taken possession of by the Swedish troops. Without authorisation from Saumarez Newman now sent von Rosen a letter demanding the return of *Dasher*, her crew and the captured Danish privateer. The second incident to test Anglo-Swedish relations took place four days later when Captain Acklom of *Ranger* boarded and spiked the guns of the Swedish schooner *Celeritas*. Finally, on 20 September *Ranger* entered Stralsund and captured the French privateer *Wagram*. The Swedish government protested about all these incidents and Krusentjerna sent a letter of complaint to Saumarez suggesting that Newman's actions were 'contrary to the intentions of the British government and to the orders they might have received from your Excellency'.[17] Saumarez countered that, whilst Newman was wrong to attack the enemy in a Swedish port, the governor of Marstrand should not have been protecting Danish vessels. He also asserted that, whilst Acklom's actions were not justified, *Ranger*'s captain had been under the impression that *Celeritas* was providing protection for French ships fitting out in Swedish ports. Von Rosen was uncertain whether Saumarez was in a 'good or hostile mood'[18] and, worried that the affair might quickly escalate with the sequestration of Swedish then British ships, he asked for advanced warning so that 'those involved will have time to hide away their possessions'.[19] Thankfully, after an exchange of letters Krusenstjerna eventually passed on his government's satisfaction with Saumarez's reprimands of his captains and his assurances that trade between the Swedish mainland and her Pomeranian provinces would continue unmolested so long as her harbours were not used by French privateers. On 26 September von Rosen wrote: 'Thank God, that the Marstrand incident turned out so well. I have really been worried about sequestration measures, which thus are no more to be feared.'[20]

On 19 October Yorke wrote to Saumarez to congratulate him on his handling of both these incidents together with his 'prudent and proper manner'[21] with Krusenstjerna over the election of Bernadotte. Saumarez did not expect the new Crown Prince to cross into Sweden until after the British had departed at the end of the season but nevertheless had taken measures to intercept the Bernadotte should he attempt to enter Sweden either from Stralsund or across the Belts. With that year's deployment coming to an end Saumarez ordered three ships, *Plantagenet*, *Minotaur* and *Africa*, back to England with the last convoy of the season and on 10 October he left Hanö Bay to rendezvous with Reynolds at Wingo. On his way through the Great Belt Saumarez received a request to allow a Swedish yacht carrying Bernadotte to pass from Jutland to Sjaelland. Saumarez did not refer the matter back to London but instead allowed the unarmed yacht carrying a Marshal of France free passage to Sweden. Bernadotte's arrival had coincided with the arrival in mid-Belt of two homeward-bound convoys and a fleet of 600 ships that had been held up at Gothenburg by easterly winds. On 14 October Bernadotte's yacht, flying the flag of the Swedish crown, passed within a mile of *Victory*, surrounded by six ships of the line and a further six frigates protecting an immense collection of over 1,000 merchant ships. No salutes were given, no signals exchanged. Bernadotte later confessed that, 'it was the most beautiful and wonderful sight he had ever beheld, being one of which he never formed an idea'.[22]

Bernadotte arrived in Hälsingborg on 19 October. From there he travelled to Stockholm, arriving in the Swedish capital on 2 November. As required by the Swedish constitution Bernadotte had already adopted the Lutheran religion of his adopted country, citing his mother's Huguenot connections and his associations with the Lutherans of Anspach. He had also renounced his French citizenship, military rank and titles and taken the name Karl Johan. On 5 November Bernadotte met the Riksdag and was confirmed as the new Crown Prince of Sweden. After their first formal audience with Bernadotte the initially sceptical Queen Hedvig-Charlotte, wife of Charles XIII wrote: 'The prince is splendid; he is big, holds himself well and has a presence so noble and so dignified that he appears born into the rank that he now occupies.'[23] Whilst Bernadotte quickly became popular at court the same could not be said for his wife. According to the Queen, Désirée Clary could at times be good-hearted and generous but generally acted like a spoilt child who hated all demands upon her and disliked and complained about anything that was not French, and consequently she was not well liked.

In-mid October the French consul in Gothenburg, Ranchoup, had reported to Alquier that 900 ships had recently sailed for the Baltic with colonial goods whilst a further 800 had sailed for Britain laden with Swedish goods; iron, timber and hemp. All 1,700 merchantmen sailing under Royal Navy escort. Furthermore, the packet boat service between Gothenburg and Harwich was still in operation. Alquier presented this information at his first meeting with Bernadotte and the new Swedish prince promised to investigate the matter further. Writing to Napoleon Bernadotte claimed that the reports had been exaggerated and had come from Sweden's enemies. There were, of course smugglers but they were mostly operating outside of Sweden. When questioned Engeström maintained that 300 of the ships at Gothenburg were American and a further 300 were in ballast, the remainder were Russian, Danish and German vessels. Furthermore Engeström pointed out that around 3,000 ships had lately sailed from England to Russia, which was where Napoleon should be turning his attention.

On 25 October Lagerbjelke, now Swedish ambassador in Paris, was summoned to an audience with Napoleon and informed that Sweden must declare war on Britain or find herself at war against France and her allies. The Swedish government was not overly concerned about French aggression but it was clear that an attack by Russia could not be defended against, even with British aid. Therefore, at a meeting on 15 November from which Bernadotte had excused himself, the Council of State chose the safer option and declared war against Britain. The only dissenting voice was Hans Järta, the Finance Secretary, who voted against the decision.

Even as the Swedish declaration of war against Britain was being issued on 17 November, von Rosen was meeting with a prominent merchant, John Morduant Johnston, to inform him that 'relations between England and Sweden will continue nearly the same as they have been for the last six months'.[24] Foy also received a similar assurance from von Engeström. For the time being the import of colonial goods would temporarily cease until more discreet ways of continuing the trade could be found and British merchant ships would be detained, but not confiscated or sequestered. The packet boat service between Harwich and Gothenburg could also continue, albeit discreetly. Von Rosen was instructed to give assurances that it was not the Swedish government's intention to follow the declaration with any act of hostility towards Britain and in London Rehausen obtained an assurance from Wellesley that Britain would also refrain from hostile acts so long as Sweden did likewise. In a private letter von Rosen assured Saumarez that the declaration ran 'contrary to the sentiments of the Swedish government, and particularly those of the Crown Prince'.[25]

Before his departure for home Saumarez noted that the Swedish naval force at Gothenburg, thirty-three oared gunboats, had been hauled out of the water for the winter and were partially dismantled. Confident of the Swedish government's peaceful intentions Saumarez decided 'against taking measures relative to the Swedish trade which I should otherwise have been justified in'.[26] He left instructions for Captain Dundas, in charge of the British fleet during his absence, 'to oppose any attack that may be mediated against you; but you are not on any account to commence hostilities against the Swedish flag or the trade of that country until you receive orders for that purpose'.[27] Sailing from Gothenburg on 28 November, Saumarez arrived at the Downs on 3 December. Travelling to London to report to the Admiralty, Saumarez was one of the numerous visitors to St James's Palace enquiring of the health of King George who was now suffering another bout of madness, triggered by the death of his beloved daughter, Princess Amelia, in early November.

Chapter 21

The Carlshamn Cargoes: February–December 1811

Following its capture in 1809 the Danish island of Anholt had been commissioned as a Royal Navy 'vessel' and placed under the command of Captain James Maurice, who had similarly commanded HMS 'Diamond Rock' in Martinique in 1804–5. The occupation of Anholt, which was used as a navigational aid, an assembly point for homeward-bound convoys and as an emergency source of water, had been a constant source of humiliation to the Danes and Frederick VI had declared the recapture of the island to be of the highest priority. On 24 March 1811 a Danish naval officer, Lieutenant Holstein, arrived on Anholt under a flag of truce in order to secretly reconnoitre the island. Anholt was garrisoned with a 'crew' of 450 sailors and Royal Marines; her main defences consisted of Fort York, which protected the lighthouse, and the Massarene Battery. The island was also serviced by a tender, *Anholt*, but this vessel was considered of little consequence by Holstein. By early 1811 the preparations for an invasion had been completed. A force of 1,000 soldiers, sailors and local militiamen, led by Major Melstedt, would be transported to the island aboard a collection of fishing vessels and coastal craft; these would be protected from British attack by a dozen armed galleys. The attack had been timed for mid- to late March, after the ice had disappeared from the Danish coast but before the bulk of the Baltic Fleet had arrived from England.

In early February Maurice learned of the build-up of Danish forces in Gierrild Bay and requested additional naval support. On 20 March Saumarez dispatched the 32-gun frigate *Tartar* and the 16-gun-brig-sloop *Sheldrake* to the island. The two vessels arrived on 26 March and were at anchor on the north side of the island when Maurice received word a day later that Danish landings were taking place to the south under the cover of fog. The garrison was quickly mobilised, but, realising they were outnumbered, fell back to the Massarene Battery.

Melstedt's men attempted to outflank the British position but were beaten back by concentrated musketry and grapeshot from the battery's guns. However, as the fog cleared the Danish galleys were able to move in and support the men ashore.

Alerted to the attack by a signal from the lighthouse, *Tartar* and *Sheldrake* were attempting to sail south but were being delayed by contrary winds and the need to avoid the dangerous offshore reefs. Meanwhile the support from their galleys allowed the Danes to attempt a full frontal assault on the British positions. However, they were met with intense defensive fire and retreated in disarray with many dead, including both Melstedt and Holstein. The tender *Anholt*, Lieutenant Baker, now arrived and began firing into the Danish flank, causing further confusion and eventually forcing the Danes to surrender. As *Tartar* came into view around the headland the Danish transports and galleys hoisted their sails and attempted to head for the Swedish coast. As anticipated this brought them within range of the waiting *Sheldrake* which began an engagement with the galleys that lasted until 8.00pm and resulted in the capture of one vessel and the sinking of another. Meanwhile *Tartar* was busy engaging the Danish transports, capturing two vessels before the presence of shoals close to the Danish shore forced her to abandon her pursuit.

Retreating to the west of the island, the Danish troops on Anholt remained in an uneasy standoff with the British forces until they were finally evacuated aboard those transports that had managed to return to the island. The British victory had resulted in the loss of just two killed and thirty wounded to the Danish losses of forty dead and twenty-five wounded, including almost all their commanding officers. In addition a further 500 soldiers and 200 sailors had been taken prisoner. Shortly after the victory Captain Maurice wrote to the Danish government, offering to parole all his prisoners in exchange for the ninety-four survivors of the sloop *Pandora*, lost in February off the Skaw, along with any other British prisoners in Danish hands. From London Saumarez sent his congratulations to Maurice: 'I most heartily congratulate you on the brilliant success of the brave garrison under your command in having repulsed an attack of the enemy's select troops … I can only assure you that this gallant affair is the theme of ever one's praise, and has excited the admiration of all, and I have no doubt but your services upon this occasion will be duly appreciated by the Admiralty.'[1]

Confirmed as commander-in-chief of the Baltic fleet for a fourth season, Saumarez hosted his flag aboard *Victory* on 2 April and received his final instructions from the Admiralty ten days later. There were concerns that the growing naval forces in the Scheldt, the Texel and Helvout (twenty-four ships of the line and a similar number of frigates) might be directed into the Baltic if they could escape the British blockading squadrons and Saumarez was therefore directed to station himself at Wingo Sound with as many ships of the line as he could spare from operations elsewhere.

Sailing from the Downs on 28 April Saumarez arrived off Gothenburg on 2 May. Reynolds, in command of the ships in Hanö Bay, had arrived aboard his flagship *St George* in company with *Hero*, *Plantagenet*, *Vanguard* and *Courageux* ten days earlier and Dixon, in command of the squadron in the Belt, arrived several hours after Saumarez aboard *Vigo*. Saumarez soon received word from Fenwick that the Danes were fitting out more than double the number of privateers and armed vessels than the previous year and were also preparing for another attack on Anholt. However, of more concern to Saumarez was the news that the sixty merchantmen at Carlshamn were being sequestered by the Swedes and their cargoes discharged and sent up country.

During the closing weeks of the 1810 season, merchantmen flying a range of flags, including those of Prussia, Denmark and Melcklenburg, had put into several Swedish ports to avoid the ice and deteriorating weather. Lloyds of London estimated that the cargoes at Gothenburg were worth around £72,420, those at Ystad £80,227 and at Carlshamn £759,003. The Swedish government claimed the cargoes at Carlshamn had been sequestered in order to obtain compensation for Swedish merchants whose property had been confiscated in Danish, Prussian and Mecklenburgian ports. No action had been taken against the cargoes in other Swedish ports and the Swedes continued to supply Saumarez's fleet, but many in Britain saw this move by the Swedish government, which still had a strong pro-French faction, as clear evidence of their hostile intentions towards Britain. Yorke was particularly wary of the new Crown Prince: 'My own opinion is that Bernadotte is playing us false, and at any rate I for one should dread to see an consolidation of the Swedish and Norwegian power ... considerable distrust appears to prevail here about the ultimate views of the Swedish Government – a little more time will develop their plans in all probability.'[2] However, on 15 May Consul Smith wrote to Saumarez to inform him that the sequestration was 'merely a demonstration to appear as having adopted the Continental System but on no account to confiscate the Property which is equally safe in our possession as on board the ships, and which most likely will be returned in a very short time'.[3] Saumarez himself thought it 'a very dubious crisis, and I trust soon to be better informed of the sentiments of the

Swedish government towards us; at the same time I have no reason to believe they are more hostile than last year'.[4]

On 17 May Smith was sent aboard *Victory* by von Rosen to gauge Saumarez's mood and to determine whether or not he would oppose the actions of the Swedish government. Saumarez informed Smith that he would do nothing without first receiving authorisation from London. He requested a full explanation of the Swedish government's actions and gave Smith an assurance that nothing short of the full restitution of the property would be accepted. Baron Tawast, the military commander of Gothenburg, now arrived aboard *Victory* under a flag of truce for a prearranged meeting regarding an exchange of prisoners. However, he had also been briefed by von Rosen to discuss the issue of the Carlshamn cargoes. Tawast informed Saumarez that 'it was the earnest wish of the Swedish government to keep upon the most amicable terms with Great Britain ... the appearance of any hostile measures was only intended for demonstration, and in order to elude the vigilance of French spies who might be dispersed in the Country'.[5] Saumarez sent Ross to obtain written confirmation of Tawast's assurances, which he sent to Saumarez on 25 May. Dissatisfied by Tawast's letter, which differed from their earlier discussion and only mentioned limited indemnities, Saumarez wrote to Smith requesting that he inform Tawast 'that government will naturally expect that the British merchants will be indemnified for whatever property belongs to them which has been landed from vessels in Sweden'.[6] Saumarez now wrote to Yorke suggesting that two persons, authorised by the British merchants and underwriters, go to Stockholm to assert their claims. He further suggested that the two bomb vessels earmarked for Baltic service be sent immediately: 'Their appearance alone would have the best effect in intimidating the Swedes to a compliance with our just demands.'[7] Having received his instructions from an unusually expeditious Wellesley, on 30 May Saumarez sent the following letter to Tawast: 'I have been directed to remonstrate in the strongest manner against measures so deeply affecting the interest of his Majesty's subjects, and at the same time to signify to the Swedish government that I cannot permit such proceedings, under whatever pretext they may be disguised, and that if acts of so injurious a tendency are persevered in, I shall be obliged to depart from the indulgent course I have hitherto pursued towards Sweden.'[8] Saumarez told Martha he thought that the Swedes were 'adopting measures against our mercantile interests that they know must fall upon their own heads'.[9] Martha declared that the Swedes, struggling to upset neither Britain nor France, stood 'between two fires either of which is likely to consume them'.[10]

In response to Saumarez's letter of 30 May, Baron Tawast explained that the sequestration of cargoes at Carlshamn had not been intended as a hostile act and that the Swedish government's hand had been forced. Tawast was certain that the English merchants would ultimately be indemnified but asked Saumarez not to send his remonstrance to the Swedish government as Baron von Essen, aide-de-camp to the Crown Prince, would be arriving soon to explain the situation properly. This had all the appearance of the Swedes playing for time and Saumarez insisted his remonstrance be sent to the Swedish government through Baron von Essen. Saumarez had, by now, been made aware that the entrance to Carlshamn had been lined with blockships and that the Swedes had begun strengthening the defences of Karlskrona and several other ports and was yet to be convinced of the Swedish government's true intentions.

On 25 June von Rosen met with Saumarez aboard *Victory*. As Britain and Sweden were now officially at war the meeting would have to remain as secret and so von Rosen arrived aboard Saumarez's flagship 'in the most private manner and earnestly requested that his visit and the communication he had been directed to make to me should be kept secret'.[11] Von Rosen assured Saumarez that Sweden wanted to break with France but was fearful of what action Russia might take should France and Russia come to an accord. Saumarez told von Rosen that his Majesty's Government would take no action so long as Sweden kept to the assurances she had previously made but that he had the authority to use all in his power to resist any aggression on the part of Sweden. Von Rosen was satisfied with this response and promised to convey it to Bernadotte. He later wrote: 'Admiral Saumarez's way of thinking and attitude regarding Sweden are quite the same as they so far have been. He protects our trade, lets our ships sail with or without convoys or licences, allows export of colonial merchandise.'[12] Saumarez came away from the meeting equally satisfied, any lingering doubts as to the sincerity of the Swedish government having been finally removed by his conversation with von Rosen.

On 20 July the French minister, Alquier, wrote to Engeström to complain about Tawast's visit to *Victory* in May, stating that Consul Smith had been present during the meeting and had promised Saumarez 600 head of cattle. Alquier also complained about the convoys gathering off of Wingo and the Swedish supplies being sent to the English on Anholt. Overstepping the mark, Alquier informed the Swedish foreign minister that if his government continued on its present course it would 'find itself in the situation that produced the disaster of the last Gustav'.[13] As Alquier's irritation over what he saw as Swedish deceits concerning their implementation of the Continental System grew he was becoming less and less diplomatic in his dealings with Swedish ministers, even managing to irritate those who, like Engeström, belonged to the Francophile party within the government.

On 16 August Yorke responded to the news of the meeting between Saumarez and von Rosen aboard *Victory*, writing that 'the affair of the Carlshamn cargoes is considered here a matter of much more nicety and difficulty than first appeared … it seems highly desirable to gain as much time as possible and to avoid coming to any rupture with Sweden'. Yorke expected the Swedes to restore all the sequestered goods but he also sounded a note of caution. 'We cannot altogether entertain (at least to the same extent) the favourable opinion you seem to possess of the fair and amicable intentions of the Swedish government.'[14]

On 9 September Engeström proposed a solution to the Carlshamn cargoes. The sequestered goods should be sold in Sweden and the merchants involved reimbursed through a payment to the British government. This mirrored a proposal set out by Saumarez in early May when he had suggested the issue be resolved 'through an agreement by an experienced merchant from Stockholm on one side, and on the other by an English envoy under the name of a merchant'.[15] In December Saumarez received word from the Board of Trade that two representatives of Lloyds, John Atkins and Isaac Adalbert, would shortly be arriving in Sweden. Saumarez was advised to give them 'every information and assistance in [his] power, in promoting the object of their enquiries, without making His Majesty's Government a Party to their transactions'.[16]

In December 1810 Napoleon annexed the north-west German Duchy of Oldenburg, whose sovereign, Peter, was the Tsar's uncle. The annexation having violated the Treaty of Tilsit, Alexander's response was an order closing Russian ports and markets to French products. As France and Russia drifted further apart during the course of 1811 Napoleon further heightened tensions in the region by increasing his armies in Germany. In response Prussia had begun to rearm and to reinforce key strongholds. Napoleon now issued a warning that if the rearmament did not stop the French ambassador in Berlin would be replaced by Marshal Davout and his army. There were loud protests from the anti-Bonapartists Gneisenau and Blücher, who was busy reinforcing the fortress at Kolberg. Saumarez had already allowed Swedish ships to import corn from Riga and Libau and ships had also been sent to the Prussian port of Königsberg with building materials to help rebuild parts of the city destroyed by a recent fire. On 2 September, having received intelligence of an intended French attack on Kolberg,

Saumarez wrote to Yorke and requested instructions on how far he was to assist the Prussians should they find themselves at war with France. A week later Gneisenau wrote to Saumarez requesting assistance in the form of arms and ammunition, suggesting they be sent to Blücher at Kolberg. Gneisenau asked that his request remain secret, 'the preparations for the insurrection not having reached the stage at which the mask can be thrown off'.[17]

Having been instructed by the Admiralty to 'afford every practicable aid to the Prussian government or any of its officers in resisting the power of France'[18] Saumarez now wrote to Gneisenau to inform him that two vessels carrying arms and ammunition (10,000 muskets, 2,000,000 cartridges and 3,000 barrels of powder) had been ordered to join him and he would send them on to Kolberg under escort as soon as they had arrived in the Baltic. Ignoring Napoleon's demands to cease rearmament, Blücher had continued to train new recruits and strengthen Kolberg's defences. He now sent a request to Saumarez to allow several vessels laden with corn and iron to enter Kolberg even though their licenses were for England. Saumarez was happy to agree to this request for which he would later receive official approval from the Admiralty. Saumarez had also suggested leaving two gun-brigs at Kolberg over the winter and this was also agreed to. Yorke suggested they be placed under the command of Captain Fanshawe of *Grasshopper*, but Saumarez thought Captain Acklom of *Ranger* better qualified. (With war between France and Russia increasingly likely *Grasshopper* had arrived off Reval in August 1811 with a convoy of transports bearing arms for the Russians. The transports had been quickly turned away and Saumarez later received a complaint from the Russian government over Fanshawe's 'deplorable lack of discretion'.[19])

On 20 September the French ambassador in Berlin presented the Prussian government with an ultimatum. Their country had three days to disarm, discharge all recruits and cease all works on the fortifications. If she refused Marshal Davout would invade Prussia with all the imperial forces stationed along the Elbe. Faced with this ultimatum Frederick William ordered a halt to the mobilisation. Blücher refused this order from the King and the French demanded his recall. On 14 October Blücher was replaced as commander of Kolberg by General Tauentzien, an officer more acceptable to Napoleon.

By late October Saumarez had still not received word from Gneisenau of the anticipated Prussian insurrection and so he ordered the transports laden with arms and ammunition to Hanö Bay under the protection of *Crescent*, *Vigo* and *Orion*, forwarding instructions for Captain Dashwood of *Pyramus* to remain at Hanö with the transports for as long as the deteriorating weather would allow. Saumarez now heard rumours of a planned French attack on Guernsey and he wrote to Martha urging her to cross to England. When he next heard from his wife on the matter it was to be informed that the alarm had passed before she had even considered leaving. Besides which: 'My going would have been the signal for many other families to move also, but while the Admiral's Lady stayed they thought they could stay too.'[20]

Having received little support from Russia a vacillating Frederick William had, by now, concluded that the survival of his state would require an alliance with France. Entering into negotiations with the French the Prussians insisted they be exempted from the wars in Spain and Italy and that any Prussian auxiliary corps be placed under a Prussian general. Napoleon agreed but insisted that Blücher be dismissed. Having lost a key ally and friend Scharnhorst now requested early retirement but was placed on indefinite leave. A formal treaty between France and Prussia was signed in February 1812. Prussia joined the Confederation of the Rhine, her borders were opened up to imperial troops and she was forced to provide Napoleon with an auxiliary corps of 20,842 men.

Having by now made himself thoroughly unpopular in Stockholm, on 2 November Alquier was appointed by Napoleon as French minister to Denmark, leaving for Copenhagen without the usual courtesy of taking leave of the court. Fenwick commented: 'It is not to be wondered that M. Alquier has left Sweden in a bad humour for it is the only country from which he has gone without affecting its ruin.'[21] Many Francophiles in the Swedish Government blamed Alquier's behaviour for ending Napoleon's plans for a closer union between France and Sweden. Conversely, Saumarez had surprised many by proving himself an unexpected ally to the Swedish nation.

On 1 November 1811 a convoy of 130 merchantmen, the last of the season, left Matvik escorted by *St George*, *Defence* and *Cressy*. Reynolds was under orders from Saumarez not to delay sailing due to the dangers of ice and the rapidly-deteriorating weather but the convoy soon encountered contrary winds and was forced to turn back. During the night of 15 November, whilst anchored off Nysted, the convoy was hit by a storm. Thirty ships were driven ashore and wrecked and a large merchantman was blown across *St George*'s bows, cutting her anchor cable. As *St George* was dragged towards the shoals the other anchors were hurriedly let go but they did not hold. Reynold's flag-captain, David Guion, requested permission to cut down the ship's masts but Reynolds, concerned about possible delays to the convoy, refused to give the order until it was too late. *St George* ran aground and as the ship struck the bottom her rudder was torn away. The following morning the devastation inflicted by the storm was clear to see; twelve merchantmen were sighted wrecked on shore with countless others foundering at their anchors. It took two days for *St George* to be refloated with the assistance of *Defence* and *Cressy*. Fitted with jury-rigged masts and a temporary rudder she was taken under tow by *Cressy* to Wingo Sound.

Captain Dashwood made his last communication with Colberg on 30 November. Having still received no word regarding the transports he decided to return to Wingo, taking the transports and the ships under his command back through the Sound as he considered the Belt far too dangerous. Sailing in a strong gale with Aklom in *Ranger* leading the way three merchantmen became damaged and were forced to put in at Landskrona where their papers were seized. However, the ship's masters were soon given permission to proceed with their cargoes.

On 2 December *Cressy* arrived at Wingo towing a badly-damaged *St George* in company with the convoy of merchantmen, now reduced to just seventy-two ships. Saumarez proposed that *St George* remain at Wingo but Reynolds insisted his ship 'was as fit to make her passage with the assistance of another ship of the line as any in the fleet'.[22] Reynolds views were shared by his flag-captain, Daniel Guion, a surprise given the condition of Reynold's thirty-year-old flagship and the fact that a decade earlier Nelson had noted: '*St George* is in a truly wretched state. I had rather encounter ten painted cabins than her dreary, dirty and leaky cabin. The water comes in at all parts, and there is not a dry place, or a window that does not let in wind enough to turn a mill.'[23] Reynolds was an experienced flag officer and, perhaps ignorant of the true state of affairs aboard *St George* and with concerns that the Swedes might seize her over the winter, Saumarez yielded to his request, ordering Reynold's flagship to be escorted to the Downs by *Cressy*, Captain Pater, and *Defence*, Captain Atkins and giving charge of the convoy to Captain Newman of *Hero*.

Once again delayed by contrary winds the convoy of seventy-six merchantmen did not leave Wingo until 17 December, escorted by *Hero* and the brig *Grasshopper*. Saumarez's ships accompanied them, sailing ahead in two squadrons, one consisting of *Victory*, *Vigo*, *Dreadnought*, *Orion* and the brigs *Mercury* and *Snipe*, the other of *Cressy* and *St George*, *Defence* and the brig *Bellete*. With the ships entering the North Sea fighting strong headwinds Saumarez sent the merchantmen back to Wingo and ordered *Cressy* and *Defence* to keep close to *St George*. On 19 December Reynolds decided to return to Wingo and Saumarez lost sight of his flagship. With the weather suddenly improving, Reynolds ordered the tow from *Cressy* to be cast off. However, on the morning of 23 December *St George*'s people were observed attempting to make repairs to the ship's temporary rudder. Pater offered to restore the tow but this was turned down by Reynolds. By now the wind had shifted to the north-west and was building into a gale. With her steering now damaged beyond repair, a combination of wind and a strong southerly current began dragging *St George* towards the Danish shore. Aboard *Cressy* Pater held an emergency meeting with his senior officers. Informed that he would soon be faced with having to cut down *Cressy*'s masts and employing dangerously worn-out anchor cables to save his ship, Pater elected to wear his ship away from danger. This manoeuvre took *Cressy* close to *St George* and one last unsuccessful attempt was made to communicate with Reynolds' flagship. Whilst *Cressy* wore away from the shore and continued north-west, Captain Atkins, mindful of Saumarez's orders, chose to stay by Reynolds' flagship rather than abandon her. Atkins also hailed *St George* but again she failed to reply. There was little chance of *St George* answering *Defence* as by now her crew were all occupied in the desperate struggle to turn the ship away from the shore. However, every time they attempted to set a sail it was torn apart by the wind. Shortly after midnight on Christmas Eve, with water flooding her lower deck, *St George* went aground along the west coast of Jutland and her ageing hull immediately began breaking up. The ship's boats were launched but all were quickly dashed to pieces. Once they were lost there was no escape for her crew. Within hours the ship had been reduced to flotsam. Several men managed to cling on to the wreckage of *St George*'s cabins and stern frame but were washed overboard before the wreckage could reach the shore. Only seven men from the crew of 872 survived the sinking, rescued by the efforts of local people. Reynolds had been in his cabin when *St George* ran aground but was taken up onto the deck, seriously injured, when his ship began to flood. He died alongside his flag-captain, Guion, on *St George*'s quarterdeck.

Five hours later *Defence* also ran aground, not far from Reynolds' flagship. Atkins and six of his crew made it onto dry land where locals were waiting to help them but high waves pounded into the British Third Rate, quickly tearing the ship apart and making further evacuation impossible. The remaining crew, 560 in all, perished and Atkins died from exposure soon after. Bodies would continue to wash up along a part of the coast now known as 'dead men's dunes' for days after the storm.

Having returned to Wingo, the seventy-six merchantmen under *Hero* and *Grasshopper* had departed again once the weather began to improve on 18 December. The ships soon divided, the merchantmen bound for the north of England headed west under the sloop *Egeria* and the armed ship *Prince William*, whilst those that were destined for London and Portsmouth sailed south-west in company with *Hero* and the brig *Grasshopper*. These ships soon encountered heavy sleet and snow. By the evening of 23 December visibility was so bad that there were only fleeting glimpses of the other ships in the convoy. *Hero* and *Grasshopper* came within hailing distance of one another and Newman announced that, having estimated their position to be in a region known as the Great Silver Pits, he had decided to take the convoy south-south-west in order to pick up the prevailing winds which would carry them to the Channel. Unfortunately Newman had miscalculated the convoy's true position which was in fact around ninety miles further east and they were now headed not for the Channel but towards the dangerous Haak Sands on the Dutch coast. Early on the morning of 24 December lookouts aboard *Grasshopper* suddenly reported the appearance of breakers. The ship's anchor was hastily let go and as she came to a halt her people could hear the sound of distant signal guns, at the same time blue distress lights flickered alarmingly in the darkness.

The distress signals were coming from *Hero* which had run aground on Haak Sands during the night and had been dismasted. A rescue attempt had been made by the Dutch but the sheer ferocity of the storm was preventing a flotilla of vessels from the Texel from coming to the British Third Rate's assistance. Only twelve men from *Hero*'s crew of 530 made it ashore by the time the storm finally tore the ship apart, the rest were all lost. Grasshopper was in a less dangerous situation but she had passed over a sandbar and was now trapped in the Dutch Helder. At first light *Grasshopper*'s boats were lowered but they were not able to make it through the heavy surf. With no way of escape Captain Fanshawe was forced to surrender his ship.

In the space of twenty-four hours over 2,000 British sailors had been lost at sea, a figure higher than the combined losses of Cape St Vincent, the Nile, Copenhagen and Trafalgar. Losses amongst the other merchant ships brought this figure up to an estimated 5,000. It was the worst disaster to befall the Royal Navy during the entire Napoleonic Wars.

Having parted from *St George* on 19 December *Victory*'s squadron was beset by baffling winds and heavy weather. On 22 December it blew a strong gale from the north-west and the weather grew steadily worse over the next twenty-four hours. Longitude was now taken and most of Saumarez's captains estimated their position to be well to the west of that taken aboard *Victory* but Saumarez elected to sail according to his own ship's reckoning, unlike Newman keeping his fleet well away from danger. At the height of the storm no readings could be taken off the ships' chronometers but by soundings taken on 23 December it was estimated that the squadron was in a region of the North Sea off the Suffolk coast known to mariners as the Broad Fourteens. The following day the storm eased and the squadron passed the entrance to the Thames Estuary. On Christmas Day the ships entered the Channel and that evening anchored in St Helen's. There had still been no news concerning *St George* but Saumarez was certain that in the face of worsening weather Reynolds would have returned to Wingo. However, writing from Spithead on 26 December he admitted his uneasiness over the possible fate of Reynolds' flagship.

Chapter 22

Baltic Fleet: Final Season:
January–December 1812

Following his return to Britain Saumarez travelled directly to London and on 3 January 1812 had a lengthy meeting with Yorke at the Admiralty. A week later the first reports began to arrive in Britain regarding the loss of *St George*, *Defence* and *Hero*. As the scale of the disaster became known, the officers and crew of *Argo*, then at Spithead, agreed to give two days' pay to the widows and orphans of the men who had been lost and urged other Royal Navy ships to follow suit. In the House of Commons on 16 January Samuel Whitbread, the MP for Bedford, asked why large ships such as *St George* had continued to operate so late in the season in the dangerous Baltic waters. The First Lord replied that Admiralty orders had been for all ships to be ready to sail by 1 November but that Reynolds' convoy had been delayed by bad weather and could not sail until 17 November. Yorke insisted that the Admiralty had not failed in its duty to provide *St George* with all that was necessary to operate safely and that the disaster was 'entirely the effect of the weather, and circumstances which no human foresight could provide against'.[1] Satisfied with this answer, Whitbread observed that 'the calamities were the effect of misfortune alone, and that it was a consolation to reflect that no blame could be imputed to anyone'.[2] All this was of little consolation to Saumarez, who for many months remained deeply affected by the loss of so many lives under his command.

In October 1811 Edward Thornton had returned to the Baltic in secret in order to carry out joint negotiations with Sweden and Russia. Wellesley had originally considered giving Saumarez the authority to sign the preliminary articles of peace but the Prime Minister, Perceval, was worried it might betray 'too great an eagerness and forwardness'[3] on the part of the government to employ Saumarez in this role and as such be counterproductive. It was therefore decided that the former

British envoy, Edward Thornton, would carry out the joint negotiations with Sweden and Russia, Thornton's mission was so clandestine that his ship, *Oberon*, had no pilots aboard familiar with the coast of Sweden and as a consequence was almost lost on the rocks north of Wingo. Safely aboard *Victory*, Thornton was eventually smuggled ashore at Gothenburg as a servant of Lieutenant John Ross. Following a meeting with von Rosen, Thornton, travelling as an American merchant, Ebenezer Thompson, met with the Russian commissioner Netzel at Åmål, a small town north of Gothenburg on the edge of Lake Vänern.

Obedience to Napoleon's Continental System had proved to be a disaster for Russia's economy and Alexander, facing increasing opposition to his rule, had been seeking to end his alliance with France since 1810. Prior to the Treaty of Tilsit Britain had purchased around 70 per cent of all Russian hemp produced and around 90 per cent of its flax. Now the markets for these commodities had all but collapsed. Most worrying of all were the effects on Russian agriculture with exports of wheat down by a crippling 80 per cent. Her economy in ruins, Russia sent a clear message to her ally France by increasing the tax on goods brought in by land (affecting French imports) and relaxed the taxes on goods brought in by sea (British and colonial goods under neutral flags). When Napoleon's Russian ambassador, Armand de Caulaincourt, returned to Paris in June 1811 he was immediately summoned by the furious Emperor. Asked if the Tsar was intent on making war against France Caulaincourt insisted Alexander wanted to maintain peaceful relations with Napoleon. Citing continual infringements of his Continental System, Napoleon responded that 'the Tsar was treacherous [and] that he was arming to make war on France'.[4]

Russia and France spent the winter of 1811/12 organising their forces. By 1812 Napoleon had assembled an army of 448,000 men; raised from every corner of his empire they included Dutch, Italians, Poles, Austrians and Spaniards. Meanwhile, the new Russian Minister of War, Barclay de Tolly, had almost doubled the size of the Russian army to around 480,000 men. In January 1812 Napoleon ordered Marshal Davout to occupy Swedish Pomerania 'where not only English smuggling is tolerated, but recent facts show that Sweden takes an active part in it'.[5] Napoleon also instructed his brother Jerome, the King of Westphalia, to prepare his army to counter the Russian forces which had evacuated from the Danube, partially withdrawn from Finland and massed on the borders of Warsaw, threatening Napoleon's newly-established Grand Duchy.

During the winter, command of a reduced Baltic fleet had passed to Captain Dashwood of *Pyramus*. The Swedes had been busy fitting out eight ships of the line and five frigates at Karlskrona and Consul Smith passed on a request from the Swedish government that that these ships should not be attacked. In anticipation that his order would receive the approval of Saumarez, Dashwood informed his cruiser captains to 'treat the Swedish flag with the respect and attention due a great nation and on no account whatever to molest them'.[6]

Re-appointed to command of the Baltic fleet for a fifth season, Saumarez requested the services of Admirals Byam Martin and James Morris, who was called upon to replace Reynolds. Morris was the son of Captain John Morris, killed aboard *Bristol* during the attack on Sullivan's Island in 1776. Hope had been promoted rear admiral in August 1811 and had subsequently turned down an offer from Yorke to continue in the Baltic under Saumarez. As Saumarez explained to his wife, after four years together he and his captain of the fleet had, by now, seen more than enough of one another. Now in command of a reduced fleet of just ten ships of the line Saumarez argued that, as no more than three or four ships would be together at any one time, he would not need a replacement for Hope. The new First Lord, Melville, who had only taken office on 25 March, yielded to Saumarez, but told him he would revisit the matter should his fleet grow in size.

Saumarez hoisted his flag aboard *Victory* at Spithead on 14 April, around the same time that Morris was arriving at Wingo with the advanced squadron, consisting of his flagship *Vigo*, *Mars*, *Dictator*, *Nimble* and *Hebe*. *Victory* sailed to the Downs and, having been delayed by contrary winds, on 28 April she headed out to the Baltic for the last time, arriving at Wingo in company with *Courageux*, *Orion* and *Reynard* on 2 May. Following the invasion of Swedish Pomerania Bernadotte had finally made up his mind to side with Russia rather than France and therefore had given up on Finland, turning his attention instead to Norway. On 6 May Thornton, who had returned to Sweden in early spring to continue peace negotiations, wrote to Saumarez from Örebro to inform him that an offensive and defensive treaty of alliance had been signed between Russia and Sweden and that discussions between Britain and Russia were at an advanced stage. He also told Saumarez that he had learned through von Engeström that it was the Swedish government's intention, upon the announcement of the peace, to present the commander of the Baltic Fleet with a sword ornamented with precious stones as 'a mark of their gratitude for the distinguished kindness you have on all occasions shown them, with which I assure you it is impossible to be more affected than they are'.[7]

Upon his arrival at Wingo Saumarez dispatched Morris with a detachment of ships through the Belt to Hanö to carry out convoy protection and to deter Danish attacks the islands in the Belt. On 9 May von Rosen arrived aboard *Victory* and spent two days aboard Saumarez's flagship, mixing openly with Swedish merchants in considerably less secrecy than during his previous visit a year earlier. Saumarez had arrived in Gothenburg bearing gifts of an English camp bed and two cases of Seville oranges for Bernadotte and another case of oranges for Engeström. Later he would send *Victory*'s surgeon, Valentine Duke, to treat villagers on the neighbouring islands. For this thoughtful gesture von Rosen would write to Saumarez, thanking 'M. le Baron'!' in the name of the King. During his visit von Rosen was introduced to Saumarez's son, James, who, following his return from Oxford, had embarked aboard his father's flagship for a taste of life at sea and a chance to tour the Baltic prior to his entering the priesthood. James would go on to visit Thornton at Örebro and then travel to Åbo and St Petersburg. Following his return from the Baltic James was admitted into deacon's orders and in August 1813 was ordained and appointed assistant curate of St Helen's Church at Benson in Oxfordshire.

On 12 May Consul Smith passed on a request from Nauckhoff to Saumarez for British cruisers to appear in the Sound and the Baltic for the purpose of convoy protection against the privateers that were 'swarming everywhere and committing depredations on trade'.[8] Saumarez ordered *Zealous* and *Rose* to patrol off Hälsingborg and wrote to the Admiralty asking for more cutters to help patrol the Sound. In early May Thornton had reached an agreement with the Russian government for Swedish ships to collect corn from Russian ports in order to alleviate the effects of the recent poor harvest. Through Thornton, Saumarez now received a Russian request that their ships not be molested by British cruisers should they join these Swedish convoys.

Danish gunboats and privateers remained a nuisance if not a real threat to convoys passing through the Sound. However, during the winter the Danes had completed the fitting-out of a new heavy frigate, the 40-gun *Nayaden*, which had subsequently disappeared into the Baltic. Assuming she would join the remnants of the Royal Danish Navy, four brigs known to be operating off the Skagerrak coast, Saumarez dispatched a force consisting of *Dictator* and the brigs *Calypso*, *Podargus* and *Flamer* to hunt this powerful cruiser down before she could wreak havoc on the convoys sailing through the Baltic. On the evening of 6 July *Nayaden* was discovered lying amongst the rocky islets off Mardo in company with the brigs *Laaland*, *Sampso* and *Kiel*. As *Dictator* cautiously made her way through a narrow passage towards the enemy's anchorage, her studding sail booms almost touching the cliffs either side, the British ships came under attack from Danish gunboats and both *Podargus* and *Calypso* were temporarily grounded. *Calypso* was soon re-floated but *Podargus* remained aground, and Stewart ordered *Flamer* to stand by her, ready to assist. Entering into the harbour at Lyngør Stewart surprised the Danes by deliberately running *Dictator*'s bows ashore, enabling his ship to swing round so that he could bring the full force of his broadside to bear on *Nayaden*. According to Stewart's official report, within half an hour the newly-commissioned Danish frigate was 'literally battered to atoms and the flames bursting forth from her hatchways'.[9] Shortly after the destruction of *Nayaden* the Danish brigs *Laaland* and *Kiel* were compelled to haul down their colours.

Dictator and *Calypso* were attempting to work their way out of Lyngør along with the captured brigs when they came under fire from Danish galleys newly arrived from Mardo, the Danish vessels darting in and out of the rocks so that the British could not bring any of their guns to bear. In the confusion both prizes ran aground with one briefly on fire. There being little possibility of these badly damaged vessels being re-floated Stewart realised he would have to abandon them, however, he did not follow the usual practice of setting them on fire as they both still had Danish crews aboard them. By the end of the engagement the British had suffered losses of eight killed and thirty-four wounded. Whilst the British had lost several valuable prizes the Danes had lost much more, for along with around 300 killed and wounded, the battle had also destroyed the remnants of the Danish navy, finally completing a task begun five years earlier at the Battle of Copenhagen.

On 13 May Byam Martin sailed for the Baltic aboard his flagship *Aboukir,* carrying with him the news of the death of the Prime Minister, Perceval, assassinated in the House of Commons two days earlier. The shocking news came as a blow to many, even Saumarez who had no real interest in politics. To Thornton he wrote: 'Most sincerely do I deplore an event that has deprived the country of one of the ablest of men – whose loss is irreparable and will long be felt by the whole nation.'[10] As the Prince Regent attempted to form a new government Saumarez, who had not received any fresh instructions prior to his departure, hoped that ministers would not be distracted from international affairs by domestic troubles. Saumarez assumed that Wellesley would be made Prime Minister with Canning the Foreign Secretary, but Wellesley had offended many of his colleagues by a poorly-judged posthumous attack on Percival and Canning had turned down the offer of the Foreign Office. Eventually the Secretary of State for War, Lord Liverpool, was able to gain enough support to be appointed Prime Minister, taking office on 8 June. Whilst Saumarez had still not received any fresh instructions he had, at least 'the satisfaction to be informed that the measures I am pursuing receive the approbation of the government'.[11] As Martha pointed out, the fact that ministers were now happy to leave the decision making to Saumarez was 'a great proof of their confidence in Thee and the result I hope will justify them'.[12]

Saumarez had sailed for the Baltic leaving Martha to deal with the pressing issue of their youngest daughter, Amelia's, education. Girls were expected to be able to play a musical instrument as one of their 'accomplishments', but Martha admitted that her daughter, who was being taught by her elder sisters, Mary, Martha and Cartaret, 'had so little taste for music that it would be wasting time to attempt her learning it'.[13] Saumarez seemed to have been against Amelia learning to draw but was soon persuaded to change his mind when Martha explained that 'in this Age of Talents, a young lady who neither Plays nor Draws will not be supposed to have been educated & it may be as great a disadvantage to her as the evil we wish to avoid'.[14]

On 11 June Saumarez received a report from Morris that a convoy of fifteen merchantmen had been spotted by *Courageux* headed through the Belt towards Kiel under escort by a Swedish frigate. Saumarez had refused to issue licenses to Swedish ships headed for Kiel as the goods they carried could only be intended for use in Holland and the Scheldt and he now asked Thornton to make a formal complaint to the Swedish government. Thornton was convinced that certain factions within the government were still trying to stir things up between Britain and Sweden and attributed 'much of this untoward circumstance to the negligence and to a forgetfulness which he takes upon himself, of Baron d'Engeström'.[15] By way of explanation Saumarez was informed, via Admiral Puke, that one of the merchantmen had been sailing to Kiel to pick up wine and books for Bernadotte and he received the Crown Prince's assurance that 'no convoy shall henceforth be given to vessels for Kiel and other places in Holstein or foreign places in the Baltic except Russian ports'.[16] Through Thornton Saumarez learned how appreciative the Crown Prince had been of the 'delicate and honourable proceedings'[17] of Saumarez and his captains.

On 6 June Thornton had written to Saumarez informing him he had been given 'full powers to sign a Treaty of Peace with Russia'[18] and that he hoped to have a response from Alexander within ten days. Thornton's return to the Baltic meant that Saumarez now had less influence in diplomatic matters and this shift in power evidently caused some friction between the two men. On 17 June von Rosen wrote to Engeström: 'The day after tomorrow I will go out to Saumarez. The old man is in a very irritable mood, angry about our convoy, about the wickedness of the English ministry, yes I believe even with Mr Thornton himself.'[19] A month later he wrote 'I am fairly certain in supposing that Saumarez and Thornton do not get on very well. They were together with me for 6 hours and during that time they did not say one word to each other.'[20] Thornton had told von Rosen that Saumarez would soon sail for the Baltic. When Saumarez heard this he replied: 'He may want that, but I will stay here as long as I can. I believe it is in the interests of Sweden, that if we need to co-operate, it must be I who should direct the operations of my fleet.'[21]

On 24 June Napoleon finally launched his invasion of Russia. His main army consisted of 450,000 men in three infantry corps under Marshals Davout, Ney and Oudinot, together with the 50,000 seasoned veterans of the Imperial Guard. To the main army's rear there were two smaller auxiliary armies of 80,000 men each, one of which was commanded by his brother Jerome, the King of Westphalia. The final elements in Napoleon's invasion force were his flank armies. His right, or southern, flank was an Austrian corps of 34,000 men commanded by Prince Schwarzenberg, whilst his left, or northern, flank was a corps of 32,500 men, mostly Prussians and Poles, led by Marshal Macdonald

Macdonald's corps had been ordered to advance on Riga and as his Polish and Prussian divisions swept through northern Germany the merchant ships gathered at Libau and Windau hurriedly made their escape. Byam Martin was off Libau at the beginning of July when he received a request for assistance from General Essen, the Governor of Riga, which had been under a state of siege since 29 June. *Aboukir*, together with the sloops *Ariel* and *Reynard*, arrived off Riga on 7 July. Martin had brought several of *Orion*'s carpenters with him as it had been agreed that he would equip a squadron of gunboats under Captain Henry Stewart, commander of *Reynard*, to patrol the Dvina River to prevent Macdonald's troops making a crossing there. Martin also gave permission for the export to Britain of 'an immense quantity of corn, hemp, flax, masts and iron'[22] both to promote trade between Britain and Russia and to prevent these goods falling into enemy hands. By 17 July sixty-seven Russian merchant ships had sailed for England with corn and hemp and a further eighty-seven were in the process of being loaded.

The appearance of Martin's squadron, small though it might have been, off Riga had greatly affected the French war effort in northern Russia. Communications by sea were effectively severed and supplies to Macdonald now had to go overland rather than by ship to the Gulf of Riga. On 15 July Saumarez wrote to Martin, approving all that he had done so far but reminding him to pay attention to his health and not 'run the risk to impair it by over-fatigue or too much exertion'.[23] Having recently spoken to Thornton, Saumarez was able to advise Martin that the long-awaited peace between Sweden and Russia would soon be settled.

After months of discussions on 17 July Thornton was finally able to report to Saumarez that 'I have this day signed a treaty of peace with the Swedish and Russian plenipotentiaries'.[24] Saumarez immediately dispatched his nephew, Flag-Lieutenant Dobree, in the sloop *Drake* with Thornton's dispatches. The peace had been anticipated by the government and the newly appointed ambassador to St Petersburg, Earl Cathcart, was already on his way out to the Baltic aboard the frigate *Aquilon* when Dobree arrived at the Admiralty on 31 July

Thornton was eager for Sweden's support in the war against France but she proved reluctant to provide any assistance to her former enemy. Saumarez, who was growing impatient at the lack of co-operation between Sweden and Russia and the 'unprecedented circumspection'[25] of Thornton, was eventually ordered to cut off Sjaelland in Denmark to prevent any Franco-Danish attempt to invade Sweden. This would involve patrols by at least nine of Martin's ships. The previous winter's disasters still fresh in his memory, Saumarez was already becoming concerned that Martin's ships might become trapped by the encroaching winter ice and was eventually able to arrange for a small Russian squadron to take their place.

The already troubled relationship between the Thornton and Saumarez now took another turn for the worse with the arrival of Thornton's heavily pregnant wife aboard *Victory* which forced Saumarez out of his cabin into a smaller one recently vacated by his son. When von Rosen arrived aboard *Victory* in mid-July he found Saumarez 'his <u>usual self</u> and the other worse than before … we were both angry'.[26] Von Rosen was clearly as relieved as Saumarez when Thornton, who had clearly been distracted from his duties, finally left *Victory* for England along with his 'odious wife on whom nothing but her teeth are sufficient, in physical and moral terms. Poor man, he has got a vixen. I have had a lot of trouble with her.'[27]

Having ignored Thornton's suggestion to sail for the Baltic, Saumarez was at Gothenburg to greet Lord Cathcart upon his arrival. On 9 July he attended a party at von Rosen's held in the British minister's honour. (Saumarez was, by now, a frequent visitor to the governor's house.) Saumarez spent the night ashore but by 9.30am the following morning was back aboard his ship. From Gothenburg Cathcart proceeded to Abo to attend a meeting between Alexander and Bernadotte, the result of which was a military agreement between their two countries. A Russian army stationed in Helsingfors was to be transferred to Riga and a joint attack on Zealand, under Bernadotte's command, was also proposed. (This attack never materialised due to Russian forces being tied up elsewhere.)

In late August Byam Martin learned that Marshal Oudinot at Danzig was preparing to send reinforcements, including a siege train, to Macdonald. Martin hastily assembled a force made up of his own squadron, the Russian frigate *Amphitrite*, two sloops and several transports with 430 soldiers aboard and on 21 August he weighed anchor. Sailing into Danzig under the Swedish flag, Martin approached the port's lower fort and, with many of his own sailors dressed as soldiers, made as if he was preparing to land troops. Pushed onto the defensive, Oudinot's forces were prevented from marching until it was too late in the season to make an advance on Riga. On 14 September Martin sent the sequestered transports back to Riga and sailed with the remainder of his squadron to join Morris at Hanö

As Napoleon's forces pushed further into Russia and drew inexorably closer to Moscow, Alexander had become increasingly concerned over the safety of his fleet and had informed Cathcart that he wished to pull his ships out of the Baltic and Arctic and have them winter in British ports. The Russians were concerned about their ships passing through Danish waters and requested British assistance, Saumarez was able to provide officers and pilots to assist in their passage through the Belt.

Saumarez's time in the Sweden was now coming to an end but there was time for one last sightseeing tour of the country he had done so much to protect. In early September Saumarez and von Rosen travelled north to visit the Falls of Trollhättan and von Platen's pet project, the Gota Canal, construction of which had begun in the 1800s with the help of British foremen, tools and equipment. Soon after their return to Gothenburg a fire broke out in the dockyard which Saumarez helped to fight, tackling the blaze, von Rosen noted, with the energy of a young midshipman.

On 9 October James returned from his tour of the Swedish, Finnish and Russian capitals; however it was not a happy reunion between father and son for James brought with him the news that Saumarez's eldest daughter, Mary, had died suddenly, aged just nineteen, on 25 September. Saumarez was grateful that the news had come from James whose presence over the following days did much to comfort his father. Once again he found strength in God, writing to his brother, Richard, of his 'resignation to the will of an all merciful Being who carries us through this vale of sorrows to make us more perfect for an inheritance in his everlasting Glory'.[28] Whilst Saumarez was grateful to have his eldest son with him he could not help but worry about Martha: 'If I could be assured of Lady Saumarez's welfare', he wrote to his brother. 'I should feel more tranquil, but I know too well the keenness of her feelings. the anxiety she suffers on my account will I fear, put to the test her practise of those pious virtues we all know her to possess, and of which she sets so bright an example.'[29] A post-mortem showed that Mary, who had complained of brief chest pains, had died from fluid on the lung. The Admiralty agreed to Saumarez's request to return home but first a replacement with suitable experience had to be found from the list of rear admirals. On 22 October Melville wrote to Saumarez to inform him that he would be replaced by Rear Admiral Hope, who was expected to sail for the Baltic within days.

Having dispatched *Briseis* with dispatches for Lord Cathcart, Lieutenant Ross returned to Hawk Road with news that Moscow had been abandoned by Napoleon and that the French were now in full retreat. Alexander immediately recalled his fleet but his orders never reached Admirals Tait and Crown who were already en route through the Belt with their respective squadrons. (Russian ships began arriving in British ports in December 1812 and they would remain in British waters until July 1814.) Forwarding the necessary instructions to Morris for escorting the Russians through the Belt, on 26 October Saumarez shifted his flag to *Pyramus* to allow *Victory* to return home and James transferred to *Aquilon* prior to her departure for England. On 28 October *Victory* sailed from Hawke Road and two days later Hope arrived in the Baltic aboard his flagship, *Egmont*. Saumarez handed command of the fleet over to Hope and *Pyramus* sailed from Hawke Road on 5 November, arriving back at Yarmouth Road on 10 November. The following day Saumarez travelled to London where he had a lengthy interview with the First Lord at the Admiralty, followed by a meeting with ministers in Downing Street. From London Saumarez travelled with Martha to Cheltenham, the couple intending to stay with their eldest son James for Christmas and the New Year. Whilst in Oxford Saumarez received a letter from Byam Martin whom he had not heard from since his return to England. Glad to find his colleague in good health Saumarez wrote: 'I can truly say that I have ever felt happy in doing justification to the zealous exertions and to your abilities and judgement on all occasions, but particularly in the defence of Riga when closely invested by the enemy. And it will ever be to me a source of the highest satisfaction that I had it in my power to select you for that important service.'[30]

Prior to his final departure from the Baltic Saumarez had been presented with an elegant sword, the handle of which was wound with a wide gold filigree band inset with diamonds, estimated to be worth around £2,000. Baron von Essen, who presented the sword to Saumarez, also delivered a letter from Bernadotte thanking Saumarez for his services to Sweden but apologizing for not being there to hand the sword over in person, being otherwise detained (negotiations with Russia were then still ongoing). At around the same time Saumarez also received a letter, much more effusive in its praise, from von Rosen:

> At length I rejoice, my dear Admiral. you have been the guardian angel of my country; by your wise, temperate, and loyal conduct you have been the first cause of the plans which have formed against the demon of the Continent … Buonaparte will be defeated, humanity will breathe again, and Europe will be once more raised up. With Wellingtons, Moreaus, Bernadottes against him, what hopes! I shall not fail to communicate to you the first news of importance, for once more I must tell you, that you were the first cause that Russia had dared to make war against France: had you fired one shot when we declared war against England, all had been ended, and Europe would have been enslaved.[31]

Writing the following January, Saumarez insisted that it was the frequent clarifications and verbal assurances from von Rosen during the Carlshamn Cargoes incident, when tensions between Britain and Sweden were at their highest, that had persuaded him to act peacefully towards Sweden whilst he awaited instructions from Government and that these instructions had themselves been formed by the reports Saumarez had sent to London stressing the mutual interests of Britain and Sweden. Saumarez later wrote: 'It will be the greatest happiness of my life if my endeavours have any way tended to establish a fixed and permanent alliance between our respective nations.'[32]

Chapter 23

Final Command:
December 1812 – May 1827

By early 1813 Napoleon had raised a new army, 250,000 strong, to replace the 500,000 men he had lost in Russia. Quickly pressed into action, his army of raw recruits was crushed by the Allied forces, including Bernadotte's Swedes, at the Battle of Leipzig in October 1813. Decisively beaten in battle for the first time, Napoleon returned home and the victorious allies, Great Britain, Russia, Austria and Prussia, signed an agreement not to negotiate separately with France. As Napoleon's troops began to desert en masse his foreign minister, Talleyrand, took control of a provisional government and began planning for the restoration of Louis XVIII. On 6 April 1814 Napoleon bowed to the inevitable and abdicated. Under the Treaty of Fontainebleau he was exiled to the island of Elba with an annual allowance of 2 million francs. At the Congress of Vienna, held from September 1814 to June 1815, France was restored to its pre-1792 boundaries.

On 24 June 1813, at a ceremony at Carlton House, the Prince Regent invested Saumarez with the insignia of a Knight Grand Cross of the Swedish Order of the Sword. Saumarez swore an oath to defend the Evangelical-Lutheran religion, to faithfully serve the King of Sweden and to defend the country from all foes. At the same ceremony Rear Admiral Bertie received a knighthood and was also invested with the insignia of a Knight Commander of the Swedish Order of the Sword.

In May 1814 Saumarez discovered his name had been omitted from the list of officers awarded peerages for their services during the war. To add further insult he discovered that Pellew, an officer who had not commanded a ship in a general action and who was not even a Knight of the Bath, was the only navy officer ennobled and was now Baron Exmouth. Saumarez and fellow admiral John Duckworth, who had also been overlooked, requested an interview with Lord Melville, and asked that they be considered for the same honour. Melville told Saumarez that there was little he could do on this occasion but he had discussed the matter with the Prime Minister, Lord Liverpool, and would recommend him should there be a further extension to the peerage. Saumarez also wrote to St Vincent to ask for his support, declaring: 'Your Lordship will judge of my feelings at finding an Officer, junior to me, advanced to the Peerage, and my long and zealous services entirely neglected upon this occasion.'[1] St Vincent agreed to support Saumarez, though he told his secretary, Tucker, that Saumarez's mode of application would 'end ill' adding 'surely, with such a high mind and unrivalled pretensions, a peerage is an object beneath him'.[2]

Having heard no further on the subject from Melville, Saumarez now wrote to Liverpool with letters of support from several colleagues to request that the Prime Minister discuss the matter of his peerage directly with the Prince Regent, declaring: 'I owe it to myself, to my family, as well as to the naval service, to which I have had the honour to belong upwards of forty-four years, to take the proper means, with every due respect, that my long and faithful services are laid before his Royal Highness.'[3] His appeals to St Vincent and various government ministers came to nothing, for Saumarez was now informed that the Prince Regent felt it was 'quite impossible, under all the circumstances'[4] to agree to Saumarez's request. By way of explanation Saumarez was told that his flag had not been flying at the end of the war whereas Pellew had been Commander-in-Chief of the Mediterranean Fleet, a position to which Saumarez might have been appointed had his command in the Baltic not been extended from the normal three years. Noting the cool treatment towards him in public, Saumarez began to realise that the real obstacle to his 'services being done justice to'[5] was in fact the Prince Regent. George was well known to favour the army over the navy, as Byron had noted: 'The Prince is all for the land service, forgetting Duncan, Nelson, Howe and Jervis.'[6] He also disliked the Whigs, whom St Vincent supported, and had a troubled relationship with the Prime Minister, snubbing him on one occasion.

With the apparent conclusion of the war the Prince Regent had invited the Tsar of Russia and the King of Prussia to England to celebrate their joint victory over Napoleon. On 6 June 1814 the Second Rate *Impregnable* arrived in Dover flying the Russian Eagle from her foremast, the Duke of Clarence's flag from her mainmast and the Prussian Eagle from her mizzen. The arrival in Britain of Tsar Alexander, King Frederick William III of Prussia and an entourage that included Marshal Blücher, General Yorck and General Bülow caused scenes of wild jubilation. Amidst cries of 'Blücher forever'[7] the elderly field marshal was pulled from his horse and almost carried to London.

Whilst Frederick William took up residence at Clarence House the Tsar took a suite with his sister, the Duchess of Oldenburg, at the Pulteney Hotel in Piccadilly and Blücher took quarters at St James's Palace.

On 15 June Saumarez accompanied the Prince Regent and the royal party on a visit to Oxford. Following the Allied sovereigns' departure for London a ceremony was held at which honorary law degrees were conferred upon Lords Kenyon, Sidmouth and Canning and Admirals Warren and Saumarez. On 19 June, in the midst of the celebrations, Saumarez received word that his daughter Carteret had died, aged just seventeen. Cartaret had taken to her bed with a severe fever a week earlier and her condition had steadily worsened. At times she was barely lucid and seemed not even to recognise members of her own family. Even for Martha, a woman of seemingly infinite resilience, the sufferings of her daughter had at times been too much to bear, especially with her husband still absent in London.

Following the departure of the Allied sovereigns on 26 June Saumarez wrote to Liverpool, listing the personal thanks or letters of approbation he had received from the Emperor of Russia, the King of Prussia, Count Metternich, Gneisenau, Viscount Cathcart and Thornton. The Tsar had publicly commended Saumarez before the Prince Regent during the celebrations but this would have done little to improve his chances of a peerage for George held Alexander in particularly low regard, making several derogatory remarks about the Tsar in private.

On 5 October Saumarez's eldest son James, then twenty-five, married Mary Lechmere, daughter of the late Vice Admiral William Lechmere, at Steeple Aston, Oxfordshire. The following month Saumarez was at Weymouth for the visit to town of Princess Charlotte, the Regent's only child. In January 1815 Saumarez was appointed a Knight Grand Cross when the Order of the Bath was expanded. The expansion of the Order into two divisions (military and civil) of three classes had been requested by the Prince Regent in order 'that those officers who have had the opportunity of signalising themselves by eminent services during the late war may share in the honours of the said order'.[8] The existing Knights Companion, of which there were sixty, now became seventy-two Knights Grand Cross, in addition there were 160 Knights Commander and a further 500 Knights Companions. Many felt that the expansion had reduced the prestige of the Order and when St Vincent received a letter congratulating him on his new award he returned the envelope marked: 'Why persecutest thou me with GCB?'[9]

On 1 March 1815, whilst the Allied sovereigns were busy restoring France to its pre-1792 boundaries at the Congress of Vienna, Napoleon left Elba with around 1,000 men and landed near Cannes. Advancing through the foothills of the Alps the deposed French Emperor and his followers arrived at Grenoble on 4 March. Louis XVIII immediately dispatched Marshal Ney with 6,000 men to intercept and capture Napoleon but Ney quickly switched allegiances when reunited with his former commander-in-chief. When Napoleon arrived in Paris on 20 March Louis XVIII had already fled the capital for Ghent.

Following a renewal of the Treaty of Chaumont between Austria, Russia, Prussia and Britain in April, Wellington was made the Supreme Commander of the 112,000 British and 116,000 Austrians stationed in Belgium. On 12 June Napoleon left Paris and crossed the Belgian border with an army of 124,000 men. Following battles between the French, Prussians and British on 16 June the Prussians retreated to Namur and the British were forced back to a position above Charleroi at Waterloo. Leaving Marshal Grouchy to pursue Blücher's Prussians, Napoleon advanced towards the British with the remainder of his army and his reserves, around 72,000 men. Realising he was outnumbered Wellington positioned his 68,000 men behind a ridge from where he could hold his ground until the arrival of the Prussians. The Battle of Waterloo began at 11.30am on 18 June. Wellington's British and German troops repulsed repeated French attacks but by 6.30pm his main position at La Haye Sainte had been overrun. Sensing victory, Napoleon sent in his Imperial Guard but Wellington's men held firm and were now joined by Blücher's 50,000 Prussians who had finally fought their way through the French lines. Now it was the Allies' turn to advance and, suddenly outnumbered, the French were quickly routed. Realising the battle was lost Napoleon fled the field and returned to France. Unable to raise support for a further military campaign Napoleon was eventually forced to abdicate. Louis XVIII was restored to the throne and Napoleon was exiled to the remote British held island of St Helena.

The 'Hundred Days', as it was known, was a purely land-based affair. During the crisis Saumarez was one of several admirals who applied to have *Victory* as his flagship but his services were not required and he remained in Guernsey, attending to island affairs. Whilst English was now becoming widespread across the island, the language of the church remained French. Saumarez had been quick to spot that this would cause a problem for the increasing numbers of English labourers, merchants and soldiers arriving on the island and had first conceived the idea of building an Anglican church in St Peter Port for the performance of services in English as early as 1807, purchasing the land behind his house in town, Square House, situated close to the Royal Court on St James Street. Little more had been done whilst Saumarez remained on active service but on 20 September 1815 a building committee met at Saumarez's house and this was followed by a public meeting at Coles Hotel on 3 October with Saumarez in the chair. On 3 August 1816 Saumarez and the Bailiff, Peter de Havilland, petitioned the Prince Regent in Council, stating that the only church in the parish, the Town Church, could not contain more than 1,500 persons while the population of the parish was estimated at more than 12,000, one-third of whom were English residents. The petition also stated that the lack of an English-speaking church was leading the English residents to defect to the Nonconformist chapels 'to the great prejudice and danger of the Established Church'.[10] Permission for the new church was granted on 29 August 1816, and the architect John Wilson was engaged. On 1 May 1817 Saumarez laid the church's new foundation stone following a formal procession of States' members from the Market Square. Building continued apace and in August 1818, in what was the first visit to Guernsey by an Anglican bishop, John Fisher, the Bishop of Salisbury, arrived on the island to consecrate the newly-completed church. Neo-clasical in design and intentionally named after St James the Less, the church had cost around £7,000 to build, of which Saumarez provided over £1,000. This included £400 for pews for the poor and a further £120 for the completion of the tower and cupola. When completed there was space in the church for 1,300 persons, this included 200 free seats for the poor and a further 200 seats for the National School children.

In January 1818 Saumarez had written to complain to Lord Liverpool that he had been overlooked for the vacant Major-Generalship of Marines in favour of Keats, a more junior flag officer. However, on 18 July 1819 Saumarez was appointed Rear Admiral of the United Kingdom, taking the position previously held by Sir William Young who was now a Vice Admiral of the United Kingdom. Also known as the Lieutenant of the Admiralty, this was an important office that had previously been held by the likes of Anson, Rodney, Howe and Hood. A month later Saumarez received his automatic promotion to Admiral of the White.

On 29 January 1820 a now permanently mad George III died in seclusion at Windsor Castle. A week later, on 4 February, the Prince Regent was proclaimed George IV. In Bath the proclamation was read out across the city. That evening there was a dinner at the Guildhall at which the new king's health was drunk. There were various toasts and Saumarez proposed 'The Wooden Walls of Old England'. One month later Saumarez, Martha and their two daughters, Martha and Amelia, were amongst the 600 guests who attended a ball at York Club, Bath, held in honour of the King. In May Saumarez attended a meeting of the Bible Society at Freemason's Hall, London, along with the Duke of

Gloucester, Lord Radstock, William Wilberforce and Admiral Gambier. The meeting ended with an address by two converts to Christianity who had recently arrived in London from Ceylon (Sri Lanka).

Saumarez had continued to petition senior ministers and the Regent's advisors over his lack of a peerage but so far his efforts had met with little success. He continued to work his way up the Admirals' List and on 21 November 1821 was made Vice Admiral of the United Kingdom following the death of Sir William Young.

In May 1822 Saumarez and the Lieutenant-Governor of Guernsey, Sir John Colborne, helped raise £500 to assist those worst affected by a famine which had recently struck the south and west of Ireland. Later that year Saumarez's eldest son James travelled from his vicarage in Staverton, Northamptonshire, to Guernsey to officiate at the wedding of his younger sister Amelia to William Herries, of Spottes Hall, Galloway, the marriage ceremony being held on 8 September at St James Church.

On 13 January 1824 Saumarez and Martha set off from London in a chaise and four to visit Admiral Sir John Orde in Beckingham. Three miles from the Green Man turnpike their trunk, carrying Saumarez's diamond star of the Order of the Bath and Martha's jewellery collection, together worth around £1,000, was discovered to be missing from the rear of their coach. Saumarez immediately reported the loss to the police at Bow Street and later issued hand bills for the trunk's recovery. The trunk was eventually discovered empty and discarded in a field by the side of the road. Martha was so distressed at the loss of all her jewellery that Saumarez had the diamonds removed from the hilt of his Swedish sword and replaced with paste in order to make new items.

On 24 March 1824 Saumarez was appointed Port Admiral at Plymouth. Arriving aboard his flagship the 120-gun *Britannia*, Philip Pipon, anchored in the Hamoaze, on 14 April, Saumarez received several copies of the Admiralty statutes, books of instructions, standing orders and various charts from the outgoing Port Admiral, Alexander Cochrane. Saumarez had been appointed a secretary, John McArthur, but McArthur had to retire after barely a month in the post due to ill health and was replaced by Cochrane's secretary, Joseph Edye. Saumarez's regular letters to the Secretary of the Admiralty, John Croker, detailed the comings and goings of ships to and from the harbour, the raising of crews and their movements between ships and the promotion of officers. Manning was always problematic and there were never enough men to go round, delaying the sailing of ships. However, smugglers operating along the coast were frequently captured by the ships under Saumarez's command and these men were sent to the flagship where they were given the choice of jail or serving under Saumarez. As commander-in-chief Saumarez also had the unenviable task of forwarding to the Admiralty letters from his captains and commanders requesting court martial procedures against seamen and officers who had variously transgressed against the Articles of War. Whatever their content, Saumarez's letters were all answered by Croker using the long-established tradition of folding a corner of the letter and writing (or in Croker's case, scrawling) on it whatever their Lordships had decided.

In May the Duke of Clarence undertook a tour of the south coast ports. On the morning of 27 May the royal yacht was becalmed whilst off Torbay en route to Plymouth and Saumarez had to dispatch the steam packet *Cambria* to tow *Royal George* into port. The following morning the Duke embarked aboard the packet for a visit to the Eddystone lighthouse and a tour of the new breakwater that was under construction. Returning to the Hamoaze the Duke went aboard *Britannia* where he was received with a royal salute of twenty-one guns. Following a visit to *San Josef* to meet Captain Ayscough, commander of the ships in Ordinary, the Duke and Saumarez landed at Richmond Walk. From there they proceeded by carriage to Whiddon's Royal Hotel for a dinner held in the Duke's honour. The following day the Duke reviewed the Royal Marines and dined with senior army officers and the Lieutenant-Governor Sir John Cameron. On 30 May *Cambria* took the Duke on a tour of St Germans Lake and on 2 June he dined with Saumarez and other members of the Plymouth Royal Navy Club at the Royal Hotel. Having towed the royal yacht out of harbour prior to the Duke's departure on 4 June the owners of *Cambria* presented Saumarez with a bill of £100 for loss of earnings during the period the packet had been employed in the Duke's service.

On 16 February 1825 Saumarez presided over a court martial held aboard his flagship for Constantine O'Friell, assistant surgeon of the survey vessel *Shamrock,* who was accused of insolent behaviour towards his superior officer, Lieutenant Henry Denham. O'Friell was found guilty and was sentenced to be dismissed from the service. Shortly after the trial Saumarez went on leave to Bath and Commodore William Cumberland hoisted his broad pennant aboard the 74-gun *Genoa.* Saumarez returned from his four weeks' leave on 19 March.

Later that month Saumarez wrote to the Home Secretary, Robert Peel, regarding the question of Catholic Emancipation. The staunchly Anglican Saumarez was convinced that the idea would prove 'destructive to the discipline of the Navy'[11] as no Catholic commander could comply to the regulations that required services aboard ship to be performed to the Anglican liturgy but would, instead, want: 'Mass and other Rites perform'd according to the tenets of the Church of Rome'[12] which would 'undermine and subvert all Naval Discipline'.[13] Responding to Saumarez's letter Peel agreed that if a Roman Catholic officer were appointed to a ship of which the majority of the crew were also Roman Catholic 'religious differences might seriously affect the discipline of the ship'.[14]

On 7 April Saumarez called a meeting at the Guildhall, Plymouth, to discuss setting up a local branch of the newly-established National Institution for the Preservation of Life from Shipwrecks (founded in March 1824 by William Hillary with the King as patron). Saumarez read a letter he had received from the Institution stating that, subject to the outcome of the meeting, they would send a lifeboat and Captain Manby's newly-developed equipment (a rope fired by a mortar). It was decided to set up a committee to investigate the matter further and Saumarez was appointed president and the mayor vice-president. At the next meeting, held at the Town Hall on 18 May, Cawsand Bay was chosen as the most suitable location for a lifeboat station in Plymouth.

On 6 August 1825 Saumarez attended a Royal Navy Club dinner at Whiddon's. Having proposed a toast to the health of Earl Grey, the Earl, who had briefly served as First Lord in Grenville's administration, stood up to thank Saumarez for his kind words then proceeded to give a speech in which he noted Saumarez's lack of recognition for his services to the country:

> I cannot but remind those about me of the merits of my noble friend – I wish I could call him my *noble* friend (noble, I mean, in rank, as he is already noble in mind) – I wish I could see him enobled by my Sovereign, as his services entitle him to be, for who would deny him that honour, who recollects the career which he has run from Rodney's glorious day, the battles of Cape St Vincent and the Nile, down to his own brilliant exploits in the Crescent and as commander-in-chief at Algeciras, and not say, that if ever a name should or would have graced the peerage, it should have been that of Saumarez?[15]

Embarking on *Britannia*'s tender, *Royalist*, Lieutenant Robilliard, on 22 June 1826 Saumarez went on his annual tour of the south coast ports under his jurisdiction, Falmouth and Milford, leaving Captain Edward King of *Windsor Castle* in temporary command of the Plymouth station. At Falmouth Saumarez learned that the packet boat crews had gone on strike as they had not been paid and were encouraging other crews to join them as their vessels arrived in port. Saumarez ordered *Bramble*, *Leveret* and *Nightingale* from Plymouth to take over from the Falmouth packets, but by the time these vessels arrived the dispute had been resolved and the striking seamen had returned to work.

In August Lord Exmouth, now retired from active service, arrived in Plymouth where he had been port admiral between 1817 and 1821. This was the first meeting between Pellew and Saumarez since their falling-out over prize money more than thirty years earlier and, their argument now long forgotten, a rapprochement of sorts was said to have been achieved between the two men. In late December Saumarez received a petition from John Fox, a seaman aboard the frigate *Blanche* who had been sent to the Marshalsea prison for striking a superior officer, passed midshipman Charles Hopkins. Under the Articles of War this was an offence punishable by death but Fox had narrowly avoided the noose, his original death sentence being commuted to two years' imprisonment soon after his court martial in May of 1826. Saumarez now forwarded a request to the Admiralty that Fox be released early for good behaviour.

On 8 January 1827 the death of Prince Frederick, the Duke of York, was announced. As a mark of respect Saumarez shifted his flag to *Thetis* and ordered the royal standard to be hoisted to half-mast aboard *Britannia*. The flags on *Thetis* and all the other ships in the harbour remained at half-mast until the duke's funeral on 20 January when Saumarez returned to *Britannia*. On 27 January there was a brief reunion with an old colleague, Thomas Masterman Hardy, when his flagship, *Wellesley*, stopped off at Plymouth on her way from Lisbon to Spithead. A few days later Saumarez wrote to the Admiralty to apologise for not being able to attend the upcoming court-martial of a marine accused of sodomy aboard the sloop *Nimrod* due to a sudden attack of rheumatism. (The marine was later acquitted and wrote to Saumarez asking for his accusers to be punished).

On 12 September 1826 the Admiralty had asked Saumarez to carry out experiments with a newly-developed form of lifesaving equipment. These rockets with an attached line fired from aboard ship were intended to act as an early form of breeches buoy. To begin with the tests carried out aboard *Royalist* proved unsatisfactory, with several rockets veering off course and plunging straight into the sea. Robilliard put this down to the line, supplied with the equipment, not having been properly stretched before use, resulting in kinks that prevented it running freely through the block. Eventually a rocket was successfully fired, embedding itself with some force into the cliffs off Plymouth. Robilliard's detailed report on the lifesaving equipment was forwarded to the Admiralty by Saumarez on 25 January.

In February 1827 it was announced in the press that Saumarez would soon be succeeded as Port Admiral, Plymouth by Admiral Robert Stopford. In April *Britannia* was taken into port for repairs and on 10 May 1827, two months after his seventieth birthday, Saumarez hauled down his flag for the last time and retired from the navy, bringing to a close a career that had spanned nearly sixty years during one of the most tumultuous periods in European history. Contrary to press reports Saumarez was replaced as Port Admiral, Plymouth not by Stopford but by Admiral Northesk. Later that month Saumarez attended the third annual dinner of the Royal National Institution for the Preservation of Lives from Shipwrecks, held at the City of London Tavern. Also in attendance were the Duke of Sussex and his fellow admirals, Keats, Hope and Harvey.

Chapter 24

Retirement:
May 1827 – October 1836

Having retired from the navy Saumarez returned to Guernsey where he became increasingly involved in charitable work, he and Martha reportedly spending around £1,000 a year on gifts and donations. One of Saumarez's first acts was to establish an exhibition at his alma mater, Elizabeth College. His investment of £500 allowed a prize of £15 to be awarded every four years to the best young theological and classical scholar. In 1812 Saumarez had helped found a school for the Infant Poor in St Peter Port and in 1827 work began on its replacement, a school for the National (Anglican) Society, built on the hill overlooking the Assembly Rooms.

In late August 1828 two Jesuit priests, Pierre Lavadiere and Nicholas Petit, arrived on Guernsey from France with the intention of setting up a seminary on the island. Although their proposal was submitted to the Royal Court, Jesuits were no more welcome on Guernsey than they were in France, where their colleges were now banned. On 2 September the Royal Court met and agreed to apply to the King to prevent the seminary being established. Two days later there was an island meeting chaired by Saumarez. Along with the usual objections to suspected popery the islanders were worried that, with main language of Guernsey being French, those attending the seminary would be open to sedition. Eventually several resolutions expressing the islanders' opposition to the school were agreed on, these included a declaration that 'the institution of a Jesuit seminary, under whatever form or name, is a measure fraught with the greatest danger to the security of the island and the peace and welfare of the Protestant Church'.[1] The petition was unanimously agreed upon and Saumarez forwarded it to Peel, for submission to the King. Refused permission to build their seminary, the Jesuits eventually left the island and returned to France.

Following a meeting of the States of Guernsey, held on 3 March 1829, it was announced that a full-length portrait of Saumarez was to be commissioned, the Bailiff, Daniel de Lisle Brock, declaring: 'The whole world acknowledge that he, at this moment, occupies the first rank among the heroes of the British Navy. And if that navy, and the United Kingdom feel honoured by the association of his name with the heroes who have guarded her flag, how much greater cause have we, as Guernsey-men, to be proud of his glory.'[2] Once completed the portrait, by Bridges, was hung in the Royal Court's Upper House behind the Bailiff's chair, where it remained until 1948 when it was moved to Saumarez Park.

On 1 October 1829 the Reverend James Saumarez officiated at the joint wedding of Catherine Spencer Beresford and Honora Mary Georgina, daughters of the late Lieutenant Colonel Spencer Thomas Vassal, to his own younger brother Thomas and the Reverend Edward Henslowe, at All Saints Church, Milford, Hampshire. Following their wedding Thomas, a lieutenant in the 71st Regiment, and Catherine travelled to Swanage for their honeymoon.

On 22 July 1830 Saumarez was promoted to Admiral of the Red. With the accession to the throne of King William IV the previous month his chances of a peerage now appeared to have improved. Unlike his predecessor, William was very much a navy man and had known Saumarez since his days as a midshipman in the 1780's. However, Saumarez's claim would still need the support of Government. In 1827 Lord Liverpool's administration had collapsed over the question of Catholic emancipation. Canning briefly took over as Prime Minister but died in August 1827. His replacement, the Duke of Wellington, managed to force through the Catholic Emancipation Bill but his administration collapsed over the issue of Parliamentary reform – 'rotten' and 'pocket' boroughs with tiny electorates that could be bought to gain influence in the House of Commons – and in November 1830 the Whig leader, Earl Grey, agreed to form a government.

On 23 February 1831 Saumarez and Keats attended a dinner at the Thatched House Tavern, St James Street, London, along with 100 other admirals and captains held in honour of the new first lord, Sir James Graham. Tasked by Grey with reforming the navy Graham had wasted little time introducing efficiencies into the organisation. He had removed from office twelve commissioners, with salaries of between £800 and £2,000 per year, and he had also reduced the number of royal yachts from five to two, these now solely for use by the King. However, when challenged in Parliament about the navy sinecures, the two Generals of Marines, four Colonels of Marines, a Vice Admiral

221

(Saumarez) and a Rear Admiral of the United Kingdom with an estimated combined annual salary of £4,740 per annum, Graham challenged the House to say that these salaries were misapplied 'if signal services and eminent gallantry displayed in a hundred fights had any claim upon the gratitude of the country'.[3]

On 3 March Saumarez was at St James's Palace for the investiture of a new Knight of the Bath, the Hanoverian statesman, Count Munster and on 12 April the knights returned to the palace to attend a grand dinner. At 7.30pm the King led the Duke of Cumberland, Prince Leopold, the Duke of Wellington, Saumarez and other knights into the Banqueting Room and took his seat at the centre of a table lit by five ornate ormolu chandeliers and laid for fifty-four guests. A band, stationed in an adjoining state room, played at intervals during the evening.

On 26 August Grey wrote to the King's Private Secretary, Herbert Taylor, suggesting that William might wish to mark his upcoming coronation by creating two new peers, one each for the army and navy. For the army Grey put forward General John Cradock, who had the backing of Goderich, the Secretary of State for War, and for the navy he suggested Saumarez, citing his service during the War of American Independence, his capture of the French ship *Reunion* at the start of the last war, his role in the battles of the Glorious First of June, Cape St Vincent, the Nile and Algeciras and his subsequent command in the Baltic. Having mentioned Saumarez's name to the King on several occasions Grey was by now aware that William held Saumarez, in his role as commander-in-chief of the Baltic Fleet, responsible for the loss of *St George* and *Defence* in 1811. He could not, therefore, have been surprised when Taylor wrote back on 27 August to explain that, whilst William had agreed to make Cradock a peer he persisted in his objections to Saumarez. Furthermore, the King's 'sentiments upon this point have been so strongly expressed upon many former occasions, and repeated upon this, that I am convinced that it would be quite hopeless to affect any change in them'.[4] When William next spoke to Grey regarding navy peers he pointedly made no mention of Saumarez.

In early September Saumarez arrived in London for the William's coronation, which he attended along with the other Knights of the Bath. The following day, 9 September, Saumarez had a lengthy interview with the First Lord during which Graham re-affirmed that he and Grey were still pressing William to award Saumarez a peerage. Saumarez was due to see Grey the following day but from what Graham had told him, did not foresee any favourable outcome from his interview. His meeting with the Prime Minister lasted over an hour and seemed to go more or less as expected. However, the following morning Saumarez received a letter from Grey explaining that, following their meeting the Prime Minister had, that evening, gone to St James's to lay Saumarez's services directly before the King and William had finally agreed to award Saumarez with his long-sought peerage. The Prime Minister wrote to the King to offer his sincerest thanks to William for relieving an 'old and meritorious officer, [who] has borne a conspicuous share in the most glorious actions by which the last wars have been distinguished, from an acuteness of distress such as Earl Grey has seldom witnessed'.[5]

On 15 September 1831 Baron de Saumarez was introduced and took his oath and seat at the House of Lords along with three newly appointed peers, Lord Breadalbane, Lord Cloncurry and Earl Lichfield. Having been informed that a naval peer would be created at the coronation Martha had been disappointed to discover that her husband's name had not been Gazetted. However on 28 September, the same day that sixty-four officers were sitting down to dinner at the Royal Navy Club in Bond Street to celebrate Saumarez's elevation to the peerage, she finally learned, from a friend of the family who had just arrived on Guernsey, that her husband had been made a lord.

The news that Saumarez had been raised to the peerage, the first Guernseyman to be so honoured, was announced to the island by the Bailiff in his *Billet d'Etat* on 6 October: 'The elevation of one of our citizens to one of the highest dignities in the kingdom, cannot fail to inspire us with the most lively gratification. Guernsey, which, besides the public man, recognises in him all the virtues which adorn a private station, ought, on this happy occasion, to testify how sincerely she honours his character.'[6]

On the evening of 21 October the newly-ennobled Lord de Saumarez embarked on the Southampton steam packet *Lord Beresford* for Guernsey. It would prove to be a very stormy voyage and, having reached sight of Alderney, the vessel was forced to put in at Weymouth, where she remained until 24 October. When the packet finally reached Guernsey late in the evening on 25 October Saumarez found the pier crowded with people awaiting his arrival. Cheering Saumarez as he landed, the crowd attempted to pull the horses from his carriage, intending to drag it to his house themselves. Order was eventually restored and the carriage drove off. However, upon his arrival at his town house the now exhausted admiral discovered its terrace similarly crowded with people who cheered as Saumarez alighted from his carriage and entered his house.

At 7.00am the following morning church bells began to ring out to announce Saumarez's arrival on the island. At 11.00am the States assembled at the court-house and agreed upon an address to be read out to Saumarez. Having requested an audience with the admiral the States proceeded to his town house. Saumarez, out of uniform but wearing his Star of the Bath, received the members of Guernsey's Parliament in his spacious drawing room, surrounded by Martha and the members of his family currently on the island. Bowing to Saumarez, Brock proceeded to read out the address that began:

> The history of all nations is known chiefly by the lives of their eminent and celebrated men. The life of your lordship, whilst it adorns the bright pages of England herself, cannot fail to shed lustre on the annals of this island, in which, besides the services rendered to the whole kingdom, will be inscribed your lordship's beneficence to the poor, to public improvement, and to general education.[7]

Having listened to the address, Saumarez declared that he had been highly gratified by the obvious pleasure his fellow countrymen had taken from his elevation to the peerage. Having won victories of some importance, the honour which had been conferred on him by the King had been universally hailed. The King had also expressed his satisfaction at the title he had chosen, Baron de Saumarez, of the island of Guernsey. Saumarez declared that he had been so taken aback by the flattering mark of respect paid to him by the States that he could not say all he might have done on such an occasion and begged the members of the States, and the other gentlemen present, to accept his most cordial thanks for the honour they had bestowed on him. Having been offered refreshments the States then took their leave.

Saumarez returned to London but was back in Guernsey on 14 February 1832 to attend the funeral of his elder brother John who had died on 2 February aged seventy-seven. On 15 February 1832 Saumarez was made General of Marines following the death of the previous holder of the position, Sir Richard Bickerton. At £1,728 15s per annum it was one of the most expensive naval sinecures and to guard against any criticism the First Lord, Sir James Graham, stated that it had been awarded to Saumarez in recognition of his 'eminent public services'.[8] Saumarez was succeeded as Vice Admiral of the United Kingdom by Lord Exmouth.

By October 1831 Earl Grey's Reform Bill had failed its first two readings in the House of Lords. In order to ensure the Bill's passage Grey now persuaded William IV to use his constitutional powers to create additional Whig peers in the Lords. Alarmed by this move the Tory's abstained from voting during the Acts third reading in April

1832, allowing the bill to be passed but avoiding the creation of more Whig peers. The newly-ennobled Saumarez had voted by proxy in favour of the Bill for its second reading in October 1831 but was in the House to vote for it in person for its third and final reading. As a result of the Act fifty-six rotten boroughs were disenfranchised, forty-two new boroughs were created and the electorate was increased from 366,000 to 650,000. However real change for the working classes, many of whom were still not eligible to vote, would only come with the emergence of the Chartists in 1836.

In 1828 Captain John Ross had persuaded the distiller, Felix Booth, to fund an expedition by a steam vessel to the Arctic. The vessel chosen was a Liverpool steamer, *Victory*, which was specially adapted for the voyage. Ross chose his nephew, James Clark Ross, to sail as his second-in-command and the expedition set off from London on 23 May 1829 with enough fuel and provisions for 1,000 days. By late 1832 Ross and his men had not been heard of in England for three summers. On 15 October Saumarez, Keats and Viscount Goderich attended a meeting held at the offices of the publishers Pinnock and Maunder in the Strand at which it was resolved to fund an expedition to find out what had happened to the expedition and if possible to bring the men back home. By February 1833 the Arctic Land Expedition had raised £3,000 by private donations and, on the promise that the expedition would also carry out scientific research, the government had pledged a further £2,000, enough to fund a two-year expedition to the Arctic.

On 7 February Saumarez was at St James's Palace for an investiture of the Order of the Bath at which fellow Nile veteran Davidge Gould was made a Knight Grand Cross and Admiral Charles Hamilton a Knight Commander. Later that month Saumarez attended the King's levée and in early April Saumarez and Martha both attended a party given by the Duchess De Dino, the wife of Talleyrand, the French ambassador, at their home in Hanover Square. The 200 guests included the Duke of Gloucester and ministers from Naples, Prussia and Sweden.

However impressive it might have been, the reception at the Talleyrands' was intimate compared to the grand state ball at St James's Palace that Saumarez and Martha attended on 17 May. The state rooms had all been opened for the occasion, the Throne Room included, and each room had a temporary orchestra. Ices and other refreshments were served from the Portrait Gallery and card tables had been set up in the King's Closet. The ball began at 10.30pm and at 1.00am around 700 guests sat down to dinner at long tables running round three sides of the Banqueting Room. The diners were treated to foods of every description, including exotic fruits grown at Kensington and Kew. Following dinner the dancing continued until 3.00am

In mid-October Captain Ross finally returned to England from the Arctic. Ross had become the first European to enter the Gulf of Boothia but his expedition had been beset by bad weather and his ship, *Victory*, had spent four winters trapped in the ice. The expedition was aided by local Inuit who made camp near *Victory* and shared their food with Ross and his men. The area to the west and north of Boothia was extensively explored and in June 1831 Ross's nephew, James Clark Ross, became the first European to discover the North Magnetic Pole. In August 1833 the ice finally broke up for long enough to enable Ross and his men to set out in *Victory*'s boats. A few miles west of Navy Board Inlet a sail was sighted and Ross and his men were finally rescued, returning to Stromness aboard the whaler *Isabella* on 12 October. Arriving in London Ross was given the freedom of the city. In December Ross travelled to Tunbridge Wells to visit Saumarez and Martha at their home, Clarence Villa. Ross was alarmed to see that Saumarez's health had deteriorated greatly since the last time he had seen his old commander-in-chief, sadly noting that 'it was but too evident that his constitution was broken'.[9] Saumarez was now suffering from prolonged pains in his right leg, probably gout, which was preventing him from walking. He frequently travelled to Bath, both for health reasons and to visit his brother Richard who had retired there in 1818.

In early January 1834 Saumarez and Martha travelled with Ross to London where Ross had lodgings, Saumarez and Martha taking rooms at Bryant's Hotel, Bond Street. On 6 January Saumarez and Ross attended a meeting of the Royal Naval Charitable Society at the Thatched House Tavern. Admiral Robert Stopford was elected President of the Society and after petitions from ninety-four orphans and widows were read out £571 was voted for their relief. On 13 January Saumarez, Martha, Ross and Stopford visited the Leicester Square studio of artist John Burford for a private viewing of a recently completed painting entitled *Panorama of Boothia* based on drawings made by Ross during his recent Arctic expedition. Burford was a popular artist specialising in panoramas and his painting remained on display to the public until May 1834.

On 5 April the Governor of Greenwich Hospital, Sir Richard Goodwin Keats, died, aged seventy-seven. Keats, who had served with Saumarez both in the Mediterranean and Baltic, was a firm favourite of the King and William had ordered all available sea-officers to attend his funeral, which was to be held on 12 April. Coincidentally, 12 April was the anniversary of Rodney's victory over de Grasse at the Battle of the Saintes, it was also the date chosen for a ceremony at which Saumarez was to be enrolled as an Elder Brother of Trinity House, a society set up in 1514 to ensure the safety of ships and seamen. Having already written to Byam Martin to inform him that he intended to go to Keats's funeral Saumarez subsequently sent his excuses to the organisers of the service for not being able to attend, being otherwise engaged. Keats's funeral was almost a full state affair, attended by the King, the Lords of the Admiralty, fifteen admirals, nineteen captains and commanders in full dress uniform and 100 pensioners of Greenwich hospital. Saumarez, who had previously agreed to be a pallbearer, was conspicuous by his absence. When Saumarez next attended the King's levée on 7 May he was publicly berated by William. Having failed to explain why he had missed Keats's funeral he was reprehended sharply by the King at both the levée and at the subsequent queen's drawing room, which he attended with Martha. The king's remonstrances at this latter function where enough to reduce the highy emotional Saumarez to tears. According to the Clerk to the Privy Council, Charles Greville, the King had started showing signs of irritability prior to his argument with Saumarez, publicly berating members of his court for little reason and inspecting the barracks of his Horse and Foot Guards, making them perform their drills before him. Saumarez resolved to write a letter to the King expressing his wounded feelings but he was persuaded against this by Byam Martin who recommended he throw the letter into the fire. Saumarez's actions were eventually explained to the King by Lord Camden, who along with Byam Martin was a fellow Elder of Trinity House, and by the time of the next levée cordial relations had been restored between the two men.

On 23 May Saumarez attended the first annual general meeting of the Royal Naval School, held at the Horticultural Society rooms in Regent Street. The school had been set up to provide education for the sons of less well-off naval and marine officers and to those whose fathers had been killed in their country's service. The original establishment had been for 150 boys but at this meeting the possibility of taking on 230 boys was now discussed. The meeting was chaired by Stopford who also chaired a meeting on 19 June held at the London Tavern to discuss the setting up of a Marine Temperance Society. Saumarez and Jahleel Brenton, who had also attended the earlier meeting of the Royal Naval School, both spoke of the loss of life through ships not sailing under 'temperance regulations', suggesting that the recent loss of the East Indiaman *Kent* and the passenger ships *Rothsay Castle* (whose captain was discovered drunk) and *Hibernia* had all been for this reason, leading to the loss of around 390 lives.

On 4 July Saumarez and Martha's world was once again thrown into turmoil by the death of their second son Thomas, aged just thirty-one.

Thankfully Saumarez was able to take some comfort from the way his son had borne what had apparently been a severe illness with 'meek and patient resignation'.[10] To his eldest son, James, Saumarez wrote: 'It has been to me, as yourself and your dear Mary will readily believe, a most distressing and truly painful trial; but it has pleased God to support me through the whole of this sorrowful time far beyond what I could have ever thought myself to have been equal to, and I trust that your dear mother and beloved brother and sister will continue resigned to the will of Providence.'[11] Saumarez now travelled to Thomas's home in Tunbridge Wells to make arrangements for the funeral. On 12 July Thomas's body was taken to Guernsey aboard the steamer *Salamander*.

Following the collapse of Earl Grey's government and the return of the Tories under Wellington Saumarez had stopped visiting the House of Lords but on 11 August he voted by proxy in favour of the Irish Tithe Bill. The Bill intended to reduce the amount of tithes payable by tenant farmers (mostly Roman Catholic) to the Irish Anglican Church for the upkeep of the clergy, most of whom were no longer resident in the parishes from which they drew their income. The Bill was opposed by supporters of the Irish Church including the Archbishop of Canterbury and Wellington, who was also an Irish peer, and was defeated in its first reading.

On 7 October the Swedish Foreign Minister, Count de Wetterstedt wrote to Saumarez to inform him that Bernadotte, now Charles XIV of Sweden, was sending him a life sized, full length portrait of himself with the inscription 'Charles XIV Jean, to James, Lord Saumarez, in the name of the Swedish nation'. Wetterstedt wrote that the portrait was intended as 'unequivocal proof ... of the enlightened views of the British government at a critical and memorable period of European history, and of the noble loyalty with which they were carried into effect by your Lordship'.[12] Charles had been intending to send Saumarez the portrait for some time but the opportunity had finally presented itself with the arrival of the steam vessel *Lightning* which had just conveyed the Foreign Office diplomat Sir Edward Disbrowe to Stockholm.

On 27 January 1835, Saumarez's younger brother Richard died aged seventy following a two-day illness at his home in The Circus, Bath. Of all his brothers and sisters Richard was perhaps the sibling that Saumarez was closest to. The two had stayed in regular contact over the years, indeed when Saumarez was in London he had often stayed with Richard and his first wife, Martha, (an unabashed admirer of her brother-in-law, Martha had died of consumption in 1802) before Richard had closed his lucrative London surgery and retired to Bath at the behest of his second wife, Elizabeth, in 1818. At seventy-eight Saumarez was already in poor health, and the loss of his brother, coming as it did so soon after the untimely death of his son, was a blow that could only have helped hasten his decline.

On 7 May Saumarez was at St Paul's Cathedral for the Anniversary Festival of the Sons of the Clergy, a charity set up in 1655 (and still in existence today) to help members of the clergy and their families in need of financial assistance. Amongst those attending were the Duke of Cumberland, the Archbishop of Canterbury, the Lord Mayor, Sir James Graham and Herbert Taylor. The festival included recitals of 'Zadok the Priest', 'The Hallelujah Chorus' and 'Te Deum'. The festival was followed by a dinner, held at the Merchant Tailors' Hall in Threadneedle Street.

In May 1836 Saumarez was contacted by Thomas White, a fellow naval officer who was preparing an account of the Battle of the Saintes. Prior to its publication White sent Saumarez a copy of his 'Naval Researches' which, Saumarez was dismayed to discover, repeated the oft-stated theory that the surrender of *Ville de Paris* was primarily due to the attack by *Canada* and not his ship, *Russell*. Recollecting the events of that day, Saumarez concluded: 'I shall only add, that I am convinced that no officer who was on board the *Canada* … will assert that she was engaged with the *Ville de Paris* at the time stated. The present Admiral Gifford was, I believe, one of the lieutenants, to whom I wish to refer you.'[13] (Gifford agreed with Saumarez's statement, declaring, 'I am of the opinion the *Canada* was engaged with the *Ville de Paris* earlier in the day than the *Russell*.'[14]) Although the battle had taken place nearly sixty years earlier, for Saumarez, always touchy on points of honour, this oft-repeated misconception clearly still rankled.

On 16 June the 79-year-old Saumarez made his last public appearance when he laid the foundation stone for the church of St John's at Les Amballes. Designed by Robert Payne this church was intended to serve the northern end of the parish of Castel and Saumarez had given around £200 towards its completion, another example of his desire to promote Anglican rather than Methodist worship on the island. Sadly he would not live to see the completion of the church.

In the autumn of 1836 Saumarez fell ill, suffering a debilitating loss of appetite and had trouble retaining his food. By 30 September he seemed to have recovered somewhat and several friends visiting the family commented on his successful convalescence, but Saumarez later confided that his apparent good health was just an illusion as he really felt quite ill. On Sunday 2 October Saumarez was too poorly to attend church and took to his bed, which he would not leave again, and had the service brought to him. By the following morning his condition had worsened still further and it became clear to his family that he would not recover. Thursday was the last day on which he enjoyed the full power of speech and he spent most of the day in meditation and prayer but during the next two days he had increased trouble breathing. October 8th was the Saumarez's forty-eighth wedding anniversary but sadly he no longer seemed to recognise his wife, who remained by his side, praying for him. The following day, Sunday, was the birthday of the couple's eldest son, James, who had unfortunately been prevented from being at the bedside of his father by his own poor health and the bad weather but at midday his youngest son John arrived from England. When John made his appearance in Saumarez's bedchamber his father was seen to stir a little in his bed. Saumarez's breathing grew weaker during the day and he passed away a few minutes before midnight on 9 October surrounded by members of his family.

Saumarez's numerous achievements had merited a state funeral in either St Paul's or Westminster but he had requested a much simpler affair and was instead buried in his parish church in Castel following a simple funeral on 13 October. Prior to the funeral the Lieutenant-Governor of Guernsey, Major General Ross, had arranged for minute guns to be fired, first from Castle Cornet then from Fort George, from 12.45pm until 1.00pm. Nearly all the shops on the island had been closed and the ships in the harbour, as well as the Sailor's Chapel (of which Saumarez had been the patron) had their flags at half-mast. The funeral cortege left Saumarez Park at midday and the simple oak coffin was carried one mile to Castel Church. The pallbearers; Major White, Captain Durell de Saumarez, Colonel Gardiner, Captain Mansell, Captain Mauger, Lieutenant Colonel Cunningham, Colonel Guille and Major General Ross, were followed by a long procession that included family members, the bailiff, the jurats of the royal court, the principal of Elizabeth college, members of the island militia and around fifty seamen, many of whom had served with Saumarez aboard *Crescent* and *Orion* and who carried a Union Flag at half-staff at their head as a mark of respect.

At around 12.50pm the coffin was carried into Castel Church which was now draped in black, the pews filled to bursting. The Reverend Durand, rector of the parish, read the thirty-ninth and ninetieth psalms together with the fifteenth chapter of Corinthians after which the coffin was carried out into the churchyard, now crowded with over 1,000 people wishing to pay their last respects. Following the burial service Saumarez was interred in a simple but elegant white marble tomb on the south side of the church, beneath the spire and close to other members of his family.

Saumarez provided for Martha in his will through an annual allowance of the interest earned on his capital, £24,000 in three per cent consols. Saumarez also gave instructions for this interest to be divided equally between his daughters, their heirs and his nephews and nieces if his youngest son, John, died with no male heir. His children, Amelia, Martha and John received £15,000 each in three per cent consols and James, the second Lord de Saumarez, received his Swedish sword together with the various pieces of plate he had been awarded during his long career. Saumarez left £100 to each of the ten parishes on Guernsey to help the poor and £20 to each of his household servants. The Royal Naval Charitable Society received £100 and his surviving brothers and sisters received £100 each. Finally Saumarez requested that a simple memorial recording his naval career be erected in the Town Church.

Martha outlived her husband by thirteen years. In June 1838 she received a Royal Command to attend the Coronation of Queen Victoria along with her son, the second Baron de Saumarez in January 1840 von Rosen wrote to thank her for a recent letter and to express his continued fondness and appreciation for Saumarez and his family. Von Rosen had just finished reading Ross's recently-published biography of Saumarez. Whilst undoubtedly welcome, the Swedish count felt that Ross's work fell short of what the late admiral deserved. Saumarez's family were similarly unhappy with Ross's biography and the reviews were also bad, the *Literary Gazette* being particularly disparaging.

Martha died on 17 April 1849, her funeral, held the following month, was attended by Lords Northwick and Dunnalley, Lady Arbuthnot and various officers who had served under Saumarez, including Captain Mansell. Her coffin was taken from her home, Montpellier Lodge, in Gloucester and taken to the family vaults of the Lechmere's in Hanley, Worcestershire. (The Lechmere's were her daughter-in-law's family.) Her coffin was later moved and interred next to her husband at Castel Church. Sadly Martha was only survived by two of her children, James and his younger brother, John, Amelia having died from consumption in December 1838 and her older sister Martha in January 1848. John's son, Saumarez's grandson, James St Vincent, became the fourth baron on his father's death in 1891. His great-grandson, Eric Douglas Saumarez, is the seventh, and current, Baron.

Shortly after Saumarez's death, and as per his will, a memorial plaque was commissioned by his family from William Whitelaw of London. With side figures, the family crest above and a scene depicting the capture of *Reunion* beneath, the plaque, with its brief description of Saumarez's naval career, was placed in the Town Church where

Saumarez had been baptised almost ninety years earlier. In 1842 Parliament ordered a group of three monuments to naval heroes of the French Wars of 1793–1815; Sir Sidney Smith, Lord Exmouth and Saumarez. Saumarez's statue depicts him stood next to a short cannon and dressed in a boat cloak over his admiral's uniform, wearing his Order of the Bath, two gold medals and his Swedish Grand Cross. The statue was originally intended for display in the Painted Hall, Greenwich, but now resides a short distance away in the upper gallery of the National Maritime Museum. On 1 August 1876 (the anniversary of the Battle of the Nile) the foundation stone for a ninety-foot obelisk was laid on top of Saumarez's favourite hill in Delancey Park, Guernsey. When completed the following year the monument was visible for over ten miles in all directions.

Even after his death Saumarez continued to serve his country. In November 1943 the Delancey Monument was destroyed by the occupying German forces as it was being used as a navigational aid for British bombers and also interrupted the field of view of nearby gun emplacements (Despite recent campaigns the monument has never been rebuilt.) In that same year the Royal Navy launched the destroyer *Saumarez*. In December 1943 *Saumarez* provided the escort to *Duke of York* prior to the sinking of *Scharnhorst* (helping to disable the German battleship) and in May 1945 she led a flotilla which attacked and sank the Japanese cruiser *Hagura*. Saumarez has not been forgotten in Sweden, Bernadotte, showing Saumarez's portrait to his grandson (later King Oscar II) sometime during the 1840s, was said to have declared 'Look at the man who saved Sweden'.[15] In May 1910 the Swedish cruiser *Fylgia* visited Guernsey to place a wreath on the Delancey monument. However, a return visit in 1914 was cancelled due to the outbreak of the First World War. Another Swedish warship did visit Guernsey in 1936 to mark the centenary of Saumarez's death and as recently as 1975 a plaque to the British admiral was unveiled in Gothenburg Town Hall by King Carl Gustav and Lord Louis Mountbatten.

Chapter 25

Summation

Born in 1757 shortly after the commencement of the Seven Years War, Saumarez, like many of his contemporaries, owed his long and successful career to fortuitous timing. He was made a lieutenant shortly after war with the American colonies had broken out allowing him an almost immediate opportunity to display his abilities and by the time he had made post Britain had begun a lengthy war against France and her allies. The younger generation, the men that followed Nelson and Saumarez, were less fortunate, as with Europe once more at peace they lacked the same opportunities to display their abilities.

Whilst Saumarez displayed no lack of initiative in battle, the accusation has been made, with some justification, that that he lacked the killer instinct of an officer like Nelson. At the Battle of Cape St Vincent in February 1797 Saumarez had come close to capturing the Spanish flagship *Santísima Trinidad* but had been forced to break off the attack by Jervis to support another part of line. A more aggressive captain such as Nelson might perhaps have pretended not to see the signal until he had men aboard the Spanish flagship and her capture had been secured. (At Copenhagen Nelson ignored Parker's order to disengage the enemy, thus ensuring a British victory.) At the Nile Saumarez differed with Nelson once again, this time over the question of tactics: whereas Nelson had no hesitation in seizing the moment and doubling the line Saumarez was against such a manoeuvre as he thought it would needlessly endanger British lives and was also unnecessary due to superior British gunnery. (A more aggressive commander might have ignored the advice of his junior officers and attacked the Russians at Rogervik, but throughout his career Saumarez had repeatedly displayed a lack of enthusiasm for any attack that would lead to unacceptably high losses amongst his men.) Whilst Saumarez might have lacked a killer instinct he was blessed with superb handling skills and was able to use this ability to turn several potentially disastrous situations to his advantage. In the widely praised ship-to-ship battle of *Crescent* versus *Reunion* Saumarez had been able to maintain his ship's position under the French frigate's stern even though *Crescent* had been almost disabled through the loss of several masts. By maintaining the attack and bringing previously unengaged guns into action Saumarez was able to carry the day and capture this larger French frigate, with no loss of life aboard his own ship. Eight months later Saumarez found his ship being chased by two French ships of the line, two heavy frigates and a corvette off Guernsey. Drawing these vessels away from the other ships under his protection Saumarez was able to evade capture by heading towards Guernsey's rocky coastline and entering a narrow passage never before attempted by a ship of *Crescent*'s size, leaving the French to surmise that she surely must have been run ashore, whereas, in fact, Saumarez's ship was cautiously making her way round the north of the island back to St Peter Port.

Whilst Saumarez had proven himself to be one of the navy's best fighting captains and the ablest of sailors, he was also capable of the long slog, enduring lengthy periods of extreme tedium and hardship, as his time spent in command of the inshore squadron stationed off the Black Rocks in 1799 ably attests. For several gruelling months Saumarez had maintained his squadron's station off the coast of France, on more than one occasion using an enemy anchorage to ride out stormy weather, thus preventing the Brest Fleet from putting to sea and gaining control of the Channel. When the Admiralty was looking for an admiral to carry out a similar role eight years later Saumarez was quickly promoted in order that he could serve as second-in-command to St Vincent before taking up his own command in the Channel Islands. With Guernsey and Jersey in the front line in the war against France and dangerously prone to invasion, this was no sleepy backwater command. Saumarez's ships were regularly employed capturing enemy ships operating along the coast, putting spies ashore to glean intelligence on the enemy, even attacking the enemy port at Granville where invasion craft were gathering. It was also a dangerous command as the loss of several ships, both to the enemy and the weather, testified.

Having finished his tenure as Commander-in-Chief of the Channel Islands Saumarez was offered but turned down command of the East India Station, citing his ill health. However, with one eye on a fleet battle that would finally earn him his long-cherished peerage Saumarez was quick to accept the Baltic command when it was subsequently offered. The five years spent in command of the Baltic fleet would see Saumarez transition from a capable second-in-command to gifted commander come diplomat, with skills that few in his profession possessed, able to foster, maintain, even enhance relations with several countries that Britain was officially at war against.

British Baltic policy in 1808 had been vague to say the least. Over the ensuing years it evolved in response to reports sent in by Saumarez who on occasion chose not to implement policies coming out from London as he felt they would be detrimental to British interests. It is therefore fair to say that Saumarez did much to mould British foreign policy in the Baltic. Also, having successfully maintained the flow of trade in and out of the Baltic and, just as importantly, relations with both Sweden and Russia, creating a massive breach in the Continental System, Saumarez can claim much credit for Napoleon's fateful decision to invade Russia, a decision that turned the war on its head. Russia allied herself with Britain and Napoleon's invasion ended in disaster, the destruction of his army, once and for all, ending its usefulness as an offensive weapon.

Returning from the Baltic with the thanks of the Swedish government and a Swedish knighthood the much sought-after peerage, which by now had been earned several times over, had still not been forthcoming, even at the end of the when other officers, with more dubious claims to the award, were being so honoured. As we have seen Saumarez took matters of honour very seriously and it is no surprise that he campaigned so vigorously to get this omission, what he saw as a slight against his character, reversed. Biographers such as Mahan have seen this need for recognition as some sort of character flaw. However, as David Shayer points out in his recent biography Saumarez set himself extremely high standards and the lack of a peerage could only have meant that somehow, somewhere he must have fallen short of these exacting standards. After their superb victory over the French at Battle of the Nile Saumarez had still confided in Martha that he had not been satisfied with elements of his own command and, following the failure of the first Battle of Algeciras, he had shut himself away in his cabin for several days whilst he examined his own performance and was finally able to convince himself that nothing more could have been done to turn avert the failures that had beset his squadron that day. His later annoyance at being overlooked for command of an enlarged Cadiz squadron having defeated the combined Franco-Spanish squadron, followed by his refusal to serve as third in command of the Channel Fleet where once he had been second in command under St Vincent were all of a piece. Saumarez saw anything that seemed to question or belittle his abilities as a stain against his character and an affront to his honour.

During those periods when Saumarez questioned his own abilities or was simply weighed down by the burden of his command, he was heavily reliant on letters from home to restore his spirits. The effects of Martha's letters on her husband during the blockade of Brest, when he could not leave the deck during the night due to the ever-present dangers and could only snatch a few moments of sleep during the day were noted by many, including his flag-captain, Jahleel Brenton:

> During the long winter nights, we could all observe the effects of this most trying situation upon the Admiral's appearance, who, having alone the responsibility for the safety of the ships under his command, suffered in proportion to its amount. It was, at the same time, a subject of general remark, how every trace of fatigue and anxiety instantly vanished on the arrival of a letter from his family. it would have been natural to suppose that, deeply as he felt the happiness of home, so in proportion would have been his distaste for a service that deprived him of it; but the moment he was assured of the welfare of the objects of his affectionate solitude, his countenance was lighted up by the utmost gratitude to the Giver of all blessings, and he again devoted himself to the fulfilment of his arduous duties with renewed energy ... I believe he was most powerfully stimulated to great and good actions, by the consideration of the share those dear to him would enjoy in their results. and, certainly, no energy whatever was wanting to get his ship, or squadron, ready for sea, ... however it might curtail the period of his domestic enjoyments; everything gave way to duty, and every possible degree of energy and zeal was brought into action for the execution of it.[1]

Saumarez and Martha were a devoted couple. As previously noted, they wrote to one another several times a week if not every day when they were apart, something Saumarez's fellow officers were well aware of, often to their own chagrin. Whilst Nelson was convalescing at home in Bath following the disaster at Santa Cruz he had paid a visit to Martha with his wife Fanny. 'Do you know,' Martha wrote to her husband, 'that he accused thee of spoiling all the wives of Thy brother officers on your station? Yes truly, by thy attention in writing so constantly to thy own that it made all the others murmur. He says that till you came among them he thought he was a very punctual correspondent, but that you outdid everybody. Think whether my heart did not thank Thee.'[2]

Close contact with his family remained important to Saumarez throughout his career, indeed it was one of the reasons why he turned down the East India Command, where it could take up to a year from sending a letter home to hearing the reply, in favour of the Baltic, where letters generally took around a fortnight to travel from Guernsey to Wingo. When the immediate support of his family was not available Saumarez turned to the other great prop in his life, his Anglican faith. For all the great trials in his life, both personally and professionally, he would bow to the will of God, always trusting in divine providence. Saumarez did not have the religious zeal of a blue light like Gambier or Pellew but he came close, ensuring, through bibles and religious tracts, that the word of God was available to anyone under his command who sought it. During his first year in command of *Crescent* divine service was performed at least once a month and, as previously related, *Orion* was one of the first ships to hoist the Church Pennant following the Battle of the Nile. Saumarez's interest in religious observance was not just limited to his ship but extended to whole fleets; in June 1800, whilst on blockade duty off Brest, he had written to Spencer, the First Lord to enquire: 'We have signals to denote that the ship's companies will have time for breakfast or dinner; why should there not be one to signify that they will have time for the performance of Divine service?'[3] Saumarez, like Nelson, understood the important role that religion played aboard ship, both as a moral support for the crew and as an aid to discipline. In the same letter to Spencer he had noted; 'I know nothing that will contribute more to keep seamen in the right line of their duty than a proper attention to religious duties.'[4] In addition Saumarez would later observe that he had found religious sailors to be particularly courageous in battle.

Closely tied to his religious faith was his interest in the welfare of others who were less fortunate. From 1789 (the year of the French Revolution) Saumarez was a member of the Society for Promoting Christian Knowledge (SPCK), a charity founded in 1699 for the establishment of Charity and Sunday Schools for the children of the poor. The charity also distributed bibles to Royal Navy ships and *The Seaman's Monitor*, a book offering moral guidance, to its sailors. At that time the SPCK was strongly Anglican, anti-Dissenting organisation that emphasised personal piety, bible study and prayers. In addition to the charity work already described, Saumarez helped establish separate girls' schools in Castel, St Peter in the Wood and the Capelles. He also gave £300 in Navy five per cent annuities to help pay for a female teacher for the Castel School. (A National School for girls was eventually established on Guernsey in 1830.) Saumarez was President of the Royal Navy Charitable Institution, the Naval and Military Bible Society and the Guernsey branch of the British and Foreign Bible Society. Unlike the SPCK the Bible Society was a non-denominational organisation, catering for both Anglicans and dissenters alike and Saumarez was known to have requested bibles from the society. In 1822 Saumarez helped set up a savings bank for the poor of Guernsey (later the Guernsey Savings Bank) and he and Martha gave clothing and money to the poor of the island every Christmas. Saumarez was also a patron of the Provident Society and the Church of England Missionary society and in 1818 made donations through the SPCK to help found a Christian college in India.

During his sixty-year career Saumarez served in almost every major theatre of Royal Navy operations; the east coast of America, the Caribbean, the Mediterranean, the Channel, the North Sea and of course the Baltic. He participated in an unrivalled number of major fleet actions and battles, eight in total, along with numerous minor engagements, his career bearing witness to a tumultuous period in world history, the loss of the American colonies, the fall of a Bourbon king and queen, the creation of the French Republic and the rise and ultimate fall of Napoleon. By the time of his death the navy in which he had served dominated the seas around the world, a position which would remain unchallenged for the next hundred years, Royal Navy sailors displaying levels of gunnery, seamanship and discipline unmatched by any other navy, allowing a tiny island off the coast of Europe to punch well above its weight in international trade and politics.

Naval biographies of the Napoleonic Wars have, for the past 200 years, inevitably focussed on Nelson, his godlike status in the national consciousness ensured by his tragic death in battle at Trafalgar. Only recently have historians begun to look further afield with works on frigate captains, Pellew, Cochrane and Moore by authors Stephen Taylor, David Cordingly and Tom Wareham. Nelson's Band of Brothers, Ball, Hood, Troubridge, Saumarez et al, have been dealt with in multi-biographical works by Peter Le Fevre, Richard Harding and others and whilst authors A. N. Ryan, Tim Voelcker, John Grainger and James Davey have focussed on Saumarez's period spent in command of the Baltic Fleet, David Shayer's recent work for the Société Guernesaise gives a brief, but interesting and entertaining overview of his life and career. However, for nearly 180 years Ross's two-part 1838 biography has remained the only in depth study of Saumarez's career. Rather poorly written and littered with inaccuracies, as von Platen pointed out it really does not do full justice to the man. Hopefully this new study will finally reveal Saumarez, the husband, father, God-fearing warrior diplomat, in his full worth.

Notes

Chapter 1
1. Stevens-Cox 1999, p.135.
2. Knight 2005, p.16.
3. Ross 1838, Vol. I, p.22.

Chapter 2
1. Shayer 2006, p.13.
2. Ross 1838, Vol. I, p.39

Chapter 3
1. Ross 1838, Vol. I, p.53.
2. SA 3/2/2/12 Saumarez Diaries, 1781.
3. ibid.
4. Ross 1838, Vol. I, p.54.
5. Voelcker 2008, p.26.
6. Willis 2008, p.78.
7. Ross 1838, Vol. I, p.62.
8. ibid., p.63.

Chapter 4
1. SA 3/1/2/12 Saumarez to mother, 9 February 1782.
2. Ross 1838, Vol. I, p. 77.

Chapter 5
1. Ross 1838, Vol. I, p.88.
2. Voelcker 2008, p.218.
3. Shayer 2006, p.29.

Chapter 6
1. Adams, J. (ed) 2009, p.30.
2. Ross 1838, Vol. I, p.108.
3. ibid., p.105
4. ibid., p.117

Chapter 7
1. Ross 1838, Vol. I, p.136.
2. ibid., p.140.
3. ibid., p.143.
4. SA 3/1/2/1 Martha to James Saumarez, 9 July 1794.

5. SA 3/1/2/1 Martha to James Saumarez, 22 August 1794.
6. SA 3/1/2/1 Martha to James Saumarez, 3 September 1794.
7. Ross 1838, Vol. I, p. 144.
8. SA 3/1/2/1 Martha to James Saumarez, 7 October 1794.
9. SA 3/1/2/1 Martha to James Saumarez, 5 November 1794.
10. Ross 1838, Vol. I, p.148.
11. ibid.
12. ibid., p.149.
13. Voelcker 2008, p.216.

Chapter 8
1. Ross 1838, Vol. I, p.160.

Chapter 9
1. Ross 1838, Vol. I, p.172.
2. ibid., p.175
3. ibid.
4. Shayer 2006, p.48.
5. Ross 1838, Vol. II, p.416.
6. Ross 1838, Vol. I, p.179.
7. ibid., p.180.
8. ibid., p.187.

Chapter 10
1. Colville and Davey 2013, p.130.
2. Knight 2005, p.235.
3. ibid.
4. Kennedy 1951, p.83.
5. ibid., p. 100.
6. Colville and Davey 2013, p.149.

Chapter 11
1. Knight 2005, p.270.
2. Kennedy 1951, p.108
3. Nicholas 1845, p.19.
4. Ross 1838, Vol. I, p.198.
5. James 1847, Vol. III, p.153.

6. Ross 1838, Vol. I, p.200.
7. ibid., p.203
8. Lavery 1998, p.115.
9. ibid.
10. Ross 1838, Vol. I, p.207.
11. Shayer 2006, p.55.

Chapter 12
1. Lavery 1998, p.181.
2. Adkins 2011, p.33.
3. Nicholas 1845, Vol. III, p.61.
4. Knight 2005, p.297.
5. Ross 1838, Vol. I, p.116.
6. ibid.
7. ibid, p.227.
8. ibid.
9. ibid.
10. ibid.
11. ibid., p. 37.
12. Kennedy 1951, p.143.
13. Ross 1838, Vol. I, p.241
14. Kennedy 1951, p.140.
15. Knight 2005, p.299.
16. Lavery 1998, p.272.
17. Kennedy 1951, p.141.
18. Tucker 1844, p.371.
19. Ross 1838, Vol. I, p 275.
20. ibid., p.276.
21. ibid.

Chapter 13
1. Kennedy 1951, p.145.
2. ibid., p.146.
3. Ross 1838, Vol. I, p.288.
4. ibid.
5. Adkins 2008, p.366.
6. Ross 1838, Vol. I, p.294.
7. ibid., p.292.
8. ibid., p.291.
9. Tucker 1844, p.104.
10. Davey 2015, p.35.
11. Kennedy 1951, p.209.
12. Ross 1838, Vol. I, p.301.
13. ibid., p.302.
14. ibid.
15. Ross 1838, Vol. I, p.303.
16. ibid., p.307.
17. ibid., p.308.
18. ibid., p.311.
19. Richmond 1924, p.375.
20. Ross 1838, Vol. I, p.306.
21. Tucker 1844, p.106.
22. Ross 1838, Vol. I, p.312.
23. ibid., p.313.
24. Kennedy 1951, p.213.
25. Tucker 1844, p.40.
26. ibid.
27. Ross 1838, Vol. I, p.316.

Chapter 14
1. Ross 1838, Vol. I, p.326.
2. ibid., p.343.
3. ibid.
4. ibid.
5. ibid., p.345.
6. ibid., p.352.
7. ibid., p.391.
8. ibid., p.398.
9. ibid.
10. Kennedy 1951, p.253.
11. Raikes 1846, p.114.
12. Kennedy 1951, p.255.
13. ibid.
14. ibid.
15. Ross 1838, Vol. I. p.410.
16. Kennedy 1951, p.256.
17. Ross 1838, Vol. I. p.421.
18. ibid., p.414.
19. Kennedy 1951, p.256.
20. Ross 1838, Vol. II, p.6.
21. Kennedy 1951, p.257.
22. Ross 1838, Vol. II, p.4.
23. Shayer 2006, p.86.
24. Kennedy 1951, p.259.
25. Ross 1838, Vol. II, p.33.
26. Kennedy 1951, p.259.
27. Voelcker 2008, p.30.
28. Kennedy 1951, p.258.
29. Shayer 2006, p.90.

Chapter 15
1. Kennedy 1951, p.257.
2. Ross 1838, Vol. II, p.49.
3. Shayer 2006, p.29.
4. ibid.
5. Shayer 2006, p.91.
6. Ross 1838, Vol. II, p.61.
7. Kennedy 1951, p.268.
8. Shayer 2006, p.87.
9. Adkins 2006, p.103.

Chapter 16
1. Ross 1838, Vol. II, p.82.
2. ibid., p.87.
3. Nicolas 1846, Vol. VII, p.130.
4. Tucker 1844, p.312.
5. Voelcker 2008, p.24.
6. Tucker 1844, p.313.
7. Cobbett 12 December 1807, p.929.
8. ibid.
9. Ross 1838, Vol. II, p.97.
10. ibid., p.99.

Chapter 17
1. Voelcker 2008, p.23.
2. Ross 1838, Vol. II, p.101.
3. ibid.
4. Voelcker 2008, p.38.

5. ibid.
6. Ryan 1968, p.13.

Chapter 18
1. Voelcker, 2008, p.40.
2. ibid.
3. ibid., p.41.
4. ibid., p.42.
5. ibid., p.44.
6. ibid., p.209.
7. ibid., p.47.
8. ibid., p.51.
9. Davey 2012, p.109.
10. Voelcker 2008, p.52.
11. ibid., p.59.
12. ibid.
13. ibid.
14. ibid., p.63.
15. ibid.
16. ibid., p.64.
17. ibid., p. 7.
18. ibid.
19. Voelcker 2008, p.68.
20. Ryan 1968, p.46.
21. Davey 2012, p. 9.
22. Voelcker 2008, p.67.
23. ibid., p.71.
24. ibid., p.204.

Chapter 19
1. Ryan 1968, p52.
2. ibid., p.56
3. ibid.
4. Voelcker 2008, p.74.
5. Ross 1838, Vol. II, p.37.
6. Black and Woodfine 1988, p.244.
7. ibid.
8. Black and Woodfine 1988, p.245.
9. Ross 1838, Vol. II, p.137.
10. Voelcker 2008, p.88.
11. Ryan 1968, p.78.
12. ibid.
13. Bonner-Smith 1942, p.15.
14. Davey 2012, p.132.
15. Voelcker 2008, p.91.
16. ibid., p.204.
17. ibid.
18. Ross 1838, Vol. II, p.163.
19. Bonner-Smith 1942, p.10.
20. Ryan 1968, p.106.
21. ibid.

Chapter 20
1. Voelcker 2008, p.108.
2. ibid.
3. ibid., p.212.
4. ibid.
5. Ross 1838, Vol. II, p.197.
6. Voelcker 2008, p.109.

7. ibid.
8. ibid.
9. ibid., p.110.
10. Barton 1921, p.259.
11. Voelcker 2008, p.111.
12. ibid., p.112.
13. ibid., p.111.
14. Black and Woodfine 1988, p.248.
15. ibid.
16. Voelcker 2008, p.113.
17. ibid., p.115.
18. ibid.
19. ibid.
20. Voelcker 2008, p.116.
21. ibid.
22. Ross 1838, Vol. II, p.215.
23. Voelcker 2008, p.164.
24. ibid., p.123
25. ibid.
26. ibid., p.124.
27. Ryan 1968, p.165.

Chapter 21
1. Ross 1838, Vol. II, p.226.
2. ibid., p.238.
3. Voelcker 2008, p.133.
4. Ross 1838, Vol. II, p.230.
5. Voelcker 2008, p.136.
6. Ross 1838, Vol. II, p.237.
7. ibid., p.240.
8. ibid., p.242.
9. Voelcker 2008, p.137.
10. ibid.
11. ibid., p.136.
12. ibid., p.151.
13. Voelcker 2008, p.154.
14. Ryan 1968, p.187.
15. Voelcker 2008, p.151.
16. ibid., p.168.
17. Ryan 1968, p.190.
18. ibid., p.191.
19. Ryan 1968, p.199.
20. Voelcker 2008, p.217.
21. ibid.
22. Ross 1838, Vol. II, p.256.
23. Nicholas 1846, p.202.

Chapter 22
1. *Belfast Commercial Chronicle*, 25 January 1812.
2. Ross 1838, Vol. II, p.267.
3. Aspinall 1959, p.97.
4. Davey 2012, p.191.
5. Bingham 2010, p.143.
6. Voelcker 2008, p.189.
7. Ryan 1968, p.233.
8. Voelcker 2008, p.189.
9. *Hampshire Chronicle*, 20 July 1812, p.4.
10. Voelcker 2008, p.192.

11. ibid., p.184.
12. ibid.
13. ibid., p.217.
14. ibid.
15. ibid., p.193.
16. Ryan 1968, p.231.
17. Voelcker 2008, p.194.
18. ibid., p.195.
19. ibid., p.194.
20. ibid.
21. ibid.
22. Grainger 2014, p.206.
23. Ryan 1968, p.238.
24. Voelcker 2008, p.195.
25. ibid.
26. ibid.
27. Voelcker 2008, p.195.
28. Blake 2008, p.130.
29. Ross 1838, Vol. II, p.29
30. Ryan 1968, p.265.
31. Ross 1838, Vol. II, p.293.
32. Shayer 2006, p.116.

Chapter 23
1. Tucker 1844, p.407.
2. ibid., p.408.
3. Ross 1838, Vol. II, p.302.
4. ibid., p.301.
5. Shayer 2006, p.117.
6. McDonald and McWhir 2010, p.1067
7. Leggiere 2014, p.366.
8. Adolphus 1818, p.XVIII.

9.   Kennedy 1951, p.345.
10. Shayer 2006, p.127.
11. Blake 2008, p.144.
12. ibid.
13. ibid.
14. ibid.
15. Ross 1838, Vol. II, p.309.

Chapter 24
1. *Morning Post*, 9 September 1828.
2. Anon 1837, p.185.
3. *Devizes and Wilshire Gazette*, 21 February 1833.
4. Grey 1867, p.342.
5. ibid., p.351.
6. ibid.
7. Duncan 1836, p.319.
8. *North Devon Journal*, 23 February 1832.
9. Ross 1838, Vol. II, p.316.
10. ibid.
11. ibid.
12. Duncan 1836, p.316.
13. Ross 1838, Vol. I, p.78.
14. Ross 1838, Vol. II, p.395.
15. Voelcker 2008, p.3.

Chapter 25
1. Ross 1838, Vol. II, p.328.
2. Voelcker 2008, p.216.
3. Ross 1838, Vol. II, p.318.
4. Shayer 2006, p.122.

Bibliography

Text Permissions

Excerpts from *Nelson and his Captains* (© Kennedy, L. 1951) are reprinted by permission of HarperCollins Publishers Ltd.

PRIMARY SOURCES

Suffolk Record Office, Ipswich
SA 3/1/2/1 Letters between James and Martha Saumarez.
SA 3/1/2/12 Letters from Saumarez to parents 1775, 1777, 1782.
SA 3/2/2/1 *Winchelsea* Captains' Log-Book.
SA 3/2/2/4 *Levant* Captains' Log-Book.
SA 3/2/2/5 *Spitfire* Captains' Log-Book.
SA 3/2/2/8 *Russell* Captains' Log-Book.
SA 3/2/2/12 Saumarez Diaries 1770–1820.
SA 3/2/7/2 Martha Saumarez Journal 1812.

Northamptonshire Record Office, Northampton
Rye X 7244 Naval Papers and Letters of Peter Rye 1770–1814.

National Archives, Public Record Office, Kew
ADM 1 Admiralty Correspondence and Papers:
ADM 1/223 Letters from Commanders-in-Chief, Channel Islands (Guernsey) 1805–7.
ADM 1/849-852 Letters from Commanders-in-Chief, Plymouth 1824–7.
ADM 1/5310 Courts Martial Papers, July 1778 – December 1778.

ADM 6 Commission and Warrant Books:
ADM 6/22/26.
ADM 6/22/33.

ADM 36 Muster Books:
ADM 36/7500 *Solebay.*
ADM 36/7472 *Pembroke.*
ADM 36/11852 *Crescent.*
ADM 36/11856 *Orion.*

ADM 51 Captains' Log Books:
ADM 51/1002 *Tisiphone.*
ADM 51/1060 *Winchelsea.*
ADM 51/1159 *Crescent.*
ADM 51/1175 *Orion.*
ADM 51/2934 *Victory.*
ADM 51/4432 *Crescent.*

ADM 52 Masters' Log-Books:
ADM 52/1369 *Montreal.*

ADM 52/1515 *Winchelsea*.
ADM 52/1565 *Ambuscade*.
ADM 52/1603 *Bristol*.
ADM 52/1656 *Chatham*.
ADM 52/1832 *Leviathan*.
ADM 52/2510 *Russell*.
ADM 52/2806 *Caesar*.
ADM 52/3264 *Orion*.
ADM 52/3265 *Orion*.
ADM 52/3768 *Hibernia*.
ADM 52/3874 *Victory*.
ADM 52/3878 *Victory*.
ADM 52/4296 *San Josef*.

ADM 107 Lieutenants' Passing Certificates:
ADM 107/6 1762–77

British Newspaper Archive (Online)
Caledonian Mercury (20 January 1812).
Devizes and Wiltshire Gazette (21 February 1833).
Dorset County Chronicle (14 April 1825).
Evening Mail (19 January 1803/26 September 1817/2 March 1831).
Hampshire Chronicle (6 April 1778/15 June 1778/20 July 1812/ 9 January 1824/5 April 1824/7
    June 1824/22 May 1826).
Hampshire Telegraph (17 January 1803).
Kentish Gazette (31 January 1794).
London Courier (31 May 1824/9 June 1826/13 April 1831).
Morning Chronicle (7 February 1809).
Morning Post (10 December 1802/7 March 1820/20 September 1824/30 December 1826/14
    November 1831/15 January 1834).
North Devon Journal (23 February 1832).
Perthshire Courier (1 October 1810/8 October 1810).
Public Ledger and Daily Advertiser (26 September 1817/31 May 1824).
Royal Cornwall Gazette (21 June 1834).
Saunders' News Letter (24 February 1825).
Waterford Mail (10 September 1828).
West Kent Guardian (10 April 1845).
York Herald (16 August 1834).

Priaulx Library (Online)
December 23, 1803: The loss of the Grappler and the sufferings of its captain and crew Priaulx Library
    http://www.priaulxlibrary.co.uk/articles/ article/december-23-1803-loss-grappler-and-
    sufferings-its-captain-and-crew (Accessed March 2016).
The death of Mary Saumarez, October 1812 | Priaulx Library http://www.priaulx
    library.co.uk/articles/article/death-mary-saumarez-october-1812 (Accessed March 2016).
Jesuits, 1828 | Priaulx Library http://www.priaulxlibrary.co.uk/articles/article/
    jesuits -1828 (Accessed March 2016).

Edited Collections of Letters and Memoirs
Almon, J. (ed.), *The Remembrancer Part II* (London, 1776).
_____ and Debrett, J. (eds), *Parliamentary Register, or History of the Proceedings and debates of the
    House of Commons Vol. V* (London, 1782).
Aspinall, A., *English Historical Documents, 1783-1832* (London, 1959).
Bonner-Smith, D. (ed.), *Letters of Admiral of the Fleet the Earl of St Vincent, 1801-1804 Vol. I.* (Navy
    Records Society Vol. 55, 1922)
_____ (ed) *Captain Boteler's Recollections, 1808-1830* (Navy Records Society Vol. 82, 1942).
Clarke, J. S., and McArthur, J. (eds), *Naval Chronicle Vol. XXVI* (London, 1811).
Crawford, J. M., and Gordon Bowen-Hassell, E. (eds), *Naval Documents of the American
    Revolution Volume 11 Part 3* (Washington, 2005).

Crawford, J. M. and Conrad, D. M. (eds), *Naval Documents of the American Revolution Volume 12* (Washington, 2013).

Greville, C., *The Greville Memoirs: A Journal of the Reigns of King George IV and King William IV* (London, 1875).

Grey, H., *The Correspondence of the Late Earl Grey with His Majesty King William IV* (London, 1867).

Hamilton, R. V. (ed), *Letters and Papers of Admiral of the Fleet Sir Thomas Byam Martin Vol. III* (Navy Records Society Vol. XIX).

Nicolas, Sir N. H., (ed.), *The Dispatches and Letters of Vice Admiral Lord Viscount Nelson, volume III* (London, 1845).

_____, (ed.), *The Dispatches and Letters of Vice Admiral Lord Viscount Nelson, volume VII* (London, 1846).

Raikes, H., *Memoir of the Life and Services of Vice Admiral Sir Jahleel Brenton* (London, 1846).

Rees, T. A., *A Journal of Voyages and Travels, by the Late Thomas Rees, Serjeant of Marines* (London, 1822).

Richmond, Sir H. W. (ed), *The Private Papers of George 2nd Earl Spencer Vol. III* (Navy Records Society Vol. 58, 1924).

Ross, Sir J., *Memoirs and Correspondence of Admiral Lord de Saumarez Volumes I & II* (London, 1838).

Ryan, A.N. (ed). *The Saumarez Papers: Selections from the Baltic Correspondence, 1808-1812* (Navy Records Society Vol. 110, 1968).

Tott, F. Baron de, *Memoirs of Baron de Tott Vol. II* (London, 1786).

Tucker, J. S., *Memoirs of Admiral the Right Honourable the Earl of St Vincent* (London, 1844).

White, C., *Nelson: The New Letters* (Woodbridge, 2005).

SECONDARY SOURCES

Adams, J. (ed), 'Captain Saumarez of the *Crescent*', in *Alabama Seaport: The Official Magazine of the Alabama State Port Authority* (Alabama, 2009), pp. 26–30.

Adams, M., *Napoleon and Russia* (London, 2006).

Adkins, R., and Adkins, L., *Jack Tar* (London, 2006).

_____, *The War for All the Oceans* (London, 2008).

Adolphus, J., *The Political State of the British Empire* (London, 1818).

Anon, *Annual Biography and Obituary Vol. XXI* (London, 1837).

Anon, *George III: His Court and Family: Vol. II* (London, 1821).

Arrow, F., *The Corporation of Trinity House of Deptford Strond* (London, 1868).

Baldwin, P., *Contagion and the State in Europe: 1830-1930* (Cambridge, 2004).

Ballantyne, I., and Eastland, J., *HMS Victory: First Rate 1765* (Barnsley, 2005).

Barton, Sir D. P., *Bernadotte and Napoleon* (London, 1921).

Beaumont James, T., *The Story of England* (Stroud, 2003).

Bingham, D. A. (ed.), *A selection from the Letters and Despatches of the First Napoleon Vol. 3* (Cambridge, 2010).

Black, J., and Woodfine, P. (eds), *The British Navy and the Use of Naval Power in the Eighteenth Century* (Leicester, 1988).

Blackmore, D., *Warfare on the Mediterranean in the Age of Sail* (Jefferson, 2011).

Blake, R., *Evangelicals in the Royal Navy, 1775-1815* (Woodbridge, 2008).

_____, *Religion in the British Navy, 1815-1879: Piety and Professionalism* (Woodbridge, 2014).

Buckley, C. M., *When Jesuits Were Giants* (San Francisco, 1999).

Clark, C., *Iron Kingdom: The Rise and Downfall of Prussia, 1600-1947* (London, 2006).

Cobbett, W., *Cobbett's Weekly Political Register* (London, 12 December 1807).

Colville, Q., and Davey, J., *Nelson, Navy and Nation: the Royal Navy and the British People 1688-1815* (London, 2013).

Cust, Sir E., *Annals of the Wars of the Eighteenth Century: Vol. IV* (London, 1859).

Davey, J., *The Transformation of British Naval Strategy: Seapower and Supply in Northern Europe, 1808-1812* (Woodbridge, 2012).

_____, *In Nelson's Wake: The Navy and the Napoleonic Wars* (Greenwich, 2015).

Davies, D., *A Brief History of Fighting Ships: Ships of the Line and Napoleonic Sea Battles 1795-1815* (London, 1996).

Douglas-Morris, K., *Naval General Service Medal Roll 1793-1840* (London, 1982).

Duffy, N. (ed.), *The Naval Miscellany Vol. VI* (Navy Records Society Vol. 146, 2003).

Duncan, J. (ed.), *Guernsey and Jersey Magazine* (Guernsey, 1836).
Ekins, C., *The Naval Battles of Great Britain* (London, 1828).
Freemont-Barnes, G., *Nelson's Sailors* (Oxford, 2005).
_____, *The Royal Navy 1793-1815* (Oxford, 2007).
_____, *Nile 1798* (Oxford, 2011).
Fuller, W. C., *Strategy and Power in Russia 1600-1914* (New York, 1992).
Gardiner, R. (ed), *Fleet Battle and Blockade: The French Revolutionary War 1793-1797* (Chatham, 1996).
_____ (ed.), *Nelson against Napoleon: From the Nile to Copenhagen 1798-1801* (Chatham, 1997).
_____, *The Sailing Frigate: A History in Ship Models* (Barnsley, 2012).
Goodwin, P., *The Ships of Trafalgar: The British, French and Spanish Fleets, October 1805* (London, 2005).
Grainger, J. D., *The British Navy in the Baltic* (Woodbridge, 2014).
Hoare, P., *Nelson's Band of Brothers: Lives and Memorials* (Barnsley, 2015).
Jacob, J., *Annals of Some of the British Norman Isles Constituting the Bailiwick of Jersey Part I* (Paris, 1830).
James, W., *The Naval History of Great Britain, Volumes I to VI.* (London, 1837).
Kennedy, L., *Nelson and his Captains* (London, 1951).
Knight, R., *The Pursuit of Victory* (London, 2005).
_____, *Britain against Napoleon: The Organisation of Victory, 1793-1815* (London, 2013).
Lavery, B., *Nelson and the Nile: The Naval War against Bonaparte 1798* (London, 1998).
_____, *Nelson's Victory: 250 Years of War and Peace* (Barnsley, 2015).
Leggiere, M. V., *Blücher: Scourge of Napoleon* (Norman, 2014).
_____, *Napoleon and the Struggle for Germany: The Franco-Prussian War of 1813* (Cambridge, 2015).
Macdonald, D. L., and McWhir, A. (eds), *The Broadview Anthology: Literature of the Revolutionary Period. 1770-1832* (Ontario, 2010).
McGrigor, M., *Defiant and Dismasted at Trafalgar* (Barnsley, 2004).
Morriss, R., *The Foundations of British Maritime Ascendancy: Resources, Logistics and the State, 1755-1815* (Cambridge, 2011).
Mudie, J., *Historical and Critical Account of a Grand Series of National Medals* (London, 1820).
Muir, R., *Britain and the Defeat of Napoleon, 1807-1815* (London, 1996).
Musteen, J. R., *Nelson's Refuge: Gibraltar in the Age of Napoleon* (Annapolis, 2011).
Roberts, A., *Waterloo: Napoleon's Last Gamble* (London, 2006).
Robson, M., *A History of the Royal Navy: The Napoleonic Wars* (London, 2014).
Roger, N. A. M., *The Wooden World: Anatomy of the Georgian Navy* (London, 1986).
_____, *The Command of the Ocean* (London, 2004).
Shayer, D., *James Saumarez: The Life and Achievements of Admiral Lord de Saumarez of Guernsey* (Guernsey, 2006).
Stevens-Cox, G., *St Peter Port, 1680-1830: The History of an International Entrepot* (Woodbridge, 1999).
Sugden, J., *Nelson: A Dream of Glory* (London, 2005).
Syrett, D., *The Royal Navy in European Waters during the American Revolutionary War* (Columbia, 1998).
Taylor, S., *Commander: The Life and Exploits of Britain's Greatest Frigate Captain* (London, 2012).
Tracey, N., and Robson, M. (eds), *The Age of Sailing: The International Annual of the Historic Sailing Ship Volume 2* (London, 2003).
Trew, P., *Rodney and the Breaking of the Line* (Barnsley, 2006).
Voelcker, T. *Admiral Saumarez versus Napoleon: The Baltic, 1807-12* (Woodbridge, 2008).
Warner, O., *The Battle of the Nile* (London, 1960).
Willis, S., *Fighting at Sea in the Eighteenth Century* (Woodbridge, 2008).
_____, *The Fighting Temeraire* (London, 2009).
_____, *In the Hour of Victory: The Royal Navy at War in the Age of Nelson* (London, 2013).
Winfield, R., *British Warships in the Age of Sail 1714-1792* (Barnsley, 2007).
_____, *British Warships in the Age of Sail 1793-1817* (Barnsley, 2007).
Woodman, R., *The Victory of Seapower: Winning the Napoleonic War 1806-1814* (London, 1998).
_____, *The Sea Warriors: Fighting Captains and Frigate Warfare in the Age of Nelson* (London, 2001).

Index

Ships with identical names have their dates of launching or type of vessel included in brackets. Abbreviations used to show nationalities of foreign ships are: (Den) Danish, (Fr) French, (Ned) Netherlands, (Rus) Russian, (Sp) Spanish, (Swe) Swedish.

248